Editor
Stephanie Jona Buehler, Psy.D.

Managing Editor
Ina Massler Levin, M.A.

Editor-in-Chief
Sharon Coan, M.S. Ed.

Illustrator
Ken Tunell
Sue Fullam

Cover Artist
Barb Lorseyedi

Art Coordinator
Kevin Barnes

Art Director
CJae Froshay

Imaging
Rosa C. See

Product Manager
Phil Garcia

*Poems contributed
by Barbara Knarr Ramming*

Publishers
Rachelle Cracchiolo, M.S. Ed.
Mary Dupuy Smith, M.S. Ed.

Pre K–1

Author
Mary Ramming Chappell

Teacher Created Materials, Inc.
6421 Industry Way
Westminster, CA 92683
www.teachercreated.com

ISBN-7439-3289-7

©2003 Teacher Created Materials, Inc.

Made in U.S.A.

The classroom teacher may reproduce copies of materials in this book for classroom use only. The reproduction of any part for an entire school or school system is strictly prohibited. No part of this publication may be transmitted, stored, or recorded in any form without written permission from the publisher.

Table of Contents

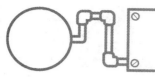

Introduction

One of the primary goals of early childhood education is to prepare young children for school. Among the skills that children acquire in their home environment, preschool, and kindergarten are early literary skills. Children with well-developed reading readiness skills exhibit

- oral language skills
- background knowledge
- motivation to learn
- appreciation for literature
- phonological awareness[1]
- print awareness[2]
- letter knowledge

Early literacy experiences provide foundations for future literacy success. Children's concepts about literacy are formed from the earliest years by observing and interacting with readers and writers, as well as through their own attempts to read and write (Sulzby and Teale, 1991). As a result, a child's environment should be rich in language— children should see, hear and use language throughout their day.

The Goals of This Book

The goals of this book are to assist early childhood educators with creating language rich environments by

- reading aloud to their classroom every day using quality children's literature.
- using a variety of techniques to introduce letter-sound associations.
- including phonemic awareness skill-building activities in a balanced curriculum.
- creating a language-rich environment in which the students have opportunities to play, explore, discover and construct knowledge.
- integrating literacy skills across the curriculum.

As a result, students will

- develop an appreciation of literature.
- build reading comprehension skills.
- understand that each letter is associated with a particular sound (or sounds).
- understand that each letter is formed in a particular and unique way.
- practice forming the letters.
- develop motivation to learn how to read and write.
- build early phonemic awareness skills.

---

[1]*Phonological awareness* is the awareness that oral language contains three characteristics: Sentences are made up of words; words are made up of syllables; words and syllables are made up of phonemes.

[2]*Print awareness* is the awareness of how print works and how it looks. Letters are written in a unique and particular way, the letters are associated with a particular sound or sounds, text is read from left to right across the page, and books are held in such a way that print can be read and interpreted.

- experience reading and writing for a variety of purposes.
- explore characteristics of numbers.
- develop an interest in the natural world (science).
- develop an interest in the people and places of the world (social studies).
- express themselves through creative play and artistic mediums.
- use music, movement, rhythm and rhyme to reinforce developing literacy skills.

How to Use this Book

The activities in this book are designed for preschool, kindergarten and first grade classrooms, or for students ages three through seven. The expectation is that teachers will modify the curriculum according to their students' learning needs. For example, a class of three-year-old children would not be able to write words in a booklet, but they may be able to dictate those words for the teacher to write. Furthermore, three-year-olds would have little need of activities in the phonemic awareness section, but they would certainly benefit from saying nursery rhymes, thereby beginning to build their phonemic awareness skills.

Curriculum Map

The core book provides the focal point—the theme—of the unit. All of the activities are directly related to either the core book or to the theme. The Read-Aloud Section of the core book should be the first activity of a new unit. The Phonemic and/or Phonological Awareness Activities, Letter Formation Activities, and Letter/Sound Association Introduction take place early on in the unit so that these concepts can continue to be reinforced across the curriculum and throughout the unit. The Art Connections culminating activity should end the unit. The remaining lesson plans and activities could be conducted at anytime throughout the week. Lesson plans include the following:

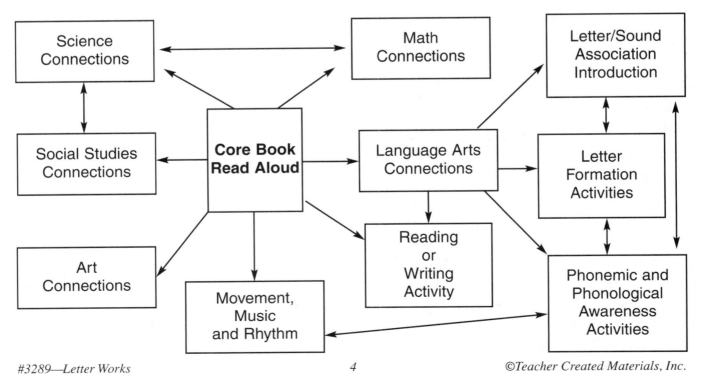

Integrating Phonemic Awareness Activities

Part of a language-rich environment, particularly in kindergarten classrooms, must include specific phonemic awareness[3] instruction in order to build reading readiness skills (Cunningham, et al, 1998; Fletcher and Lyon, 1998). The phonemic awareness and letter-sound association sections are to be taught as mini-lessons—short skill-based lessons no longer than ten minutes. These activities are based on the theory that phonemic awareness develops in different stages (Opitz, 2000; Christena, 2000), progressing from the awareness that words have similar patterns (rhyming) to the most difficult tasks, in which learners segment and manipulate phonemes[4] to create new words.

Balance is the key in teaching of phonemic awareness skills effectively. Early literacy skills cannot be developed solely via phonemic awareness activities. Phonemic awareness will not teach a child to love literature, or build networks of knowledge that provide background information. It simply provides explicit instruction on how oral language works.

Time Line and Curriculum Connections

Each letter unit is designed to be taught over approximately one week. Teachers have the option of teaching in the traditional alphabetical order of the letters. As an alternative, teachers who prefer to teach thematically could extend individual units into other letter units, thereby creating a flow from one theme to another. In doing so, teachers could extend the entire curriculum from twenty-six weeks to a full year. Conversely, most of the individual lessons can also be taught independently, so teachers could select parts of the *Letter Works* curriculum to complement their own or district mandated curricula.

Following is a chart of possible curriculum connections.

A Apples	V Vegetables	L Leaves	Y Yellow	R Rain	H Hats	U Underwear and Uniforms
K Kings	Q Queens	N Nursery Rhymes	J Jack and the Beanstalk	P Pigs	F Farm	X Fox
D Dogs	Z Zoo	G Gorilla	E Elephant	T Trees	S Salamanders and Snakes	M Mouse
I Insects	C Caterpillars	B Butterflies	O Octopi in the Ocean	W Whales in the Waves		

[3] Phonemic awareness is the awareness that spoken words or syllables are made up of phonemes. Phonemic awareness is a sub-category of phonological awareness.

[4] A phoneme is the smallest unit of sound that can be heard in a language.

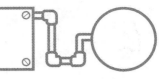

Citations

Burns, Susan; Griffin, Peg, and Snow, Catherine (eds). (1999.) *Starting Out Right: A Guide to Promoting Children's Reading Success*. Washington, D.C.: National Academy Press.

Christena, Karol (M. Ed) and Lynch, Mary Ann (M. Ed.) (2000.) *A Guide to Teaching Beginning Reading*. Westminster, California: Teacher Created Materials.

Cunningham, James A; Cunningham, Patricia M.; Hoffman, James V; Yopp, Hallie Kay. (1998.) *Phonemic Awareness and the teaching of Reading: A Position Statement from the Board of Directors of the International Reading Association*. Delaware: International Reading Association.

Fletcher, Jack M. and Lyon, G. Reid. (1998.) "Reading: A Researched-Based Approach." In Williamson, M. Evers (ed.) *What's Gone Wrong In America's Classrooms*. Stanford, California: Hoover Institution Press.

International Reading Association. (2000.) *Making A Difference Means Making it Different: A Position Statement of the International Reading Association*. Delaware: International Reading Association.

Opitz, Michael. (2000.) *Rhymes and Reason: Literature and Language Play for Phonological Awareness*. Portsmouth, New Hampshire: Heinemann.

Owocki, Gretchen. (2001.) *Make Way For Literacy: Teaching the Way Young Children Learn*. Portsmouth, New Hampshire: Heinemann.

Sulzby, E. and Teale, W.H. (1991.) "Emergent Literacy." In R. Barr, M.L. Kamil, P. Mosenthal, and P.D. Pearson. *Handbook of Reading Instruction, Vol. 2*. New York: Longman. 9

Apple

Overview

Celebrate fall with a study of apples. In this unit, explore the sounds of A through apple art, apple pie, and apple trees. Begin with an apple story, such as *How to Make an Apple Pie and See the World* by Marjorie Priceman (Alfred A. Knopf, 1994). Integrate math, science, social studies and language arts.

A natural follow-up to this unit is "V—Vegetables." Just as fruits and vegetables go together, so do the shapes of "A" and "V." Read *Apples and Pumpkins* by Anne Rockwell (Macmillan Publishing Company, 1989) to transition from one unit to the next.

Apple

Language Arts Connections

Core Book

Priceman, Marjorie. *How to Make an Apple Pie and See the World.* Alfred A. Knopf, 1994.

You head to the market to buy ingredients for an apple pie, but discover that the market is closed. What to do? Travel the world and collect everything you need: grab a French chicken for the finest eggs, cut a few stalks of sugar cane from Jamaica, and for the cinnamon, don't forget to peel bark from a kurundu tree in India.

Read-Aloud Activities

Prior to Reading

- Ask students who have made apple pie to describe how they did it.
- Tell the students that in this story, making an apple pie becomes an adventure.
- Read the title and author's name, and show the cover illustration to the class.
- Ask students for ideas on what the title of the book tells them about the story's plot.

During Reading

- Stop when the character discovers that the market is closed. Ponder aloud, "The market is closed. I wonder what she'll do now. I guess there won't be apple pie today. But wait, the story isn't over yet . . . let's keep reading. What do you think will happen next?"
- Call attention to the illustrations and discuss them during the reading.

After Reading

- Ask for student responses to the story. What part did they like best?
- Model responses with comments such as, "I really liked the part where she got the bark from the kurundu tree. I thought that picture was very funny."
- Make an apple pie following the recipe in the back of the book or the one provided on page 14.

Additional Books

Stock the class library with books about apples. Students will enjoy looking at the illustrations and "reading" them to each other. Also, make a recording of yourself reading from the core book. Then put the tape and the core book in a literacy center so your students can listen to it time and time again.

Aliki. *The Story of Johnny Appleseed.* Prentice-Hall, Inc., 1966.

Hall, Zoe. *The Apple Pie Tree.* Scholastic, Inc., 1996.

Gibbons, Gail. *The Seasons of Arnold's Apple Tree.* Harcourt Brace Jovanovich, 1984.

LeSieg, Theo. *Ten Apples up on Top!* Random House, Inc., 1961.

Maestro, Betsy. *How Do Apples Grow?* Harper Trophy, 1993.

Rockwell, Anne. *Apples and Pumpkins.* Macmillan Publishing Company, 1989.

Silverstein, Shel. *The Giving Tree.* Harper & Row, Publishers, 1964.

Slawson, Michele Benoit. *Apple Picking Time.* Random House, 1994.

Wellington, Monica. *Apple Farmer Annie.* Dutton Children's Books, 2001.

Language Arts Connections (CONT.)

Letter-Sound Introduction

What is first sound of the word *apple*? Say *apple* slowly and deliberately, emphasizing the /a/ sound. Tell students that the letter **a** makes the /ā/ sound and /ă/. The long /ā/ says its own name, as in *ate*. The sound is long and drawn out. The long **a** usually needs help from the letter **e** to say its name. The short /ă/ is a quick sound, as in *apple*.

Phonemic Awareness

Skill: syllable counting

How many syllables, or beats, are in the word *apple*? Say the word, emphasizing the syllable breaks: *ap-ple*. Clap with the beats: *ap-ple*. Write *ap* on a square of green construction paper, and *ple* on a square of red construction paper. Hold both squares up, but push the green *ap* square forward when saying that syllable, and push the red *ple* square forward when saying that syllable.

Distribute squares of colored paper (at least four colors, to represent four syllable words) to the students. Brainstorm /ā/ and /ă/ words with the students (*ate*, *map*, *ladder*, etc.). Read the words, and have the students use the colored paper squares to represent the number of syllables in the words.

Letter Formation

After reading the core book and introducing the letter-sound association, reinforce the association between the letter formation and its sound by drawing the **A** and **a** into a drawing related to apples. For example, the **A** can be drawn into a ladder leaning up against an apple tree, and the **a** can be drawn into an apple shape.

These activities will help to reinforce letter formation for students of all learning styles.

- Guide students in warming up their fingers, hands, and arms by "air writing" triangular shapes for **A** and circular shapes for **a**.

- Encourage pairs of students to discover how to form **A** and **a** shapes with their bodies.

- Cut apples in halves or quarters for students to use as paint stamps. They can stamp the shapes of the letters **A** and **a**.

- Thinly slice apples into strips and circular shapes. Have students experiment with forming the letters **A** and **a** with the apple pieces.

- Put magnetic letters with similar shapes (e.g., **A**, **K**, **V**, **Y**, **a**, **b**, **d**, **p**, **q**, **o**) into a paper bag stapled shut or a closed box. Make a hole in the side of the container. Students reach into the container and feel each letter. They say its name, its sound, and then pull it out of the box or bag to check their answer.

Apple

Language Arts Connections *(CONT.)*

How to Make an Apple Pie

Baking an apple is easy, as long as you follow some simple steps. In this lesson, students will practice sequencing skills.

Skill: story sequencing

Materials:

- *How to Make an Apple Pie* story sequence sheet (page 19)
- crayons
- scissors
- glue
- construction paper

Teacher Preparation:

1. Make one copy for each student of *How to Make an Apple Pie* story sequence sheet.

Procedure:

1. After reading the story, brainstorm with students how an apple pie is made.
2. Next, distribute copies of the story sequence sheets for "How to Make an Apple Pie."
3. Have students cut out each story scene, color it, and then paste it onto construction paper in the correct order.

Follow-up Activity:

Students can prepare an apple pie by following the recipe in the back of *How to Make an Apple Pie and See the World* or following the directions on page 14.

Math Connections

Adding Apples

Ten Apples Up On Top! by Theo LeSieg (Random House, Inc., 1961) is an amusing Dr. Seuss-inspired book that can initiate many math lessons. Read the book with your class and follow up with the following lessons.

Skills: counting and adding

Materials:

- "Adding Apples" (page 18)
- lion, tiger and dog faces (pages 15–17)
- tape or Velcro© squares and felt board (The Velcro© will hold the pictures onto the felt board.)

Teacher Preparation:

1. Copy the "Adding Apples" sheet on green, yellow and red colored paper.
2. Laminate and cut out the apples.
3. Copy the lion, tiger and dog's faces on white paper.
4. Affix tape or Velcro© squares to the backs of the apples and animal faces.
5. Optional: prepare copies of the faces and apples for the students' use.

Apple

Math Connections (CONT.)

Adding Apples (CONT.)

Procedure:

1. After reading *Ten Apples Up on Top!*, retell the story using the faces of the lion, dog and tiger. Put an apple on each animal head and ask, "How many apples up on top?" Allow students to respond. Continue putting apples up on top and counting.

2. Once students have accurately counted apples on top of the animal heads, ask "How many apples all together?" Count the number of apples on the lion's, dog's, and tiger's heads. For example, "One, two, three apples up on top of the lion, and four, five, six apples on top of the dog. That makes six apples all together."

3. Now subtract apples. Put five apples up on top of one of the animal heads. Say, "Oops, he tripped and dropped three apples!" Take three apples away and say, "I have to take away three apples. Now how many apples are up on top?"

4. Restate what you did by saying, "He had five apples, and when he tripped, that took away three. Then he had two apples up on top."

5. Continue adding and subtracting apples. Involve students by having them put on and take off apples.

6. Optional extension: Students can manipulate their own apples and animal faces, either independently or in groups.

Apple Memory Game

Students match numbers in this card game. Use the apples from the "Adding Apples" math lesson.

Skills: number identification and number matching

Materials:

- laminated and cut apples from "Adding Apples" lesson. Use two colors only (for example, red and green).
- black marker
- one small container (i.e., strawberry basket) for each group

Teacher Preparation:

1. Write numbers (1 to 10, 1 to 20, odds, evens, etc.) on the backs of one color group of apple cards.
2. Draw circles (like apples) on the backs of the second color group of apples. The number of circles should correspond with the numbers (1 to 10, 1 to 20, odds, evens, etc.)

Procedure:

1. Divide class into groups of four or five. Split each group into two teams.
2. Students mix up the apple cards and place them face down on table.
3. Teams take turns selecting and turning over two apple cards, one from each color group. Teams determine whether they have a match by counting the number of apple circles and looking at the number written on the second card.
5. Matching cards are placed into an "apple basket" (the small container).

Apple

Science Connections

Comparing Seeds

Discuss how apples and other fruits have seeds that can grow into new trees. Brainstorm with the students what they think a seed would need in order to be able to grow into a strong tree (sunlight, water, soil).

Prior to class, remove the seeds from several different types of fruits and vegetables (apples, oranges, grapes, cucumbers and tomatoes). Bring samples of the same fruits and vegetables, uncut. Allow your students to examine the sets of seeds. Ask them to predict which seeds belong with which fruits and vegetables. Take a class poll. Confirm their predictions by cutting the fruits and vegetables and taking out the seeds. Compare these seeds to the seeds they have already examined.

Social Studies Connections

Seeing the World

After reading the core book, pull out a globe and show the students where the little girl went to find ingredients for apple pie. Be sure to provide a point of reference by first showing where on the globe your school is located.

Art Connections

Apple Tree Orchard

This colorful project will transform the classroom into an apple orchard.

Materials:

- green butcher paper
- brown butcher paper
- glue

- tempera paint (red, green, and yellow)
- 1 apple half (sliced vertically) per student
- soap, water, and towels for clean-up

Teacher Preparation:

1. Cut one treetop out of green butcher paper for each group.
2. Cut one tree trunk out of brown butcher paper for each group.
3. Slice apples into halves.
4. Set up tables with paint, glue, apple halves, treetop, and tree trunk.

Procedure:

1. Divide class into small groups.
2. Have students dip apple halves into paint, and stamp onto treetops.
3. Allow treetops to dry.
4. Glue treetops onto trunks.
5. Display.

Apple

Music, Movement, Rhythm, and Rhyme

Reinforce phonemic awareness skills, specifically substituting one phoneme with another, with the following "apple" songs.

Have You Ever Seen an Apple?

(Sung to the tune of "Have You Ever Seen a Lassie?")

Have you ever seen an apple, an apple, an apple?

Have you ever seen an apple so juicy and red?

In one bite, I munch it. I crunch it so loud.

Have you ever seen an apple, an apple so red?

Rolling Apples

(Sung to the tune of "Frere Jacques")

Rolling apples, rolling apples,

Down the hill, down the hill.

Dropping off the tree

And rolling down the hill,

Roll away, roll away.

Five Little Apples

Five little apples, no less, no more

One was picked and then there were four.

Four little apples, hanging on the tree

One dropped off and then there were three.

Three little apples, shiny and new

One rolled down and then there were two.

Two little apples, ripening in the sun

One was plucked and then there was one.

One little apple sitting alone

It got picked and then there were none.

Math Center

Skills: sorting and counting

Baskets of Apples

Use the cut and laminated green, yellow, and red apples from the "Adding Apples" math lesson. Set out three containers (such as strawberry baskets) to be used as apple baskets. Attach one red apple, one green apple, and one yellow apple to the outside of each container. Students sort apples into the baskets by color.

Snacks

Be sure to check with parents about allergies before serving students any food.

Mini Apple Pies

Try these sweet treats after reading *How to Make an Apple Pie and See the World* by Marjorie Priceman.

Ingredients/Materials:

- ready made pie crusts
- ready made apple pie filling
- round cookie cutter or jar lid
- oven or toaster oven
- cookie sheet

Directions:

1. Assist each student with cutting circles of pie crust (using cookie cutter or jar lid).
2. Drop a scoop of apple pie filling onto the center of the bottom crust.
3. Put the second pie crust on top
4. Crimp closed using fingers or fork.
5. Poke holes in top.
6. Bake in toaster oven for 15 minutes or at 425° in a regular oven until the crust is golden.
7. Allow to cool thoroughly before serving.

Apple Sauce

Make fresh apple sauce with a few simple ingredients.

Ingredients/Materials:

- 8 cups apples, peeled and sliced
- 2 cups water
- 1 cup sugar
- 1 tablespoon lemon juice
- cinnamon
- stove
- pan
- potato masher or food processor

Directions:

1. Cook the ingredients in a saucepan until tender.
2. Mash the mixture with a potato masher until smooth.

Note: *Apple Farmer Annie* by Monica Wellington (Dutton Children's Books, 2001) is a good resource for additional apple recipes.

 **Apple**

Lion Head

Directions: Use with the Math Connections activity "Adding Apples" on page 11. Copy and cut out the lion head. Add or take away apples to demonstrate concepts of addition and subtraction.

Apple

Dog Head

Directions: Use with the Math Connections activity "Adding Apples" on page 11. Copy and cut out the dog head.

Tiger Head

Directions: Use with the Math Connections activity, "Adding Apples" on page 11. Copy and cut out the tiger head.

Apple

Apples

Directions: Use with the Math Connections activities "Adding Apples" and "Apple Memory Game" on page 11, and with the "Baskets of Apples" center on page 13. Copy the apples onto sheets of green, red, and yellow paper. Cut into cards.

How to Make an Apple Pie: Correct Order

Directions: Color and cut the cards on the dotted lines. Put the cards into order that shows how to make a pie. Glue the cards in order on another sheet of paper.

I pick ripe red apples.

All done!

I put the apples in the pie crust.

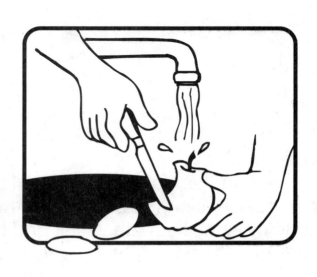

I wash and slice the apples.

Overview

Take flight with beautiful butterflies, and explore /b/ sounds and letter shapes. In this unit, students will study butterfly habitats and record their observations in a butterfly journal, use butterfly picture cards to focus on specific math skills, and decorate the classroom with brightly colored butterflies. Combine this unit with a study of "C—Caterpillars," and include both in an extended unit of "Creatures, Creepers and Crawlers" ("I—Insects," "M—Mouse," and "S—Salamanders and Snakes").

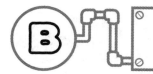 **Butterflies**

Language Arts Connections

Core Book

Ehlert, Lois. *Waiting for Wings*. Harcourt, Inc., 2001.

Follow along as eggs hatch into caterpillars and then transform into butterflies. This beautifully illustrated book has layered pages. The rhyming prose passes along just enough information to keep young readers interested.

Read-Aloud Activities

Prior to Reading

- Read the title aloud, pointing to the words as you read. Point out the illustrations on the front and back covers.
- Ask students to predict what they think the story might be about based on the title and cover illustrations. Discuss what students already know about the change of caterpillars into butterflies.
- Read the author's name. Remind students of other books by Ehlert that they may know, such as *Growing Vegetable Soup*.

During Reading

- Read the words slowly so that the students can see the layers of pictures created by the die-cut illustrations. Talk about how the layers of illustrations create new and different pictures.

After Reading

- Show the students the illustrations of butterflies in the back of the book, and ask if students can recognize any as ones they may have seen around their own environment.

Additional Books

Stock your class library with books about butterflies. Students will enjoy looking at the illustrations and "reading" them to each other. When you read a story to your class, record yourself on tape. Then put the tape and the book in a literacy center so that your students can listen to it time and time again.

Allen, Judy. *Are You A Butterfly?* Larousse Kingfisher Chambers, 2000.

Brorstrom, Gay Bishop. *A Class Trip to Miss Hallberg's Butterfly Garden*. Pipevine Press, 2000.

Bunting, Eve. *The Butterfly House*. Scholastic, 1999.

Cassie, Brian. *The Butterfly Alphabet Book*. Charlesbridge Publishing, 1995.

Gibbons, Gail. *Monarch Butterflies*. Holiday House, 1989.

Ovenall-Carter, Julie. *The Butterflies' Promise*. Annick Press, 1999.

Rosenblatt, Lynn. *Monarch Magic: Butterfly Activities and Nature Discoveries*. Williamson Publishing, 1998.

Ryder, Joanne. *Where Butterflies Grow*. Lodestar Books, 1989.

Sabuda, Robert and Reinhart, Matthew. *Young Naturalist Pop-Up Handbook — Butterflies*. Hyperion Press, 2001.

Swope, Sam. *Gotta Go! Gotta Go!* Farrar, Straus and Giroux, 2000.

Taylor, Harriet Peck. *Coyote and the Laughing Butterflies*. Simon and Schuster, 1995.

Language Arts Connections (CONT.)

Letter-Sound Introduction

What is first sound of the word *butterfly*? Say *butterfly* slowly and deliberately, emphasizing the /b/ sound. Tell students that the letter **b** makes the sound /b/. (Be careful when saying /b/ to not say /*buh*/.)

Phonemic Awareness

Skill: identifying beginning /b/ sounds

Focus on alliteration skills by having the students make up tongue twisters with beginning /b/ sounds such as the following:

A bunch of blue butterflies bought bananas before bed.

Letter Formation

After reading *Waiting for Wings* and introducing the letter-sound association, reinforce the association between the letters **B** and **b** and the /b/ sound by drawing the letter shapes into pictures of butterflies.

These activities will help to reinforce letter formation for students of all learning styles.

- Put magnetic letters with similar shapes (**B, D, E, F, P, R, a, b, d, g, j, p, q**) into a paper bag stapled shut or a closed box with a hole in its side. Students reach into the hole and feel each letter. They say its name, its sound, and then pull it out of the box to check their answer.
- Trace **B** and **b** onto sheets of cardboard. Glue bumpy textures, such as aquarium gravel, onto the letters. Have students close their eyes and feel the letter shapes, saying, "Bumpy B says /b/."

Butterfly Journals

Integrate science and language arts by making Butterfly Journals in which students record their observations of the metamorphosis of caterpillar to butterfly (see page 34 in "C—Caterpillar"). Depending upon their developmental abilities and preferences, students can record their observations in writing or with illustrations.

Skills: observation, writing, illustrating objects

Materials:

- Butterfly Journal cover (page 27)
- blank sheets of paper
- crayons and markers
- butcher paper

Teacher Preparation:

1. Make a copy for each student of the Butterfly Journal cover.
2. Assemble booklets with covers and blank sheets of paper.
3. Cut the butcher paper into the shape of a butterfly.

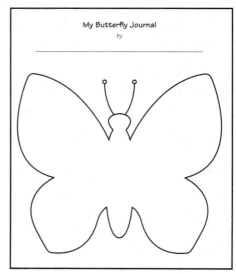

My Butterfly Journal
by
_____

 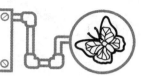

Language Arts Connections (CONT.)

Butterfly Journals (CONT.)

Procedure:

1. Have students decorate the covers of their butterfly journals and write their names on them.

2. Discuss how journals can be used to draw pictures of what the students see, to write words to describe what they see, or to record dictated stories about butterflies.

3. Brainstorm key butterfly words (*butterfly*, *caterpillar*, *chrysalis*, *cocoon*, *colors*, *fly*) that students may want to use in their journals, and record these on the butterfly-shaped butcher paper. Students can refer to this list for spelling of words when writing in their journals. Continue to add to the list throughout the unit.

4. Set a time each day during the unit in which students write in their journals, sounding out letters and phrases. If students have butterfly stories that they would like to dictate, write them in the butterfly journals.

Math Connections

All Sorts of Butterflies

Use butterfly picture cards to reinforce early math skills.

Skills: colors, following directions, sorting, counting, identifying patterns

Materials: Butterfly Cards (page 28)

Teacher Preparation: Make copies of the Butterfly Cards for students.

Following Directions Procedure:

Provide step-by-step directions on how to color the butterflies. Use the butterfly with the circle in the middle.

1. To focus on oral directions, use verbal cues, but no visual cues.
   a. Pick up the butterfly with circles.   c. Color the rest of the wings purple.
   b. Color the circle in the middle red.   d. Color the body pink.

2. To focus on visual directions, use no verbal cues.
   a. Draw a large version of the butterfly with circles on butcher paper or on the board. Use cues to indicate that students should pick it up.
   b. Hold up a red crayon. Color the circle in the center red.
   c. Hold up a purple crayon. Color the wings purple.
   d. Hold up the body. Color the body pink.

Compare the butterflies, and discuss whether it was easy or difficult for students to follow directions without pictures or without words.

Sorting Procedure:

Make many copies of the butterfly cards, cut, and shuffle. Have students sort the cards according to type of patterns on the butterfly.

Butterflies

Math Connections (*CONT.*)

All Sorts of Butterflies (*CONT.*)

Counting Procedure:

Make up counting songs about butterflies, and have the students use the cards as manipulatives. Sing to the tune of "Elephants Went Out to Play" as follows: "One butterfly went out to play, on a bright blue flower one day. It had such enormous fun, it called for another butterfly to come."

Patterns:

Make patterns using the butterfly cards. Have students identify the pattern and fill in the missing parts with the appropriate butterfly cards.

Science Connections

Butterfly Facts

At the beginning of this unit, have students brainstorm questions about butterflies. Write their questions on a sheet of butcher paper. Draw and cut out a large butterfly. Tape it to a wall next to the sheet of questions. As students discover the answers to their questions throughout the unit, write the questions and answers on pieces of brightly colored construction paper and attach these to the butterfly.

Social Studies Connections

The Flight of the Monarch

Discuss the monarch butterfly, which embarks on a journey to Mexico during an annual migration. In the fall, the monarch travels to Mexico from the United States. In February, the butterflies head north. Visit *www.learner.org/jnorth* to learn about a global study of the monarch migration. *Gotta Go! Gotta Go!* by Sam Swope (Farrar, Straus and Giroux, 2000) is a story of a monarch's migration. More books about monarchs are listed in "Additional Books" on page 21.

Art Connections

Coffee Filter Butterflies

This activity is best done over two days: One day to color, wet and dry the coffee filters, and one day to assemble the butterflies.

Materials (for each student):

- one number two cone-shaped coffee filter
- one number four cone-shaped coffee filter
- markers
- water
- glue (a glue gun works best, but must be handled only by an adult)
- chenille stem

- black paint (optional)
- two 15" (or longer) pieces of thin string or dental floss
- five ¼" x ⅝" craft stick
- small white adhesive labels or strips of white tape

Art Connections *(CONT.)*

Coffee Filter Butterflies *(CONT.)*

Teacher Preparation:

Determine how much preparation will be done prior to the lesson. Preparing the following materials ahead of time will save time and may be necessary for very young students:

1. Paint the craft sticks black and allow to dry.
2. Tie one piece of string (or dental floss) to the top front of the craft stick and one to the bottom. Optional: Secure the string with hot glue from a glue gun.
3. Cut each coffee filter in half at the seam so that a V shape is formed at the bottom center of the filter. Cut off the seam.

Procedure:

1. Have the students decorate the coffee filters with markers.
2. After the filters are brightly colored, have the students dip them in containers of water. The colors will run, creating vibrant and abstract patterns.
3. Place the students' filters on sheets of newsprint with their names on them. Allow the coffee filters to dry. This will take a few hours.
4. Distribute the dried filters, the craft sticks with strings attached, and the chenille stems.
5. To assemble the butterflies:
   a. Place the small coffee filter on one end of the craft stick (see illustration) and glue in place.
   b. Place the large coffee filter overlapping the small one (see illustration) and glue in place.
   c. Bend the chenille stems in half to form the antennae.
   d. Use the glue gun to attach the antennae at the top of the craft stick.
6. Write students' names on labels or tape and stick on to the bottom of the craft stick.
7. Students can fly their butterflies with the two strings, or use the strings to hang the butterflies from the ceiling.

Music, Movement, Rhythm and Rhyme

Butterfly in the Sky

by Barbara Knarr Ramming

Butterfly, butterfly in the sky,
Flying close, flying high.
Pretty colors on his wings
Hear happy children as they sing.
Butterfly, butterfly up above
Butterfly, butterfly full of love.
I like to follow you around
A gentle friend that I have found.

Butterflies

Music, Movement, Rhythm and Rhyme (CONT.)

Butterfly Walk

Take a nature walk and hunt for butterflies. Try to identify butterflies, talk about butterfly habitats, and discuss the importance of respecting creatures' homes in order to keep them happy and healthy. Imagine what it would feel like to really be a butterfly. Flitter, flutter, and float—fly like a butterfly!

Centers

Set up centers to encourage students to explore the theme further during a free choice period, or assign small groups to parent-guided centers while you work with other students.

Math Center

Skills: sorting, matching colors

Butterfly Flowers

Copy and cut out pictures of the flowers on page 29. Decorate the flowers with distinct colors to create patterns. Copy and cut out butterflies (page 28) and color them with the same colors and patterns as the flowers. Have students match the butterfly picture cards to the flowers.

Snacks

Be sure to check with parents about allergies before serving students any food.

Laura's Letter Pretzels by Laura Horton

Make pretzels as a center activity, bake, and then serve at snack time. Two **b**-shaped pretzels look just like butterflies! This recipe makes either twelve big fat pretzels, or twenty-five to thirty small thin ones.

Ingredients:

- 3 tablespoons yeast
- 1½ cups warm water
- 3 teaspoons honey
- topping ingredients (salt, cinnamon sugar, parmesan cheese)
- melted butter

- oven
- 4 teaspoons salt
- 4 cups flour (more if needed)
- mixing bowls

Directions:

1. Preheat oven to 425 degrees.
2. Dissolve yeast in the warm water. Add the honey and the salt.
3. Add this mixture to flour in a medium sized bowl and mix.
4. Roll pieces of dough to form letters (or traditional pretzel shapes).
5. No need to let dough rise. Brush with melted butter, then sprinkle with salt or other toppings—parmesan cheese, cinnamon sugar, etc.
6. Bake 10 minutes or until golden brown on a lightly greased cookie sheet.

My Butterfly Journal

by

_____

Butterflies

Butterfly Cards

Directions: Make multiple copies of the butterfly cards. Use with the Math Connections activity "All Sorts of Butterflies" on page 23 and with the Math Center activity "Butterfly Flowers" on page 26.

Butterfly Flowers

Directions: Make several cards of the flowers. Decorate them in several distinct patterns to match the Butterfly Picture Cards on page 28. Use with the Math Center activity "Butterfly Flowers" on page 26.

Overview

After studying "I—Insects," focus on "C—Caterpillars" and "B—Butterflies." Begin by reading *Clara Caterpillar* by Pamela Duncan Edwards (Harpercollins Publishers, 2001). Create a butterfly habitat and observe caterpillars as they turn into butterflies. Follow this unit with "B—Butterflies" or study both "B—Butterflies" and "C—Caterpillars" at the same time.

Caterpillars

Language Arts Connections

Core Book

Edwards, Pamela Duncan. *Clara Caterpillar*. Harpercollins Publishers, 2001.

Curled snuggly inside her egg case, Clara is encouraged to come out by fellow young caterpillars. She emerges and proceeds to chomp her way through cabbage, carrots, and cauliflower. As Clara and her friends cram themselves with leaves, they grow into big fat caterpillars. The young caterpillars eventually transform into butterflies, only to be threatened by a hungry crow. Clara saves the day, as only she can, and discovers that she is indeed contented and courageous.

The perfect letter **C** book, *Clara Caterpillar* is completely crammed with colorful /k/ words. Young readers love Clara's story, and selected it as one of the "Children's Choices for 2002" in the International Reading Association's Children's Choice project.

Read-Aloud Activities

Prior to Reading

- Ask the students what they know about caterpillars.
- Tell them that this book is about a caterpillar named Clara. Read the title and the author's name.

During Reading

- Speak slowly, so as to not become tongue twisted with all the /k/ words.
- Some of the vocabulary may be advanced for young listeners, but allow students to experience the story without pausing too often to explain words. During the Language Arts Connections, use the story as an opportunity to introduce new vocabulary.

After Reading

- Ask for student responses to the story. Ask, "What part did you like the best?" and "What characters in the story did you like, or which ones didn't you like?"
- Explain that this book was selected by a group of children as one of the best books of the year in 2002. Ask students if they think it deserved this honor.

Additional Books

Stock your class library with books about caterpillars. Students will enjoy looking at the illustrations and "reading" them to each other. When you read a story to your class, record yourself on tape. Then put the tape and the book in a literacy center so that your students can listen to it time and time again.

Carle, Eric. *The Very Hungry Caterpillar*. Philomel Books, 1987.

Deluise, Dom. *Charlie the Caterpillar*. Simon and Schuster, 1990.

French, Vivian. *Caterpillar, Caterpillar*. Candlewick Press, 1993.

Hall, Franklin. *Wings of Change*. Illumination Arts, 2001.

Heiligmann, Deborah. *From Caterpillar to Butterfly*. Harper Trophy, 1996.

Keller, Holly. *Farfallina & Marcel*. Greenwillow, 2002.

Laurence, Michael. *The Caterpillar That Roared*. DK Publishing, 2000.

Legg, Gerald. *From Caterpillar to Butterfly (Lifecycle)*. Orchard Books, 1998.

Caterpillars

Language Arts Connections (CONT.)

Letter-Sound Introduction

What is first sound of the words *caterpillar* and *Clara*? Emphasize the /k/ sound in caterpillar and Clara. Tell students that there are two letters, **k** and **c**, that make the sound /k/. In this unit, they will be learning more about **c**. The letter **c** also makes another sound, /s/, as in celery.

Phonemic Awareness

Skills: identifying /k/ sounds in words

Caterpillars Can Catch!

Make a copy for each student of the caterpillar on page 37. Have students color and cut out their caterpillars, and glue them onto craft sticks. Tell students that the book *Clara Caterpillar* had lots of /k/ words, written with the letter **c**. When they hear one of these **c** words while you are reading the book aloud, they can hold up their caterpillars to catch the word. Note: this activity can be combined with the vocabulary lesson, "Comprehending **C** Words."

Letter Formation

After reading *Clara Caterpillar* and introducing the letter-sound association, reinforce the association between **C** and the /k/ sound by drawing the **C** and **c** as the shapes of caterpillars crawling on leaves.

The following activities will help to reinforce letter formation for students of all learning styles.

- Have students "curve" their bodies or flexible objects (rubber bands, bendable rods) into **C** shapes.
- Use "coins" to trace the "curve" of the letter **c**.
- Make vegetable stamps out of carrots, cauliflower, cabbages, and cucumbers. Dip the vegetable stamps in paint to color in **C** and **c** drawn onto butcher or art paper.

Comprehending *C* Words

Clara Caterpillar is filled with alliteration, an important tool in the development of reading skills. It also contains vocabulary that may be unfamiliar to young readers. Use the book as an opportunity to build vocabulary skills and create foundations for comprehension. The process of defining the words will occur over the course of the week.

Skills: vocabulary, alliteration, phonemic awareness skills

Materials:

- a copy of *Clara Caterpillar*
- paper
- caterpillars on craft sticks from the Phonemic Awareness activity above
- poster board strips

Language Arts Connections (CONT.)

Comprehending C Words (CONT.)

Teacher Preparation:

1. Determine whether students will define vocabulary as a class activity or as a take-home activity to facilitate home-school connections.

2. Write "Confusing **C** Words" on one poster board strip. Draw a face next to the words with a frowning mouth.

3. Write "Clear **C** Words" on another poster board strip. Draw a happy face next to the words.

4. Post the two poster board strips next to each other on the board with tape, or put them on two sides of a pocket chart.

Procedure:

1. Tell students that *Clara Caterpillar* has many big words in it that they may not understand completely. Part of becoming a good reader is learning how to figure out what unfamiliar words mean.

2. Tell students that you are going to reread *Clara Caterpillar*. When they hear a **c** word that says /k/ they should hold up their caterpillar (see page 37).

3. Begin reading. When the students indicate that they hear a **c** word by holding up their caterpillars, stop reading.

4. Write the word down on a poster board strip.

5. Ask the students if they know what the word means. If students do not appear to understand the meaning of the word, post it under the category of "Confusing **C** Words." Explain that the word will be on the "confusing" sheet until everyone is clear about what it means.

6. If the students define a **C** word properly (such as *Clara* or *caterpillar*) post it under the category of "Clear **C** Words." Consider illustrating the word with a simple drawing or symbol.

7. Consider the following options for how to have students define the confusing words:

    a. Define the words as a class activity. Take one word at a time (perhaps as a fill-in activity throughout the day) and model defining the word. Encourage students to read the sentence for context clues, look at the pictures, look the word up in the dictionary, etc., to determine the meaning.

    b. Distribute the words to groups or pairs of students to define. Assist students with looking the words up in the dictionary and finding definitions. Students can draw pictures to illustrate the meaning, or write the definition, with assistance, in simple words and phrases.

    c. Distribute words for students to take home. Ask parents to assist their children in defining the words in simple phrases. Students can either illustrate the meaning or write the definition, with parental assistance, in simple words and phrases.

9. Once the students appear to understand the meaning of the word, move it to the "Clear **C** Words" category.

Caterpillars

Math Connections

The Caterpillar Game

Help the caterpillar munch through some leaves, and then it'll be ready to build its cocoon. In this game, students solve math problems or identify numbers, according to the math skills that they are currently learning. When they correctly complete a task, the caterpillar munches through that leaf, and continues down the path. When it gets through all the leaves, it is ready to build his cocoon.

Skills: variable, depending upon student needs: number identification, value, addition

Materials:

- "Caterpillar" and "Cocoon" (page 37)
- "Leaves" (page 38)

Teacher Preparation:

1. Copy the caterpillar and cocoon on page 37. Color and cut them out.
2. Copy the leaves on page 38 onto green paper. The number depends on the number of problems the students will solve. Optional: Laminate the leaves.
3. Write numbers or equations that reinforce math skills that the students are currently working on. For example, if the students are studying number value, write numerical digits (i.e., 5) or draw quantity symbols (five circles) on the leaves. If they are focusing on addition or subtraction, write equations on the leaves.
4. Place the leaves face down on a table, the floor, or stuck onto the chalkboard so that they create a path. At the beginning of the path, place the caterpillar. At the end, place the cocoon.

Procedure:

1. Direct the students to complete the tasks on the leaf cards. For example, if they are to read the number on the card, tell them to turn the first leaf card over, and read the number.
2. Select one student to go first. The student turns over the first card and completes the task. If the student does it correctly, he or she moves the caterpillar over the card, and removes the card from the path. If the response is incorrect, assist the student until he or she is able to complete the task.
3. Continue until all the leaves on the path have been removed.

Science Connections

From Caterpillar to Butterfly

Bring caterpillars and butterflies into the classroom so students can observe the metamorphosis for themselves. Create a butterfly habitat and observe caterpillars as they change into butterflies. Butterfly habitats are available via the Internet at web sites such as *www.insectlore.com*, or from teacher supply catalogs.

Visit a butterfly garden such as the one in the book *A Class Trip to Miss Hallberg's Butterfly Garden* by Gay Bishop Brorstrom (Pipevine Press, 2000). Or, after reading books about butterflies, have students discuss what types of habitats butterflies need in order to be happy and healthy.

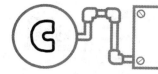

Caterpillars

Social Studies Connections

Every Living Thing is Beautiful

The theme in *Clara Caterpillar* is learning to appreciate diversity in physical appearance, personality, and so forth. Discuss this theme in the core books as well as when additional caterpillar-related books are read in class, and work with the students to create an environment that embraces diversity with tolerance and acceptance.

Art Connections

Caterpillar Sock Toy

Make a caterpillar toy out of single socks. Add optional wings to transform the caterpillar into a butterfly.

Materials:

- one sock per student
- chenille stem ties
- newspaper or something to be used as stuffing
- yarn and needle (with large hole to accommodate yarn)
- optional: tissue paper
- googly eyes
- paint
- glue gun (for adult use only)

Teacher Preparation:

1. Ask parents to send in clean socks. The socks should be calf high or longer.

Procedure:

1. Have students stuff the sock with stuffing material.
2. Use the glue gun or needle and yarn to close the open end of the socks.
3. Have the students decorate the body of the caterpillar with paint and allow to dry.
4. Glue on wiggly eyes and chenille stems for antennae.
5. Optional: Make tissue paper wings and have an adult glue gun these onto the caterpillar. To do so, make a wing outline out of chenille stems. Cut tissue paper in the shape of the outline. Glue gun onto the chenille stems.

Music, Movement, Rhythm, and Rhyme

Caterpillar Dance

by Mary Ramming Chappell

Caterpillar crawling on my finger,
Moving along, not stopping to linger.
Creeping slowly in the plants,
In a crunching, munching, eating dance.
Working hard by the light of the moon,
Getting ready to build your cocoon.
Sleeping soundly, changing, growing,
What you'll be we'll soon be knowing.

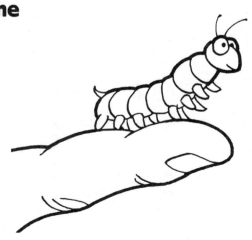

Music, Movement, Rhythm, and Rhyme (CONT.)

A Caterpillar's Life

Act out the stages of a caterpillar's life. Brainstorm these stages with the students after studying the life cycle of a caterpillar, including the metamorphosis into a butterfly, and then have the students determine ways in which to act out the stages.

Caterpillar Crawl

Form a caterpillar chain, creeping and crawling through the grass. Have students get on their knees in a straight line (from shortest to tallest). Then have them put their hands on the waist of the student before them, and slowly begin the caterpillar crawl.

Centers

Set up centers to encourage students to explore the theme further during a free choice period, or assign small groups to parent-guided centers while you work with other students.

Math Center

Skills: problem solving, attention to details

A-Maze-ing Caterpillars

Copy the maze on page 39. Have students figure out which path will take the caterpillar to the food. Then have students create their own mazes to be solved.

Snacks

Be sure to check with parents about allergies before serving students any food.

Hungry Caterpillar

After a reading of *The Very Hungry Caterpillar* by Eric Carle (Philomel Books, 1987), set out some of the foods that the caterpillar ate. Discuss which foods were healthy choices and which were not.

Ingredients:

- apples
- pears
- plums
- strawberries
- optional: salami and sausage

- oranges
- pickles
- Swiss cheese
- watermelon

Directions:

1. Slice foods into serving size pieces. Have the students sample the snacks during a reading of *The Very Hungry Caterpillar*.

Caterpillar

Directions: Copy, color and cut out the caterpillar for "Caterpillars Can Catch" on page 32 and "The Caterpillar Game" on page 34.

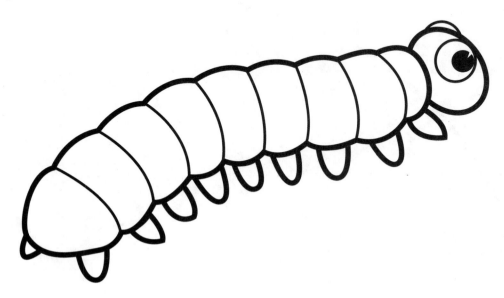

Cocoon

Directions: Copy, color and cut the cocoon for "The Caterpillar Game" on page 34.

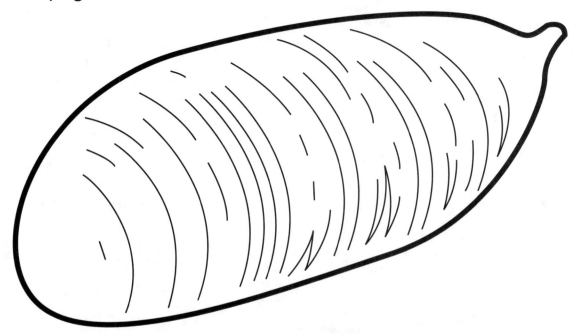

Leaves

Directions: Copy, color and cut the leaves for "The Caterpillar Game" on page 34.

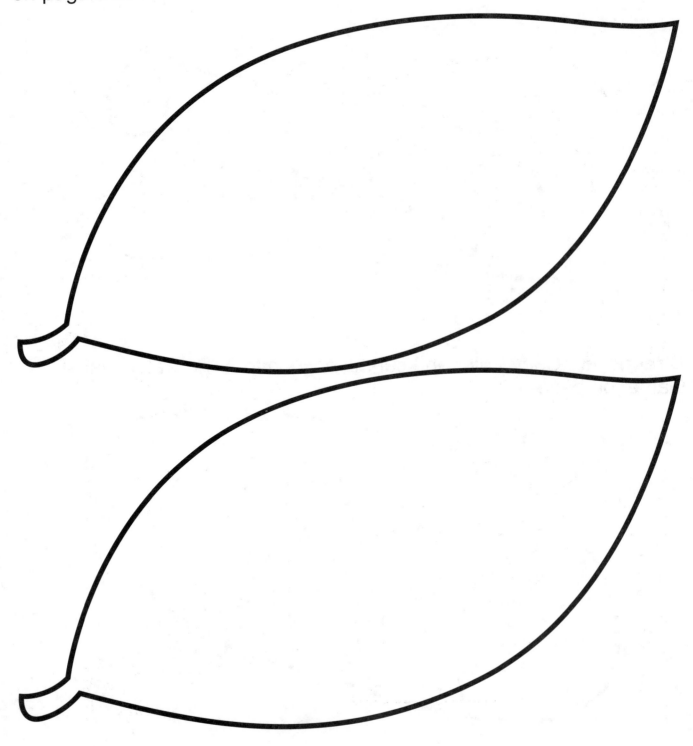

A-Maze-ing Caterpillars

Directions: Use with the Math Center activity on page 36. Help the caterpillar find his way to his food.

Dogs

Overview

Introduce the letter **D** with a study of dogs, beginning with P.D. Eastman's classic book, *Go, Dog. Go!* (Beginner Books, 1961). Identify words rhyming with dog to build phonemic awareness skills, make a rebus book, use a bar graph in the math activity, and make dog sock puppets.

This unit can be used in the extended farm unit, with "P—Pigs," "F—Farm," and "X—Fox."

 **Dogs**

Language Arts Connections

Core Book

Eastman, Philip D. *Go, Dog. Go!* Beginner Books, 1961.

Dogs, dogs, dogs! Dogs are everywhere and doing everything in this Dr. Seuss-inspired book. The illustrations are colorful, fun, and imaginative, and the text is a great tool for teaching colors, prepositions, and sizes.

Read-Aloud Activities

Prior to Reading

- Read the title, pointing to the words as you read.
- Read the author's and illustrator's names. Point out that this book has a "Cat in the Hat" symbol, just like Dr. Seuss books. Dr. Seuss did not write this book, but this author, P.D. Eastman and Dr. Seuss, wrote a book together, called *The Cat in the Hat Beginner Book Dictionary*. The same company that published Dr. Seuss' books published this book.

During Reading

- Be expressive, and remember to slow down. There are many things happening in the pictures in this story, so allow time to look at the illustrations.

After Reading

- Ask for student responses to the story. For example, ask, "What was your favorite part of this book?" Students can share their responses with the whole group or with a partner.
- Suggest a variety of ways to respond to the core book. For example, students can draw a picture of their favorite scenes, role play characters, or use music to express their reactions.

Additional Books

Stock your class library with books about dogs. Students will enjoy looking at the illustrations and "reading" them to each other. When you read a story to your class, record yourself on tape. Then put the tape and the book in a literacy center so that your students can listen to it time and time again.

Barner, Bob. *Walk the Dog.* Chronicle Books, 2000.

Boynton, Sandra. *Doggies.* Little Simon, 1995.

Brett, Jan. *The First Dog.* Harcourt, 1988.

Day, Alexandra. *Good Dog, Carl.* Green Tiger Press, 1985.

Freymann, Saxton and Elffers, Joost. *Dog Food.* Arthur A. Levine, 2002.

Frith, Michael. *I'll Teach My Dog 100 Words.* Random House, 1973.

Oram, Hjawyn. *Just Dog.* Scholastic, 1999.

Simont, Marc. *The Stray Dog.* Harpercollins, 2001.

Sis, Peter. *Madlenka's Dog.* Frances Foster Books, 2002.

Stevens, Janet. *My Big Dog.* Golden Books, 1999.

Zion, Gene. *Harry the Dirty Dog.* Harpercollins, 1956.

Language Arts Connections (CONT.)

Letter-Sound Introduction

What is first sound of the word *dog*? Say *dog* slowly and deliberately, emphasizing the /d/ sound. Tell students that the letter **d** makes the sound /d/. Note: Take care to say /d/, not /duh/.

Phonemic Awareness

Go, Dog!

Help the dog get to his bone by identifying words rhyming with dog.

Skills: hearing and identifying similar word patterns.

Materials:

- "Go, Dog!" activity sheets (pages 47–50)
- glue
- 4 squares of paper (approximately 3") for each pair of students
- craft sticks
- markers and/or crayons

Teacher Preparation:

1. For each pair of students, make copies of the "Go, Dog!" activity sheets and "Go, Dog!" word cards on pages 47–50.
2. Group students in pairs.

Student Preparation.

1. Color the Stop sign red and the Go sign green,
2. Glue the Stop and Go signs back to back on a craft stick.
3. Color and cut out the dog figure and his bone.
4. Cut out the "Go, Dog" word cards, shuffle them, and put them face down on the table. You may wish to show the cards to the students first to familiarize them with the words.
5. Put the dog on the left side of the playing area, the bone on the right, and the squares in a line in between the dog and his bone.

Game Directions:

1. The first student selects a word card.
2. If the picture represents a word that rhymes with dog, the second student holds up the Go sign and moves the dog to the first square. If it does not rhyme with dog, the second student holds up the Stop sign. The dog is not moved.
4. The second student selects a card while the first student holds up the sign.
5. The game continues until the dog has reached his bone.

Follow-up:

1. After all the pairs of students have completed the game, go through the word cards as a class. Tape a green Go sign on one side of a piece of butcher paper or the chalkboard, and tape a red Stop sign on the other side.
2. Hold up each word card. If the word rhymes with dog, put it under the Go sign. If it does not rhyme, put it under the Stop sign.

Language Arts Connections (CONT.)

Letter Formation

After reading *Go, Dog. Go!* by P. D. Eastman, reinforce the association between the letters **D** and **d** and /d/ by drawing the letter shapes into a picture of a dog.

These activities will help to reinforce letter formation for students of all learning styles.

- Provide a variety of different shapes: lines, circles, ovals, rectangles, and squares. Which shapes can be used to form the letters **D** and **d**?

- Have students look at the letters of the alphabet and pick out letters that look like **D** and **d**, such as **B**, **b**, **P**, **p**, **a**, **g**, and **q**. Next brainstorm ways that these letters look alike and different. Then, brainstorm ways in which students can remember which letter is which. For example, **b** and **d** look similar, except that one circle faces left and one faces right. When put together, the circles face each other, but only if **b** comes first. Remind students that **b** always comes first in the alphabet.

Where, Oh Where, Has My Little Dog Gone?

Practice using prepositions by making a booklet that answers the question, "Where, oh where, has my little dog gone?"

Skills: prepositions, sight word identification, rebus pictures cues

Materials:

- "Where, Oh Where?" book cover, sentence strips and pictures (pages 51-54)
- seven sheets of paper for each student
- optional: poster board strips and pocket chart.

Teacher Preparation:

1. Make one copy of "Where, Oh Where?" book cover and sentence strips and pictures for each student. Cut out the sentence strips and the pictures.
2. Assemble the materials so that the sentence strips are in order, but the pictures are not. Complete each packet by adding six sheets of paper.
3. Optional: Write the booklet phrases on poster board strips and display in the pocket chart. Make copies of the illustrations to use on the pocket chart.

Procedure:

1. Distribute a "Where, Oh Where?" packet to each student. Read the poem, "Where, Oh Where?" Have students use their index fingers to follow along.
2. Tell students that they will find out exactly where the little dog went in the booklet they will assemble.
3. Have students color the illustrations and write their names on the booklet covers of their booklets.
4. Have students find the first phrase of the booklet, "He crawled under the fence," by finding the rebus picture of the fence. Point to each word on the pocket chart strip. Students use their index fingers to point to each word on the strip.
5. Ask students which illustration goes with the first phrase. Have them find the illustration of the dog crawling under the fence.

Language Arts Connections (CONT.)

Where, Oh Where, Has My Little Dog Gone? (CONT.)

6. Have students glue the first phrase and the matching illustration onto one of the half sheet of paper.

7. Continue matching the remaining sentence strips and illustrations.

8. When complete, allow pages to dry thoroughly, then assemble.

Math Connections

What Kind of Pet?

Poll students about pets they have at home. Display results on a bar graph.

Skills: counting, comparing numbers, bar graphing

Materials:

- butcher paper
- markers
- pictures of common pets: dog, cat, hamster, fish, bird, etc.
- picture of a plant

Teacher Preparation:

1. Make the bar graph by drawing a grid with the words "Number of Students" on the vertical left, and the words "Type of the Pet" at the top.

2. Write common pet types at the top of each column, and put the corresponding picture next to each one.

Procedure:

1. Tell students that many people have pets in their homes. Some people do not have pets, due to allergies or other reasons, and instead have plants or other things that they care for.

2. Take a poll of the types of pets that students have.

3. For each type of pet, color a square on the bar graph, indicating the number of students who have that pet. Students can raise their hands more than once if they have more than one type of pet. Be sure to also poll for non-pets, such as plants, so that no students are excluded.

4. Compare the results of the bar graph.

Science Connections

All About Dogs

Discuss what all dogs have in common (fur, warm-blooded, give birth to live pups, provide milk for pups) and identify dogs as mammals (versus fish or reptiles). Talk about what dogs need in order to be happy and healthy: food and water, a safe and warm place to live and sleep, attention, and regular visits to the animal doctor, or veterinarian.

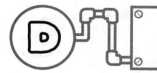

Dogs

Social Studies Connections

Dogs of a Different Color

The dogs in *Go, Dog, Go!* symbolize the diversity children find in the world: green dogs, yellow dogs, big dogs, little dogs, dogs who prefer cars, and dogs who favor skis. Talk about differences between people. What makes us the same? What makes us different?

Art Connections

Dog Sock Puppets

Make dogs out of socks, and customize them with different ears, eyes, and noses.

Materials:

- socks
- buttons
- felt
- materials that could be used for tails, ears, etc. (e.g., yarn, fabric)
- glue (glue gun recommended, for adult use only)
- permanent marker

Teacher Preparation:

1. Ask parents to send in clean, old socks and buttons.
2. Cut felt into different shapes for ears.
3. Arrange for a parent volunteer or assistant to use the glue gun.

Procedure:

1. Students select the materials they would like to use for their dog puppets: buttons for eyes and noses, felt for ears, etc.
2. Have an adult glue the materials in place with the glue gun.
3. Students draw a mouth onto the puppet with a permanent marker.

Music, Movement, Rhythm and Rhyme

Bow Wow, Says the Dog

Bow, wow, says the dog,

Mew, mew, says the cat,

Grunt, grunt goes the hog,

And squeak goes the rat.

Hoo, hoo says the owl,

Caw, caw, says the crow,

Quack, quack, says the duck,

And what cuckoos say you know.

Old Mother Hubbard

Old Mother Hubbard,

She went to the cupboard,

To fetch her poor dog a bone.

But when she got there,

The cupboard was bare,

And so the poor dog had none.

 **Dogs**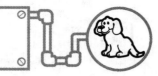

Centers

Set up centers to encourage students to explore the theme further during a free choice period, or assign small groups to parent-guided centers while you work with other students.

Math Center

Skills: sorting, counting

All Sorts of Dogs

Collect pictures of different types of dogs; dog magazines are a good resource. Students sort the pictures into different categories: smooth, fluffy, short, small, large, etc. After sorting the pictures, students glue them onto paper that can be labeled with the category. Encourage students to spell each category, or list category headings so students can copy them.

Snacks

Be sure to check with parents about allergies before serving students any food.

"Dog Biscuit" Sugar Cookies

Forgo the dog food and settle for some doggie biscuit shaped cookies! Make sugar cookie dough as a center activity, and then bake. Serve during a "dog party."

Ingredients/Materials:

- ⅓ cup butter or margarine, softened
- ⅓ cup shortening
- ¾ cup sugar
- 1 teaspoon baking powder
- pinch salt
- 1 egg
- 1 teaspoon vanilla
- 2 cups all-purpose flour
- granulated sugar, colored if desired
- dog bone-shaped cookie cutters
- cookie sheets
- oven (toaster ovens are not recommended)

Directions:

1. Beat butter and shortening thoroughly.
2. Add sugar, baking powder and a pinch of salt and mix until well combined.
3. Beat in egg and vanilla. Stir in flour.
4. Cover and chill for at least one hour.
5. Roll the dough and cut dog-bone shapes with cookie cutters.
6. Bake at 325° on cookie sheets (do not grease) for 7 to 8 minutes, or until the edges are lightly browned.

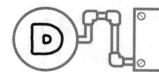 

"Go, Dog!" Game

Directions: Color the Stop sign red and and the Go sign green. Cut out the signs. Glue them back-to-back onto a craft stick. Use the signs, the dog, the game, and the word cards on pages 48-50 with the Phonemic Awareness lesson on page 42.

"Go, Dog!" Game (CONT.)

Directions: Color and cut out the dog and bone. Glue them back-to-back onto a craft stick. Use with Stop and Go signs, the dog, the game, and the word cards on pages 48–50 with the Phonemic Awareness lesson on page 42.

"Go, Dog!" Word Cards

Directions: Copy and cut out each word card. Use with the stop and go signs and the dog and bone on pages 47-48 and additional word cards on page 50. Use all with the Phonemic Awareness lesson on page 42.

frog

log

fog

hog

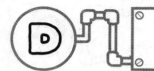 
"Go, Dog!" Word Cards (CONT.)

Directions: Copy and cut out each word card. Use with the stop and go signs and the dog and bone on pages 47-48 and additional word cards on page 49. Use all with the Phonemic Awareness lesson on page 42.

cat

sock

door

doll

"Where, Oh Where?" Booklet Sentence Strips

Directions: Copy booklet. Cut sentences into strips and match with corresponding illustrations. Glue sentence strips and illustrations onto sheets of paper, and assemble into booklets.

He crawled under the fence.

He ran across the lawn.

He walked around the sprinkler.

He jumped over the puddle.

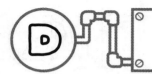 
"Where, Oh Where?" Booklet Sentence Strips (CONT.)

He squeezed between the bushes.

And then he came through the front door! Home at last!

"Where, Oh Where?" Booklet Pictures

"Where, Oh Where?" Booklet Pictures (CONT.)

"Where, Oh Where!" Booklet Cover

Where, Oh Where?

Oh where, oh where has my little dog gone?

Oh where, oh where can he be?

With his ear cut short, and his tail cut long.

Oh where, oh where can he be?

54

©Teacher Created Materials, Inc.

Elephant

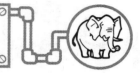

Overview

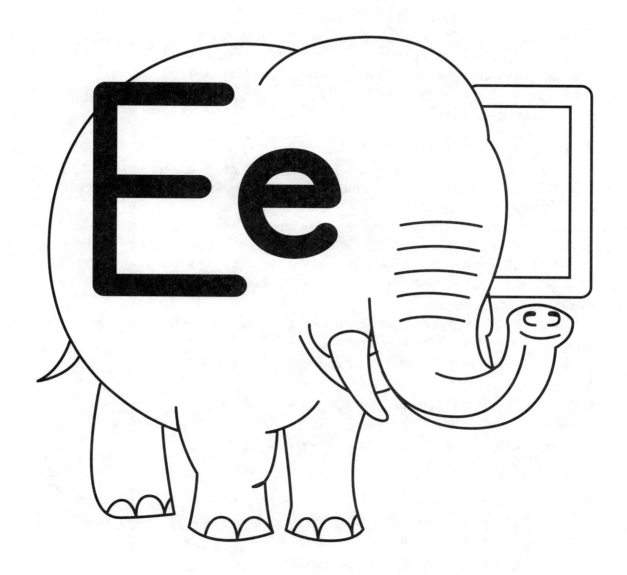

Introduce the letter **E** and its sounds with a study of elephants. Read elephant stories, such as *Horton Hatches the Egg*, by Dr. Seuss (Random House, 1966). Then make elephant head masks, integrate math and language arts with an elephant counting song, and learn about African and Asian elephants. Include "E—Elephants" in a Zoo unit with "Z—Zoo" and "G—Gorilla."

Elephant

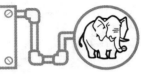

Language Arts Connections

Core Book

Dr. Seuss. *Horton Hatches the Egg*. Random House, 1966.

Poor Horton, the elephant. Mayzie the lazy bird has duped him into sitting on her egg while she flies off for a vacation. Devoted Horton perches on a teetering tree, where he withstands wind, rain, snow, and even teasing. To make matters worse, three hunters capture Horton and ship him off, egg and all, to a circus. Just as the egg is hatching, who should drop in but Mayzie, ready to take back her egg!

Read-Aloud Activities

Prior to Reading

- Read the title, *Horton Hatches the Egg*, pointing at the words as you read. Read the author's name, Dr. Seuss. Remind students of other Dr. Seuss books that you have read in class or that students may have read.
- Ask students to predict what they think the story might be about based on the title and cover illustrations. Ask students how they think an elephant is going to manage to hatch an egg? Do elephants lay eggs? Move into reading the story by saying, "Let's find out just how this elephant hatches an egg."

During Reading

- As you read, make sure that each student can see the illustrations. Hold the book that it is facing the students, and turn it slowly as you read.
- Be expressive. Use one voice for Mayzie and another for Horton.

After Reading

- Provide students with three choices for how to describe their favorite scene from story: draw a picture of the scene, retell it verbally to another student, or act it out with another student.
- Ask students what they would say to Mayzie if they were Horton.

Additional Books

Stock your class library with books about elephants. Students will enjoy looking at the illustrations and "reading" them to each other. When you read a story to your class, record yourself on tape. Then put the tape and the book in a literacy center so that your students can listen to it time and time again.

Dr. Seuss. *Horton Hears a Who*. Random House, 1954.

James, Ellen Foley. *Growing Up in Africa's Elephant Kingdom*. Sterling Publications, 1998.

Meeker, Clare Hodgson. *Hansa: The True Story of an Asian Elephant Baby*. Sasquatch Books, 2002.

McKee, David. *Elmer*. Lothrup, Lee and Shepard, 1989.

Peet, Bill. *The Ant and the Elephant*. Hougthon Mifflin, 1972

Pitau, Francisco and Gervais, Bernadette. *Elephant Elephant: A Book of Opposites*.
   Abrams Books, 2001.

Radcliffe, Theresa. *Bashi, Elephant Baby*. Puffin, 2001.

Thomas, Patricia. *"Stand Back," Said the Elephant, "I'm Going to Sneeze."*
   Lothrup, Lee and Shepard, 1990.

 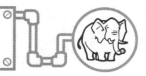
Language Arts Connections *(CONT.)*

Letter-Sound Introduction

What is first sound of the word *elephant* or *egg*? As you say *elephant* and *egg* emphasizing the /e/ sound. Tell students that the letter **e** makes the sound /ĕ/ as in *pet* and the sound /ē/ as in *emu*.

Phonemic Awareness

Skill: syllable counting

Drumming to the Beats

Make a drum out of an empty instant oatmeal cylinder or an empty coffee can with a plastic lid. Make a drum stick by swaddling cotton onto the end of a craft stick with tape. Cut out magazine pictures of zoo animals (elephant, giraffe, lion, tiger, bear, penguin, etc.). On squares of construction paper, draw pictures of one drum stick, two drum sticks, three drum sticks, and four drum sticks (if you have any pictures of animals with four syllables, such as an armadillo). Tape these squares to a wall or chalkboard.

Hold up a picture of an elephant. Say "The word *elephant* has three beats: *el–e–phant*." Beat your "drum" three times as you say *el-e-phant* again. Tape the picture of the elephant under the "three drum sticks" square of paper. After modeling the activity, invite students to select pictures of animals, beat the beats on the drum, and post the picture under the corresponding number of drum beats on the correct square.

Letter Formation

After reading *Horton Hatches the Egg* by Dr. Seuss, and after introducing the letter-sound association, reinforce the association by drawing the shapes of **E** and **e** into pictures of elephants.

These activities will help to reinforce letter formation for students of all learning styles.

- Crush eggshells (cleaned and dried) and put them in container. Students use the eggshells to glue the shapes of **E** or **e** on construction paper.

- In pairs, have students play the game, "I'm thinking of a letter." The first student closes his or her eyes, or turns so he or she is not facing the second student. The second student picks a magnetic letter out of a bag and does not show it to the first student. The second student says, for example, "I'm thinking of a letter. It has four lines. One line goes straight up and down, and the other three lines go across." This activity takes some practice, so you may need to model it first.

- Have the students use line shapes (craft sticks) to form **E** and circular shapes (rubber band pieces) to form **e**.

 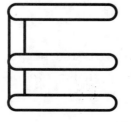 

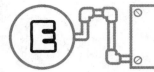 **Elephant**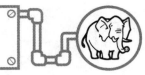

Language Arts Connections (CONT.)

Big, Gray Elephants

Introduce the use of descriptive words and phrases as students write about elephant characteristics.

Skills: using describing words, writing

Materials:

- elephant picture (page 62)
- pencils, crayons or markers
- non-fiction elephant books (see page 56 for recommendations)
- large piece of butcher paper (optional: cut paper in an elephant shape)

Teacher Preparation:

1. Make a copy of the elephant picture for each student.

Procedure:

1. Read non-fiction books about elephants such as *Little Bull, Growing Up in Africa's Elephant Kingdom* by Ellen Foley James (Sterling Publications, 1998) or *Hansa: The True Story of an Asian Elephant Baby* by Clare Hodgson Meeker (Sasquatch Books, 2002).
2. After reading books, ask students to describe elephants. Prompt responses with questions such as, "What do they look like?" "What color are they?"
3. Record these brainstormed descriptive words and phrases on the butcher paper.
4. Have students write at least one describing word on the elephant picture, followed by the word *elephant* (e.g., big elephant).
5. Discuss how to sound out the letters of the describing word by segmenting the phonemes (big: /b/ /i/ /g/). Also remind the students that they can look at the list of brainstormed words to help them spell the describing words.
6. Model the correct spelling of the word by writing it under the students' spelling.
7. Display the elephants with tails and trunks linked together.

Math Connections

The Elephant March

Have students practice adding one as they create a long line of marching elephants.

Skills: number sequencing, adding one

Materials:

- "The Elephant March" chant (page 60).
- Elephant Picture (page 61) or Elephant Headdress Mask (pages 62-63)
- crayons or markers

Teacher Preparation:

1. Make a copy of an elephant for each student or have students make the elephant head dress ears.
2. Write the words to "The Elephant March" on the chalkboard, on poster board strips, or on butcher paper.

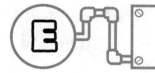 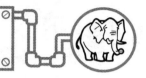

Math Connections (CONT.)

The Elephant March (CONT.)

Procedure:

1. Have students color and cut out their elephant pictures, if used.

2. Have one student hold his or her elephant while standing before the class.

3. Read "The Elephant March" to students, pointing at each word as you read.

3. After the last line, "Now there's one elephant—plus one," ask, "How many elephants are there now?" Invite a second student to come to the front, and begin, "Two little elephants marching along…."

4. Continue adding elephants.

Science and Social Studies Connections

Asian and African Elephants

Elephants are either Asian or African. See what you discover about these two types of elephants via the Internet, an expert on elephants (such as a zookeeper), or non-fiction books about elephants (see additional books for recommendations). Have your students come up with a list of questions about elephants, such as "How are Asian and African elephants alike and how are they different?" "Where do they live?" "What do they like to eat?"

Among some of the facts that you may discover:

1. The African elephant lives in central Africa.

2. The Asian elephant lives in India, Indochina, Indonesia, Malaysia, and South China. (Be sure to pull out a globe and find out where these places are.)

3. The African elephant is larger and has larger ears than the Asian elephant.

Art Connections

Elephant Headdress

With this elephant headdress, your students can imagine that they are a herd of elephants on an African savannah or in the jungles of Asia.

Materials (per student):

- 3 toilet paper rolls
- yarn or string
- single paper hole punch
- gray paint

- thin cardboard or heavy craft paper
- 2 ½" x 12" strips of heavy paper
- stapler and staples, glue, or tape

Teacher Preparation:

1. Copy the elephant ears on pages 63–64 onto white paper and cut out. Then trace ears onto cardboard or heavy craft paper and cut out. Note: You will use this as a template, so you may want to make one or two for every group of students.

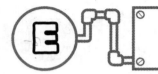
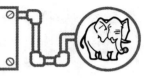
Art Connections *(CONT.)*

Elephant Headdress *(CONT.)*

Procedure:

1. Make the trunk:

   a. Punch one hole at the end of one toilet paper role.

   b. Tie on one 18" piece of string or yarn.

   c. Run the string through the remaining toilet paper rolls.

   d. Punch a hole at the end of the last toilet paper role.

   e. Tie the string off to hold the toilet paper roles together.

   f. Punch two holes into the sides of the last toilet paper role.

   g. Tie two pieces of yarn (12" each) on the role, one in each hole.

   h. Use the string to tie the trunk on to the student's head.

2. Make the head and ears:

   a. Have each student trace the ear templates onto two pieces of cardboard or craft paper and then cut out the ears.

   b. Make a headband for each student with a strip of paper with ends stapled, glued, or taped together.

   c. Attach the ears onto the headband by folding the tab so that it lies against the headband, and affix them with staples, glue, or tape.

3. Paint gray and allow to dry.

Music, Movement, Rhythm, and Rhyme

The Elephant March
by Mary Ramming Chappell

One little elephant marching along,
Swinging his tail and singing a song.
Here comes another to join in the fun.
Now there's one elephant—plus one!
Two little elephants marching along,
Swinging their tails and singing a song.
Here comes another to join in the fun.
Now there's two elephants—plus one!

Elephant Snack
by Barbara Knarr Ramming

When an elephant wants a snack,
She opens up her pack.
She finds apples to eat,
And pears that are sweet,
Bananas of yellow,
And fluffy marshmallow,
(But salty peanuts are still her favorite!)

 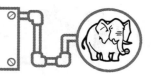

Music, Movement, Rhythm, and Rhyme (CONT.)

March Like Elephants

Have the students wear the elephant headdress masks (pages 62-63) and march around, hands linked, chanting "The Elephant March" on page 61.

Centers

Set up centers to encourage students to explore the theme further during a free choice period, or assign small groups to parent-guided centers while you work with other students.

Problem Solving Center

Skills: problem solving, fine motor skill coordination, colors

The Elephant's Trunk

Elephants do not suck water through their trunks like a straw, but they do use them to hold water. Challenge students to figure out how to use a straw to make green water.

Put out three paper cups, one empty, one partially filled with yellow water and one partially filled with blue water. (Color the water with food coloring or a small amount of tempera paint.) Also provide several tools: a pencil or crayon, a fork, and a straw (do not include a spoon, as the students could use it to scoop water). Tell the students that they need to make green water in the empty cup with water from the blue and yellow cups, but they cannot pick up or move the cups in any way or put anything in their mouths. The trick is to submerge the tip of a straw into the water, plug the exposed end, then raise the bottom end to opening of the empty cup, and let finger go.

Snacks

Be sure to check with parents about allergies before serving students any food.

Haystacks

The elephant's food of choice is grass and hay. Kids cannot eat hay, but they will love these sweet haystacks. **Note:** Check for food allergies.

Ingredients:
- 1 (11 oz.) package butterscotch chips
- ¾ cup creamy peanut butter or peanuts
- 2 (5 oz.) cans chow mein noodles

Directions:
1. Melt chips in double boiler until smooth.
2. Stir in peanut butter (or peanuts) until smooth.
3 Add noodles.
4. Drop by spoonfuls on foil or wax paper and chill.

 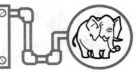
Elephant Picture

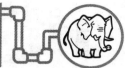

Elephant Headdress Ears

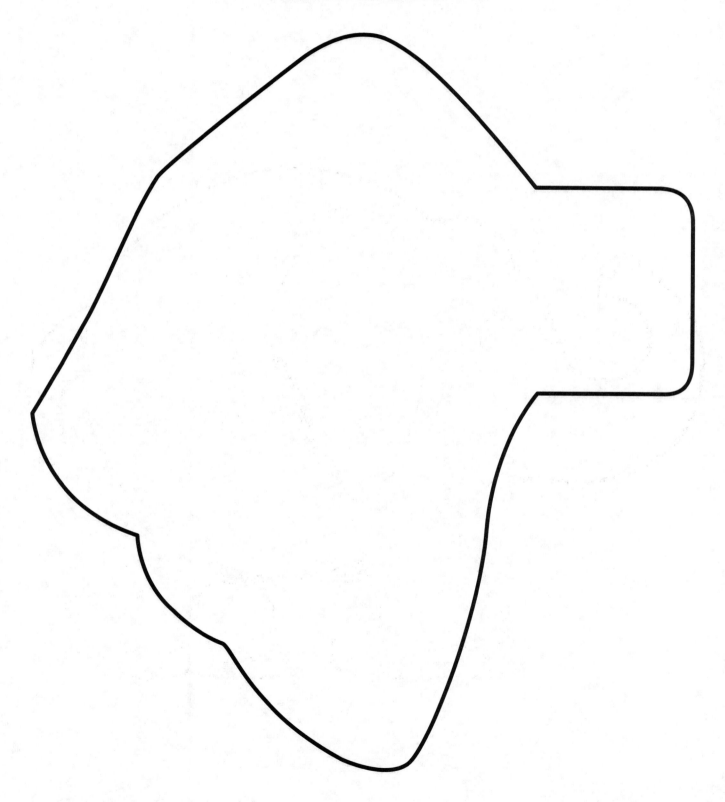

 # Elephant

Elephant Headdress Ears

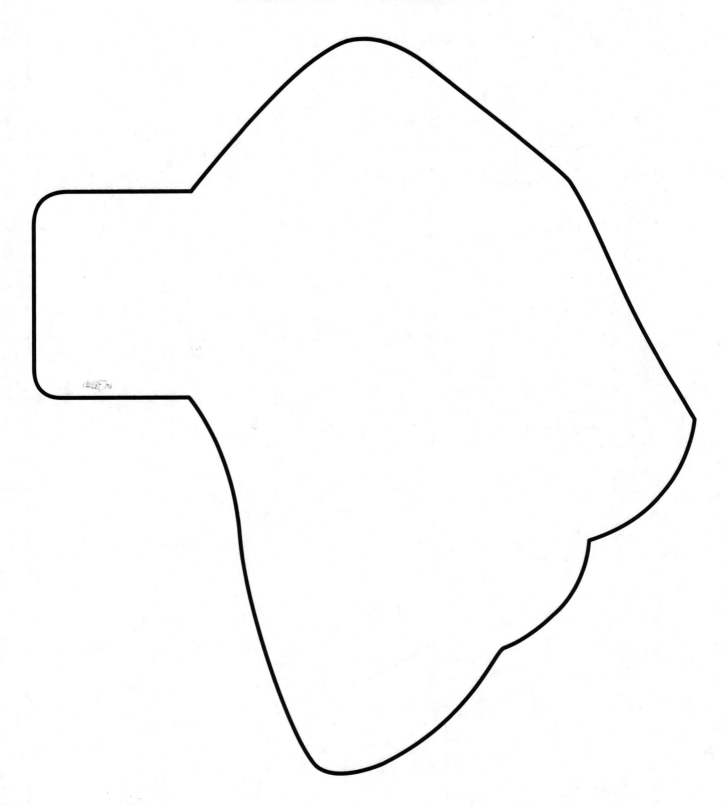

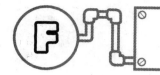 

Overview

It's farm time in the classroom! Explore the barnyard through picture books, such as the Caldecott award-winner *Click, Clack, Moo: Cows that Type* by Doreen Cronin (Simon and Schuster, 2000). Integrate language arts with phonemic awareness activities, a rebus rhyme, and other language building activities. Count Hickety Pickety's eggs in a math lesson, and use geometric shapes to create farm animal pictures for a culminating art activity. Expand this unit by including "P—Pigs," "F—Fox," and "D—Dog."

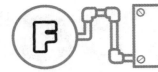

Farm

Language Arts Connections

Core Book

Cronin, Doreen. *Click, Clack, Moo: Cows That Type*. Simon and Schuster, 2000.

Farmer Brown's problems begin when the typing cows send him letters requesting blankets to keep them warm at night. When he doesn't give in to their demands, the cows go on strike, refusing to give milk.

Read-Aloud Activities

Prior to Reading

- Read the title, *Click, Clack, Moo: Cows That Type*, pointing to the words as you read. Read the author's and illustrator's names, too.
- Mention that this book was given the Caldecott Honor award for being one of the best picture books of 2000.
- Point out the illustrations on the front and back covers. Ask students to make story predictions based on the title and cover illustrations.

During Reading

- Point to illustrations and words as you read, making sure that each student can see the hilarious pictures.
- Be expressive. For example, when reading the word "moo," moo!
- Pause occasionally to create suspense, to ask for predictions, and discuss what is happening.

After Reading

- Ask students to imagine what a farm like this, with cows that type, would be like.
- Show students the second book by Doreen Cronin, *Giggle, Giggle, Quack*, and explain that it is a sequel to the *Click, Clack, Moo*. Ask if students know what a sequel is, and explain that it is the next part of the story.

Additional Books

Stock your class library with books about farms. Students will enjoy looking at the illustrations and "reading" them to each other. When you read a story to your class, record yourself on tape. Then put the tape and the book in a literacy center so that your students can listen to it time and time again.

Aliki. *From Cow to Carton*. Harpercollins, 1992.

Brett, Jan. *Daisy Comes Home*. Putnam Publishing Group, 2002.

Brown , Margaret Wise. *The Big Red Barn*. Harper Collins, 1956.

Capucilli, Alyssa Satin. *Inside a Barn in the Country*. Scholastic, 1995.

Cronin, Doreen. *Giggle, Giggle, Quack*. Simon and Schuster, 2002.

Ehlert , Lois. *Color Farm*. Harper Festival, 1990.

Gibbons, Gail. *The Milk Makers*. Aladdin Library, 1987.

Gibbons, Gail. *Farming*. Holiday House, 1988.

Hutchins, Pat. *Rosie's Walk*. Simon and Schuster, 1968.

Martin, Bill and Archambault, John. *Barn Dance*. Henry Holt and Company, 1986.

Provensen, Alice and Martin. *The Year at Maple Hill Farm*. Aladdin Library, 2001.

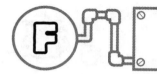

Farm

Language Arts Connections (CONT.)

Letter-Sound Introduction

What is first sound of the word *farm*? Say *farm* slowly and deliberately, emphasizing the /f/ sound. Tell students that the letter **f** makes the sound /f/.

/F/ is known as a "lip biter sound" because the top teeth gently bite the lower lip. Your students should be able to feel their throat vibrate if they place their hand against their neck. It is a "motor off" or "quiet" sound, because the vocal cords do not vibrate when producing this sound. The formation of the lips and teeth are in the same position as the /v/ sound, except that /v/ is a "motor on" sound; the throat vibrates when producing /v/.

Phonemic Awareness

Skills: phoneme blending and segmenting

Farm Time Phonemes

Segment the names of farm animals, and have your students put them back together again to practice blending phonemes. Say, "I'm thinking of a place where animals live. This place is a /f/ /ar/ /m/. What is it?" (Farm.) Next, say, "I'm thinking of an animal that lives on a /f/ /ar/ /m/. It is a /p/ /i/ /g/. What is it? Continue segmenting words into phonemes with other farm animal names. Then sing, "Old MacDonald Had a /F/ /ar/ /m/." Instead of saying the names of the animals, have the student segment them. For example, "And on this /f/ /ar/ /m/ he had a /p/ /i/ /g/." Suggestion: decide ahead of time the order of the animals, and identify the animal visually (by pointing at a picture of that animal) when the time comes to sing that verse.

Letter Formation

After reading the core book and introducing the letter-sound association, reinforce the association between **F** and **f** and the sound /f/ by drawing the **F** and **f** into the shapes of a farm with a barn, farm animals, and fields of wheat.

These activities will help to reinforce letter formation for students of all learning styles.

- Cut the **F** and **f** letter shapes out of fluffy or furry textures, such as felt, cotton batting, or fake fur. Students close their eyes and try to identify the letter shapes by feel, or look at the letter shape as they feel it.

- Draw **F** onto pieces of butcher paper. Students glue furry and fluffy objects and pieces of material on to the letter shape.

- Put magnetic letters with similar shapes (**F, f, E, L, l, T, t**) into a paper bag stapled shut or a closed box with a hole its side. Students reach in and feel each letter. They say its name, its sound, and then pull it from the box or bag to check their answer.

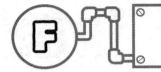

Farm

Rebus Farm Rhymes

In rebus stories, some words in the text are represented by symbols and pictures. Create a rebus rhyme using farm animal pictures in a traditional farm nursery rhyme.

Skills: tracking, sight word identification

Materials:

- "Farm Time Pictures" (pages 73–77) or "Nursery Rhyme Characters" (pages 173–179)
- pointer
- poster board strips and pocket chart
- glue

Teacher Preparation:

1. Select a farm theme nursery rhyme, such as "Old MacDonald Had a Farm."
2. Write the nursery rhyme on strips of poster board for a pocket chart.
3. In place of key words, insert a picture that symbolizes the word. For example, in "Old MacDonald Had a Farm," glue a picture of the farmer in place of "Old MacDonald," the barnyard in place of the "farm," and a pig in place of "pig."

Procedure:

1. Tell students that a rebus is a story using both words and pictures.
2. Display the rebus rhyme. Instruct students to read along.
3. Using the pointer, point at each word as you read it.

Math Connections

Hen House Counting

Recite the poem "Hickety Pickety" on page 71. Then count Hickety Pickety's eggs and put them into numerical order.

Skills: number identification, number sequencing

Materials:

- "Hen House Counting" (pages 78–79)
- construction paper
- scissors
- crayons and markers
- glue

Teacher Preparation:

1. Make one copy for each student of "Hen House Counting."

Procedure:

1. Instruct students to color and cut out the hen, the nest, and the eggs.
2. Glue the hen, on her nest, onto a sheet of construction paper.
3. Assist students with identifying the numbers, and putting them into the correct order.
4. Have the students glue the eggs, in numerical order, on construction paper.

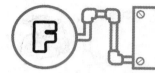 

Farm

Science and Social Studies Connections

Farm Time

Discover what life on a farm is really like. Read picture book stories about farms, and discuss student perceptions of what they think a farm is like. Record these ideas on a sheet of butcher paper, and also draw pictures representing those ideas. Guiding questions might include, "Who lives on a farm?" "What does a farmer do?" "What types of plants and animals does a farmer raise?" "What do these plants and animals need to live happily and healthily?" "How does a farmer provide plants and animals with what they need?"

After discussing these ideas of what students think farms are like, read non-fiction farming books, such as Gail Gibbons' *Farming* (Holiday House, 1990) or *Milk Makers* (Aladdin Library, 1987). Compare students' initial ideas of what they think farms are like to their ideas after reading the non-fiction book.

Art Connections

Color and Shape Farm

Color Farm by Lois Ehlert (Harper Festival, 1990) uses shapes of different colors to create images of farm animals. In this art activity, students create their own farm pictures using geometric shapes.

Materials:

- "Geometric Shapes" (pages 80–82)
- colored paper (several different colors)
- colored construction paper
- black construction paper
- scissors
- glue sticks
- *Color Farm* by Lois Ehlert

Teacher Preparation:

1. Copy the "Geometric Shapes" onto several different colors of paper
2. Cut out the shapes (or have students cut them out during as an activity to build fine motor coordination).
3. Compile bags or envelopes of various colors and shapes for each group of students to use.
4. Cut the colored construction paper into 8½" squares.
5. Cut the black construction paper into 8½" by 1½" strips.
6. If *Color Farm* will not be read, prepare an example of a farm animal shape picture.

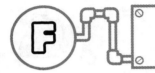 

Art Connections (CONT.)

Color and Shape Farm (CONT.)

Procedure:

1. Read *Color Farm* or display the prepared example.
2. Distribute construction paper squares and other geometric shapes.
3. Review the colors and shapes.
4. Tell students that they will use these shapes to create pictures of animals that live on farms.
5. Instruct students to first experiment with making animal pictures using the shapes before gluing them on the construction paper square.
6. Once students are satisfied with their shape pictures, they can glue them down.
8. Create frames for the pictures by gluing the black strips of construction paper on the edges of the picture.

Follow-up:

Have students dictate stories about their farm pictures.

Alternate Procedure:

Some students may need explicit guidance. As an alternative lesson, provide step-by-step directions for creating a shape picture of a pig.

1. Find a big circle.
2. Glue the big circle onto the middle of the construction paper square.
3. This is the pig's head
4. Find two small diamonds of the same color.
5. Glue the two small rhombuses onto the top half of the big circle to make eyes.
6. Find one small hexagon.
7. Cut the hexagon in half.
8. Glue the two hexagon halves on top of the pig's head, slightly to each side. These are the pig's ears.
9. Find another hexagon.
10. Glue the hexagon into the middle of the pig's head, under the eyes. This is the nose.
11. Make two dots with your marker with the hexagon with your markers to make the nostrils.
12. Find a small rectangle.
13. Glue the rectangle under the nose. This is the mouth.

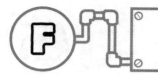 

Farm

Music, Movement, Rhythm, and Rhyme

Baa, Baa Black Sheep

Baa, baa, black sheep,
Have you any wool?
Yes, sir, yes, sir,
Three bags full.
One for master,
One for my dame,
One for the little boy
Who lives down the lane.

Hickety, Pickety

Hickety, pickety, my black hen,
She lays eggs for gentlemen;
Gentlemen come every day,
To see what my black hen doth lay.
Some days five and some days ten,
She lays eggs for gentlemen.

In the Fields

One day I saw a big brown cow,
Raise her head and chew.
I said, "Good morning, Mrs. Cow,"
But all she said was, "Moo!"
One day I saw a woolly lamb,
I followed it quite far.
I said, "Good morning, little lamb,"
But all it said was, "Baa!"
One day I saw a dapple horse,
Cropping in the hay.
I said, "Good morning, Mr. Horse,"
But all it said was, "Neigh!"

Old MacDonald

Old MacDonald had a farm, E-I-E-I-O
And on this farm he had some pigs, E-I-E-I-O
With an oink, oink here, and an oink, oink there,
Here an oink, there an oink, everywhere an oink-oink.
Old MacDonald had a farm, E-I-E-I-O
And on this farm he had some cows, E-I-E-I-O
With a moo, moo here, and a moo, moo there,
Here a moo, there a moo, everywhere a moo, moo.
Continue with animals names and their sounds:
Donkeys, hee-haw
Ducks, quack, quack
Horses, neigh, neigh

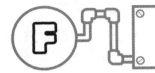 

Farm

Music, Movement, Rhythm, and Rhyme (CONT.)

Farm Time Activities

Act out stories and nursery rhymes about farms, incorporating movements. For "Old MacDonald Had a Farm," students form a circle. One student plays the part of the farmer, and stands in the center of a circle—the barnyard. With each verse, groups of "animals" join the farmer in the center of the circle until the entire class is in the "barnyard."

Centers

Set up centers to encourage students to explore the theme further during a free choice period, or assign small groups to parent-guided centers while you work with other students.

Sorting Center

Skills: sorting, categorizing

All Sorts of Animals

Make copies of "Farm Time Pictures" on pages 75–77. Color, cut, and laminate. Draw pictures for labels for predetermined categories—animals with fur and animals with feathers; animals that live in a house and animals that live in a barnyard; animals with two feet and animals with four feet; etc. Students sort them according to similarities and differences.

Are You My Mother?

Using the "Farm Time Pictures" on pages 73–77, students match babies to mothers.

Snacks

Be sure to check with parents about allergies before serving students any food.

Farm Food Snacks

Eat foods that come from farms, such as dairy products, eggs, bread, and fresh fruits and vegetables. Read books that address where foods come from, such as *Milk Makers* by Gail Gibbons (Aladdin Library, 1987) or *From Cow to Carton* by Aliki, (Harpercollins, 1992).

Ingredients:
- dairy products such as milk, cottage cheese, cheese, yogurt
- hard-boiled eggs
- farm fresh fruits and vegetables (ideally, from the farmer's market)

Directions:
1. Serve the snacks, and discuss where each food item comes from, i.e., cheese is made from milk, which comes from a cow.

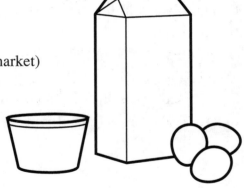

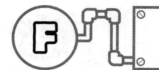 
Farm Time Pictures

Directions: Use these pictures in the Rebus Farm Rhyme activity on page 67 or as characters in oral story-telling activities.

Farm Time Pictures *(CONT.)*

Farm

Farm Time Pictures (CONT.)

Farm

Farm Time Pictures (CONT.)

©Teacher Created Materials, Inc.

Farm Time Pictures (CONT.)

Hen House Counting

Directions: Color and cut out the hen, the nest, and the eggs below. Glue the hen, sitting on her nest, onto a sheet of construction paper. Glue the eggs next to the nest in numerical order.

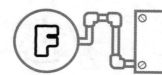

Hen House Counting (CONT.)

1 one

2 two

3 three

4 four

5 five

6 six

7 seven

8 eight

9 nine

10 ten

11 eleven

12 twelve

Geometric Shapes

Circles and Ovals

Geometric Shapes (CONT.)

Squares and Rectangles

Farm

Geometric Shapes *(CONT.)*

Triangles, Diamonds, and Hexagons

Overview

Introduce the letter **G** with a study of gorillas. Read *My Friend Gorilla* by Atsuka Morozumi (Straus and Giroux, 1997). Integrate math and language arts by making gorilla counting books, learning about gorilla habitats, and discovering Koko, the "talking" gorilla. Use this unit after "Z—Zoo" and "E—Elephants," then continue exploring animals and their habitats with the unit "T—Trees."

 **Gorilla**

Language Arts Connections

Core Book

Morozumi, Atsuko. *My Friend Gorilla*. Farrar, Straus and Giroux, 1997.

When the zoo is closed down, Daddy brings home Gorilla. At first Gorilla seems pretty big, but he's also friendly and helpful. He soon becomes a family friend. But the day comes when Gorilla needs to return to his home in Africa. His little boy misses him, but is reassured by a photograph of Gorilla in his new home.

Read-Aloud Activities

Prior to Reading

- Read the title and the author's name, pointing to the words as you read.
- Discuss the illustrations on the front and back covers. The front cover shows the little boys holding onto Gorilla's back as Gorilla climbs a tree. The back cover shows the boy and Gorilla building sand castles at the beach. Ask students to predict what they think the story might be about based on the title and cover illustrations.
- Ask students what they already know about gorillas.

During Reading

- Call attention to the changes in the boy's expressions throughout the story; at the beginning, he looks very apprehensive. What happens later? Do his feelings towards the gorilla change?

After Reading

- Respond to the story and begin a discussion with a comment and a question. For example, "The little boy seemed really nervous to have a gorilla in his house. I wonder what that would be like."
- Allow time for students to articulate responses. Wait a few moments so they can think about what they would like to say.
- Discuss what it might be like to have a gorilla living in the house.

Additional Books

Stock your class library with books about gorillas. Students will enjoy looking at the illustrations and "reading" them to each other. When you read a story to your class, record yourself on tape. Then put the tape and the book in a literacy center so that your students can listen to it time and time again.

Alborough, Jez. *Hug*. Candlewick Press, 2000.

Bornstein, Ruth. *Little Gorilla*. Clarion Books, 1976.

Buuehner, Carolyn and Mark. *The Escape of Marvin the Ape*. Dial Books, 1992.

Carle, Eric. *From Head to Toe*. HarperCollins, 1999.

Browne, Anthony. *Gorilla*. Alfred A. Knopf, 1983.

Morozumi, Atsuko. *One Gorilla*. Farrar, Straus & Giroux, 1990.

Patterson, Francine. *Koko-Love*. Dutton Children's Books, 1999.

Rathman, Peggy. *Good Night, Gorilla*. G.P. Putnam's Sons, 1994.

Simon, Seymour. *Gorillas*. HarperCollins, 2000.

Gorilla

Language Arts Connections (CONT.)

Letter-Sound Introduction

Say *gorilla* slowly and deliberately, emphasizing the /g/ sound. What is first sound of the word *gorilla*? Tell students that the letter **g** makes the sound /g/. Sometimes **g** says /j/, as in *giraffe*.

Phonological Awareness

Skill: word awareness

Provide each student with counters (beans work well) and a small container. After reading *My Friend Gorilla* by Atsuko Morozumi, select one sentence from the story. Read the sentence slowly and tell the students to drop a counter into their containers every time they hear a word. Write the sentence on the board. As you write, use a word separator, such as your hand or a chalkboard eraser, in between the words. Ask students, one at a time, to come up and circle each separate word that they see. After the words have been circled, count the number of circled words. Compare this number with the number of counters in the students' containers. Continue with the activity for up to ten minutes, using sentences from the story.

Letter Formation

After reading *My Friend Gorilla* by Atsuko Morozumi, and after introducing the letter-sound association, reinforce the association between the letter shapes of **G** and its /g/ sound by drawing a picture of two gorillas, one big and one little. The shape of **g** forms the arms of a gorilla. The shape of **G** forms the head and one arm of a gorilla.

These activities will help to reinforce letter formation for students of all learning styles.

- Make "gooey gross goop" by mixing equal parts of glue and liquid starch, (gradually mixing the starch into the glue). Have students use the goop to form the gooey letters **G** and **g**.

- Put magnetic letters with similar shapes (**O, C, G, Q, g, p, q, d, b, j, y**) into a paper bag stapled shut or a closed box with a hole in its side. Students reach in and feel each letter. They say its name, its sound, and then pull it out of the box to check their answer.

- Use "glue" and "gold glitter" to make **G** and **g** shapes on construction paper.

- Draw the letters **G** and **g** onto pieces of butcher paper. Have the students make a collage out of green objects (tissue paper, yarn, shamrocks, etc.) or paint the letters green.

Gorilla

Language Arts and Math Connections

Gorilla Counting Book

In this integrated language arts and math activity, students make their own gorilla counting books. Modify this lesson for younger students by writing out the number groups for the students rather than having them write the numbers themselves. If the students are to write their own numbers, consider extending this lesson over two days.

Skills: number writing, number quantity

Materials:

- Gorilla Picture Cards (page 88)
- "My Gorilla Counting Book" book cover (page 89)
- paper
- glue
- markers and crayons
- numbers, written both as numerals and in words (1 one) on pocket strips in a pocket chart or on the board. Suggestion: Write numerals and words on a sheet of paper, copied for each student to use at his or her desk.

Teacher Preparation:

1. Make copies of Gorilla Picture Cards. If the students are focusing on numbers one through five, each student will need a total of 15 cards. If the students are working on larger number groups, more copies will be needed.
2. Make a copy of "My Gorilla Counting Book" book cover for each student.
3. Write out the numbers and number words, either on the board or on sheets to be copied and distributed to students.
4. If students in the class are not yet writing numbers and number words, write these on single sheets (one page for 1—one, one page for 2—two, etc.) and copy a set for each student.

Procedure:

1. Read or display copies of animal counting books, such as *1, 2, 3, to the Zoo* by Eric Carle (The Putnam & Grosset Group, 1968). Introduce the activity by telling students they will be making their own gorilla counting books.
2. Have students color and cut the Gorilla Picture Cards.
3. Assist students with writing numbers, directing their attention to the numbers and number words that are written as an example.
4. If needed, review the quantities symbolized by numbers. For example, "If I am on my first number page, for the number one, how many gorillas should I put on this sheet?"
5. When students have written the numbers, they can begin to add gorillas to their pages.
6. While pages are drying, distribute copies of "My Gorilla Counting Book" book covers to be colored.
7. After pages have been "illustrated" and are thoroughly dry, assist students with compiling pages in numerical order.
8. Staple each book, using "My Gorilla Counting Book" as the book cover.

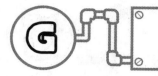
Gorilla

Science and Social Studies Connections

Koko the Gorilla

Koko is a world famous gorilla who learned to communicate with humans by using sign language. Learn more about Koko and her amazing accomplishments, and in the process, learn more about gorillas. Visit Koko's Internet website, *http://www.koko.org*, and read books about Koko, such as *Koko-Love* by Dr. Francine Patterson (Dutton Children's Books, 1999).

The Life of a Gorilla

Use books and other resources to explore gorillas' natural habitats and learn about typical gorilla characteristics. There are three types of gorillas (Western Lowland, Eastern Lowland, and Mountain) living in different parts of Africa. Locate Africa on a world map or globe with your students. Gorillas eat mostly plants, including leaves, flowers, and fruit, and live in highly vegetated areas so they have access to plenty of food. Male gorillas can eat up to fifty pounds of food a day!

Art Connections

Gorilla Hand Puppets

Use the template on page 91 and small brown paper bags to make gorilla hand puppets.

Materials

- Gorilla Hand Puppet (page 91)
- one small brown paper lunch bag for each student
- markers and crayons
- scissors
- glue sticks

Teacher Preparation:

1. Make one copy of the Gorilla Hand Puppet for each student.

Procedure:

1. Have the students color and cut the gorilla head, body, and arms.
2. Assist the students as needed with gluing the head and arms onto brown paper lunch bags.

Music, Movement, Rhythm and Rhyme

Gorilla, Gorilla
by Mary Ramming Chappell

Gorilla, Gorilla,
Under a tree.
Quietly watching,
Still as can be.
Momma Gorilla,
Gentle, kind mother,
Watching the babies
Playing with other.

Little Gorilla,
Playing in the sun,
Rolling and grunting,
Just having fun.
Gorilla, Gorilla,
Under a tree.
Quietly watching,
You're just like me.

Music, Movement, Rhythm and Rhyme (CONT.)

Silly Gorilla

by Barbara Knarr Ramming

A silly gorilla came up to me.
He asked if I could climb a tree.
I said that I could,
He asked if I would,
So away we both went,
As high as can be.

Move Like An Animal

Read *From Head to Toe* by Eric Carle (Harper Collins, 1999) and do as the animals do! If the book is not available, imitate animal movements by slithering around the classroom as snakes, stomping through "jungles" like lions, and galloping across the playground like a herd of zebras.

Centers

Set up centers to encourage students to explore the theme further during a free choice period, or assign small groups to parent-guided centers while you work with other students.

Math Center

Set up centers to encourage students to explore the theme further during a free choice period, or assign small groups to parent-guided centers while you work with other students.

Skills: Gorilla Snack Sort

Have the students sort, count and make patterns with fruits that gorillas love to eat: banana chips, grapes, sliced apple, strawberries, and pineapple chunks. Put "gorilla food" on a wooden bamboo kabob stick and make a pattern (one apple, two banana slices, a strawberry). After the math activities, have each student eat their fruit for a snack. Due to the nature of this activity, the presence of an adult is highly recommended.

Snacks

Be sure to check with parents about allergies before serving students any food.

Banana Butter

Go ape! Gorillas love fruit and other plants. Eat bananas, whole or sliced, and make banana snacks with your students. The following spread is delicious served on bread.

Ingredients:

- 1 cup peanut butter
- 3-4 ripe bananas
- cinnamon
- ¼ cup raisins
- ¼ cup chopped nuts
- bread
- 1 tablespoon shredded coconut

Directions:

1. Smash bananas.
2. Mix other ingredients
3. Spread on bread.

Gorilla

Gorilla Picture Cards

"My Gorilla Counting Book " Book Cover

Directions: Use with Math Connections Lesson on page 85.

My Gorilla Counting Book

by

_____

Gorilla

Gorilla Hand Puppet

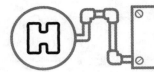 

Unit Overview

Focus on Hats during explorations with **H** and /*h*/. Read Esphyr Slobodkina's classic story, *Caps for Sale* (Scholastic, Inc., 1940). Design signs advertising hats for sale, practice math skills by helping the cap peddler organize his hats, and make and decorate newspaper hats. Do this unit as after "R—Rain" and follow it with "U—Uniforms."

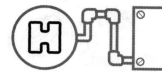

Hats

Language Arts Connections

Core Book

Slobodkina, Esphyr. *Caps for Sale*. Scholastic, Inc., 1940.

The cap peddler was not having a very good sales day, so he took a nap against a tree. When he awoke, he checked to make sure that his caps were still on top of his head, but they were gone! He looked all around, and soon discovered the culprits who had made off with his caps. A fun story that is sure to delight, it also offers opportunities to learn sequencing, colors, and patterns.

As an alternative for older students, try *The 500 Hats of Bartholomew Cubbins* by Dr. Seuss (Random House, 1989). This book is also a perfect transition from "hats" to "king."

Read-Aloud Activities

Before Reading

- Introduce the book by reading the title, the author, and showing students the front cover illustrations.
- Set the stage for the story by telling students that a long time ago, salespeople often carried what they sold in a wagon or on a cart. This is a story of a hat seller who carried his hats with him to sell. When someone wanted to buy a hat, he would simply reach over his head and pull the hat from his stack.

During Reading

- Point to the hat colors as you read them.
- Talk about the illustrations.

After Reading

- Ask students what part of the story they liked the best.
- Ask students if they have ever felt as frustrated as the cap peddler. Share your own story of a time when you felt frustrated.
- Ask the students what they would have done to make those naughty monkeys give them their hats back.

Additional Books

Stock your class library with books about hats. Students will enjoy looking at the illustrations and "reading" them to each other. When you read a story to your class, record yourself on tape. Then put the tape and the book in a literacy center so that your students can listen to it time and time again.

Agee, Jon. *Milo's Hat Trick*. Hyperion Books for Children, 2001.

Boynton, Sandra. *Blue Hat, Green Hat*. Little Simon, 1995.

Brett, Jan. *The Hat*. Putnam, 1999.

Dr. Seuss. *The 500 Hats of Bartholomew Cubbins*. Random House, 1989.

Dr. Seuss. *The Cat in the Hat*. Random House, 1957.

Morris, Ann. *Hats, Hats, Hats*. Lorthrup, Lee and Shepard, 1989.

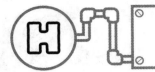

Language Arts Connections *(CONT.)*

Letter-Sound Introduction

Say the word *hat* slowly and deliberately, emphasizing the sound /h/. Ask students what beginning sound they hear in *hat*. Tell students that the letter **h** makes the sound /h/.

Phonemic Awareness

Skill: Hearing and identifying similar word patterns.

Make copies of "Hat Rhyme Time" (page 101), one for every pair or small group of students. Have the students cut the cards apart. Students can spread cards out and sort them into words that rhyme with *-at* and words that don't rhyme with *-at*. Or, they can play a structured game, such as "Rhyme Time Memory."

Rhyme Time Memory: Students turn the cards face down on the table. The first student turns two cards over. The cards are considered a match if they both rhyme with *-at* words. The student keeps any rhyming pairs. If they don't match, the student turns both cards back over in the same spot. The next student takes a turn trying to match rhyming *-at* words. The game is over once all the -at cards have been matched, and the winner is the student with the most pairs of cards.

Letter Formation

After reading *Caps for Sale* and introducing the letter-sound association, reinforce the association between the letter's formations and its sound by drawing the **H** and **h** into the shape of a hat.

These activities will help to reinforce letter formation for students of all learning styles.

- Guide your students in warming up their fingers, hands, and arms by "air writing" vertical lines and right angles.

- Encourage pairs of students to discover how to form **H** and **h** shapes using both sides of their bodies.

- Draw an **H** on butcher paper, as large as can be. Have students hunt for objects beginning with /h/ around the classroom, and then draw pictures of the objects in the interior space.

Hat Signs

Make signs advertising hats for sale.

Skills: writing, brainstorming

Materials:

- construction paper or poster board
- crayons and markers
- examples of signs or advertisements from newspapers or magazines
- chalkboard or butcher paper

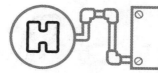 

Hats

Language Arts Connections (CONT.)

Hat Signs (CONT.)

Procedure:

1. After reading *Caps for Sale*, mention that it seems as thought the cap peddler is having some difficulty selling his hats. Ask students if they can think of any way that he could get more business.

2. Suggest that if he had some more signs advertising his caps with pictures and descriptions, perhaps he would have better luck. Show examples of advertisements from newspapers or magazines.

3. Discuss the characteristics of effective signs or advertisements: lots of color, good pictures or descriptions, good prices, etc.

4. Brainstorm key words that the students may want to use in their signs. Write these on the board or on butcher paper. Words might include *hats* (instead of caps since the focus letter is **H**), *for sale*, *colors available*, *prices*, *descriptions*, etc.

5. When writing the words on their signs, students can either sound them out and or copy them from the brainstormed chart.

6. Have students work individually, in pairs or in groups to create their hat signs.

7. Display the hats signs throughout the room when complete

Alternate procedure:

Some developing writers may not be able to copy the words, but they could probably draw pictures of hats or use some letters and numbers to convey a message.

Providing opportunities for young children to explore reading and writing skills is an important aspect of early literacy instruction.

Math Connections

The Hat Closet

Organize the hat closet by sorting the different hats according to shape, color or style. Then, pile the hats in sequence. Finally, create addition problems using the hats.

These activities can be done with individual students, pairs, or small groups of students.

Skills: sorting, sequencing, patterning, counting, adding, subtracting

Materials:

- The Hat Closet (page 102)
- empty cereal box
- roll of adhesive Velcro

Teacher Preparation:

1. Make several copies of The Hat Closet. Color the hats and laminate them.

2. Cut out hat squares.

3. Make a "closet" out of the cereal box:

   a. Cut off the top of the cereal box.

   b. Cut the cereal box open down the middle so that there are two flaps ("doors") that can open and close.

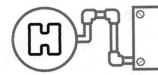
Math Connections (CONT.)

The Hat Closet (CONT.)

4. Cut off pieces of adhesive Velcro into squares. Put one side of Velcro on the inside of the "closet." Make columns of Velcro squares on the inside doors of the closet and on the back walls.

5. Put the other side of Velcro on the back of a hat square.

Sorting Activity Procedure:

1. Put hat squares face up in random order in front of the closet.

2. Tell students that this closet belongs to the hat peddler from the book *Caps for Sale*. Usually he is very tidy, but after today's experience with the monkeys, he's feeling particularly tired. He could use some help cleaning up.

3. Tell students that they can organize the hats according to size, shape, or color.

4. Assist students as needed.

Sequencing and Patterning Activity Procedure:

1. Tell students that now it's the next morning, and the hat peddler needs help stacking his hats. They need to be stacked in the right order.

2. Provide a sequence for students to replicate, for example, the white hats, then the red hats, then blue hats, and then the black hats.

3. For patterning, provide a specific pattern for your students to follow, such as red hat, blue hat, red hat, blue hat.

4. Instruct students to lay the hats on the table in front of them while getting them into order.

Counting and Adding Activity:

1. Tell students that the hat peddler wants to know how many hats he has sold and needs help counting.

2. Provide addition story problems. For example, say, "The peddler has sold one blue hat and two orange hats. How many hats has he sold all together?"

3. Demonstrate how to pull the hats out of the closet and lay them on the table as they count. "1 blue hat and 2 orange hats are 3 hats all together."

(blue hat)

(orange hat)

(orange hat)

4. Continue to provide addition story problems, and then have students come up with their own story problems.

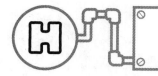

Hats

Math Connections *(CONT.)*

The Hat Closet *(CONT.)*

Subtraction Activity:

1. Tell students that the hat peddler wants to know how many hats he has left over.

2. Provide subtraction story problems. For example, say, "The peddler started out with three blue hats. He sold one. How many does he have left over?"

3. Use the hat cards as manipulatives to help students understand the concept of subtraction.

   "He started off with two blue hats and one orange hat. (Lay out two blue hats and an orange one.) He sold one blue hat. (Remove the blue hat.) How many hats does he have left?" (Two.)

Extension: "The Hat Closet" Free Choice Center: Students can continue to sort, sequence, and pattern hats using the materials from this lesson.

Science Connections

Health: What to Wear?

Bring in an assortment of seasonal clothing or accessories: snorkels and sandals; raincoats, boots and umbrellas; mittens, scarves and woolen hats; and baseball hats and sweatshirts.

On large sheets of butcher paper, draw pictures of the four different seasons: the sun, flowers, and trees for summer; yellow and brown trees, rain and clouds for fall; snow and bare trees for winter; and clouds, a rainbow, the sun, and budding flowers for spring. Label each scene with the name of the season.

Stand in front of the summer scene, and say, "Wow, it's hot! What should I wear today?" Have the students find appropriate accessories for you to wear in the summer. You can put some of the items on (i.e. sandals, a baseball cap, etc.)

Then move to the fall scene, still wearing some of the summer clothing. Rub your arms, and say, "Brr… it's getting colder. What should I wear today?"

Continue through winter and spring scenes, with your students selecting the appropriate attire for each season.

After you have modeled the activity, invite your students to help each other choose appropriate seasonal outfits.

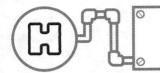

Hats

Social Studies Connections

Hats of the World

Bring in hats from cultures around the world, and discuss how they are similar to and different from hats that your students have seen and worn. If real hats are not available, then bring in pictures from magazines. *Hats, Hats, Hats* by Ann Morris (Lorthrup, Lee and Shepard, 1989) is a photographic books that shows pictures of hats used around the world for many different purposes.

Before you tell your students about the hats, allow them to brainstorm about their origins. For example, where might a woolen ski hat be from? A warm tropical island? Probably not. Maybe it's from a place where people need protection from cold and snow. How about a straw hat? It would be useful in a hot climate, where people need protection from the sun.

Keep a globe or large world map handy so that you can show your students where in the world the hats are from.

If possible, set the hats up in a costume center so your students can use them as creative play costumes during a free choice period. Provide a mirror as well.

Art Connections

Make a Hat

In moments, each student will have a custom made hat that they can decorate and personalize. This is a fun project that the whole class will enjoy. Be sure to enlist the help of a couple of parent volunteers.

Materials

- newspaper (enough for at least two full pages per student)
- masking tape
- paint
- glue
- feathers
- stickers
- glitter
- other materials to decorate the hat.

Teacher Preparation:

1. Arrange for a couple of parents to assist with creating the hats. (It takes only about two minutes to make each hat, but the more parent volunteers you have helping, the less time students will have to wait.)

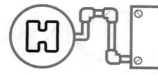 

Art Connections (CONT.)

Make a Hat (CONT.)

Procedure:

1. Have each student sit in a chair.

2. Place two pieces of newspaper on top of his or her head. Tell him or hear what to expect when the newspaper covers his or her head, i.e., it may feel a little strange, and it will sound funny.

3. If a child balks at the idea of having the newspaper cover his or her head, cover a ball (basketball, soccer ball) with paper instead.

4. Wrap the masking tape around the child's head two or three times just above the ears. Roll the newspaper up tightly to form the brim of the hat. Continue to roll until the brim is complete.

5. Secure the rim in place with three to four pieces of tape.

6. Invite students to decorate their hats with paint, glue, feathers, or collage materials.

7. Allow each hat to dry thoroughly.

8. Provide a time for students to showcase their special hats. For example, organize a hat parade in which everyone wears his or her own hat.

Music, Movement, Rhythm, and Rhyme

A Hat for a Cat

Where are you going,

My little cat?

I am going to town,

To get me a hat.

What? A hat for a cat?

Who ever saw a cat with a hat?

The Cap Peddler Says

The monkeys in *Caps for Sale* seemed to enjoy imitating the cap peddler. Your students will enjoy this version of "Simon Says."

Select one student to be the cap peddler. Everyone else can play the part of the monkeys. The cap peddler stands in front of the class and says, "Cap peddler says…stomp your feet." (He or she stomps his or her feet, then the monkeys stomp their feet.) He or she continues, "Cap peddler says…shake your fist." (He or she shakes his or her fist and the monkeys follow along, listening carefully.) When the cap peddler omits the phrase "Cap peddler says…" and just names the action, such as "Jump up and down" then the monkeys do not do the action. If a monkey is caught in the act, he or she becomes the next cap peddler.

Balancing Hats

Your students can practice their balancing skills by piling hats on top of their head, just like the hat peddler! How many hats can they manage to keep upright?

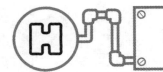 

Hats

Centers

Set up centers to encourage students to explore the theme further during a free choice period, or assign small groups to parent-guided centers while you work with other students.

Shapes and Colors Center

Skills: identification and use of shapes and colors

Shape Pictures

In the shape and color center, students use shapes to create pictures of objects. A rectangle is placed on top of an oval to form the shape of a hat. A square and a triangle become a house. Provide a variety of shape manipulatives. For example, cut shapes out of felt and set up a flannel board where students can make their shape pictures. You could also use block sets that include pyramids, cubes, cylinders, and other three-dimensional shapes. Or, provide shape stencils. Students can make their own shape sets by tracing shapes onto construction paper and cutting them out or using the geometric shape templates on pages 80–82.

Flannel Board Center

Skills: selecting weather appropriate clothing, identifying seasonal changes

What to Wear?

Set out flannel board sets featuring seasons and seasonal clothing. Students can create scenes depicting seasons and dress flannel characters appropriately.

Snacks

Be sure to check with parents about allergies before serving students any food.

Graham Cracker Hat Snacks

Kids love these quick snacks, which are similar to s'mores but without the chocolate.

Ingredients:
- large marshmallows
- graham crackers

Directions:
1. Break the graham crackers into squares.
2. Put one marshmallow on top of each graham cracker square.
3. Pop into the toaster oven and bake for a few minutes until lightly browned.
4. Allow to cool and serve.

Cheese and Cracker Hats

Ingredients:
- cheese (cubes)
- small wheat crakers

Directions:
1. Cut cheese into cubes, slightly smaller than the crackers.
2. Place one cheese cube on each cracker.

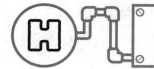 

Hat Rhyme Time

hat

bat

can

rat

mat

ham

cat

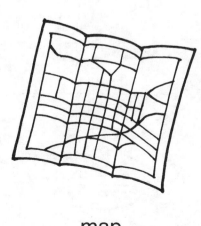

map

dog

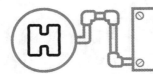 
The Hat Closet

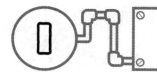 

Overview

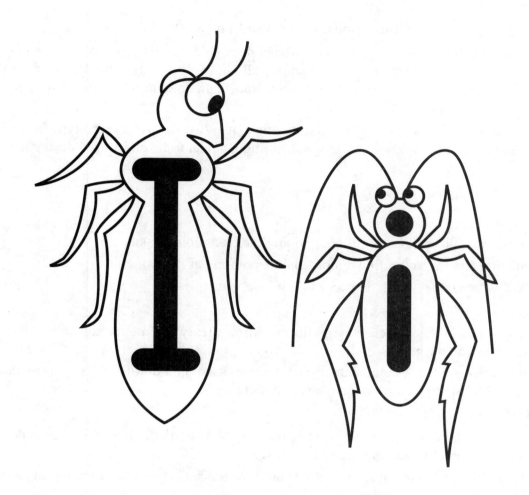

Enter the fascinating world of insects by reading *Two Bad Ants* (Houghton Mifflin Company, 1988)—a visual feast written and illustrated by Chris Van Allsburg. Discover the difference between insects and other bugs, identify parts of insects and parts of a story, count by sixes, and build phonemic awareness skills through rhythm and rhyme, music and movement.

For an extended unit study of "Creatures, Creepers and Crawlers," study "I—Insects" after "T—Tree" and "S—Salamanders." Follow it with "C—Caterpillars" and "B—Butterflies."

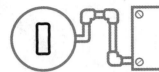 **Insects**

Language Arts Connections

Core Book

Van Allsburg, Chris. *Two Bad Ants*. Houghton Mifflin Company, 1988.

A cache of sparkling and delectable crystals has been discovered, and a group of worker ants sets out to fetch some for the queen. The mission goes well for all but two bad ants, who decide to stay behind and eat their fill. The ants suffer a series of misadventures, and long to return to the security of their colony.

Be prepared to read this book several time during this unit—*Two Bad Ants* is the type of book that can be read over and over again, and still reserve something magical to be discovered during the next reading.

Read-Aloud Activities

Prior to Reading

- Show the cover illustrations prior to beginning the read-aloud session.
- Read the title and the author/illustrator's name, pointing at the words.
- Ask students what they think the story might be about.

During Reading

- The illustrations in this book are magnificent. Allow plenty of time for students to look at them before turning the page.
- Be prepared for student's comments and encourage discussion during the reading as they attempt to figure out what the ants are seeing and experiencing.

After Reading

- Seek student responses. Since the artwork in the book is particularly striking, consider asking students to respond by drawing their favorite scene.
- Show students a scoop of sugar, and talk about how the ants must have seen the sugar, the toaster, and other objects in the kitchen.

Additional Books

Stock your class library with books about insects. Students will enjoy looking at the illustrations and "reading" them to each other. When you read a story to your class, record yourself on tape. Then put the tape and the book in a literacy center so that your students can listen to it time and time again.

Aardema, Verna. *Why Mosquitoes Buzz in People's Ears*. Scholastic, Inc., 1975.
Barner, Bob. *Bugs, Bugs, Bugs*. Chronicle Books, 1999.
Bono, Mary. *Ugh! A Bug*. Walker and Company, 2002.
Carle, Eric. *The Grouchy Ladybug*. Harper Collins Publishers, 1977.
Carle, Eric. *The Very Quiet Cricket*. Philomel Books, 1990.
Carle, Eric. *The Very Lonely Firefly*. Putnam Publishing Group, 1995.
Carle, Eric. *The Very Clumsy Click Beetle*. Philomel Books, 1999.
Gribben, Mary. *Big Bugs*. Ladybird Books, 1996.
Jenkins, Steve. *Bugs are Insects, Too*. Harpercollins Publishers, 2001.
MacQuitty, Miranda. *Amazing Bugs*. DK Publishing. 1996.

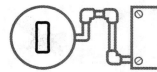 

Insects

Language Arts Connections (*CONT.*)

Additional Books (*CONT.*)

Pallotta, Jerry. *The Icky Bug Alphabet Book.* Charlesbridge Publishing, 1990.

Pinczes, Elinor J. *One Hundred Hungry Ants.* Schlastic, Inc., 1997.

Rattigan, Jama Kim. *Truman's Aunt Farm.* Houghton Mifflin Company, 1994.

Ryder, Joanne. *My Father's Hands.* Morrow Junior Books, 1994.

Letter-Sound Introduction

After reading *Two Bad Ants* by Chris Van Allsburg, tell students that ants are insects. In this unit, they will be learning all about insects. Then ask, 'What is the first sound of the word *insects*? Say *insects* slowly and deliberately, emphasizing the /ĭ/ sound. Tell students that the letter **i** makes the sound /ĭ/. The letter **i** is a vowel and also says the long **i** sound, as in **ice**.

Phonemic Awareness

Counting Sounds

Skills: syllable counting, phoneme counting, and phoneme segmentation

Make a copy of "Interesting Insects" on pages 112–113. Color and cut out the pictures. Write the name of the insect on poster board strips, and put each strip into pocket chart pockets next to the corresponding picture. Note: Arrange the insects in order of the number of phonemes, from least to greatest.

Distribute counters (e.g., beans, counters, or buttons) to students. Each student should have at least ten counters. Guide students through identifying the names of the insects displayed in the pocket chart. Mention that some insect names are short, like *ant*, while others are longer, like *grasshopper*. As you read through the names of the insects again, ask students to clap the beats (syllables) of each insect name.

After students are familiar with the insect names, tell students to say *ant* very slowly. Tell them to think about what their mouths are doing when they say the word. Their mouths are changing shapes. Demonstrate how the mouth changes shape with each change in sounds—/a/ /n/ /t/. Exaggerate the movements. Ask students how many times their mouths changes shape when saying /a/ /n/ /t/. (Three times.) Tell students to try counting the number of sounds (not syllables) of each word. They can keep track by moving a counter in front of them for each sound. Demonstrate with /a/ /n/ /t/— use three counters.

Continue, with the remaining words, depending on the students' proficiency. Some of the longer words may prove to be very challenging.

Letter Formation

After introducing the letter-sound association, write the letters **I** and **i** so that all the students can see them. Reinforce the association between the letter formations and its sound by drawing the **I** and **i** into the shapes of insects.

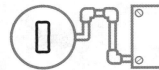 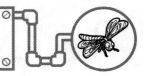
Language Arts Connections (CONT.)

These activities will help to reinforce letter formation for students of all learning styles.

- Use ice cubes (set on a towel to catch drips and prevent slipping) to form the letters **I** and **i**, or freeze water into the shape of **I** and **i**.
- Put magnetic letters with similar shapes (**I**, **i**, **J**, **j**, **L**, **l**, **T**, **t**) into a paper bag stapled shut or a closed box with a hole in its side. Students reach in and feel each letter. They say its name and sound, then pull it out to check their answers.
- Have individual students form the letter **I** and **i** with their bodies, saying, "I am I!"

Stories Have Three Parts, Too!

Just as insects have three body parts (head, thorax, abdomen), good stories have a beginning, a middle, and an ending. Introduce beginning story writers to this concept with the following activity.

Skills: identifying beginning, middle, and ending of story

Materials:

- large sheets of butcher paper
- crayons, markers, pencils

Teacher Preparation:

1. Cut sheets of butcher paper.

Procedure:

1. After reading *Two Bad Ants*, ask students to recall some story details. Record their ideas on the board or on a sheet of butcher paper.
2. Tell students that things happened in the story in a certain order. For example, first the ants had their adventure, and then they went home. What would the story have been like if they had gone home before they ever had their adventure?
3. Remind students of the story ending. (The ants went home at the end of the story.) Tell students that a good story also has a beginning and a middle.
4. Provide an example of the beginning, middle, and ending by telling a quick story. Ask students about the beginning, middle, and ending parts.
5. Have students brainstorm what is found in the beginning part of the story (introduction of characters and setting), the middle (problems), and ending (resolution).
6. Tell students that now they will have a chance to think about the beginning, middle, and ending parts of *Two Bad Ants*.
7. Tell students that you are going to read the story again, and this time, they will illustrate the beginning, middle and ending of the story.
8. Have the students fold their sheets of butcher paper into three parts: one for the beginning, one for the middle, and one for the ending. They can also draw lines, or write the numbers 1, 2, and 3 to separate the parts of the story.
9. Reread the story, allowing time for students to draw pictures from the different parts of the story.
10. At the end of the story, have students get into pairs to discuss what they drew. Circulate to check for understanding.

Insects

Language Arts Connections (CONT.)

Stories Have Three Parts, Too! (CONT.)

Follow-up Activity

After introducing the concept of the head, thorax and abdomen as three parts of an insect's body, compare them to the three parts of the story. Draw and cut out several large insects on butcher paper. On the head, write "beginning"; on the thorax, write "middle"; and on the abdomen, write "ending." After reading insect books recommended in "Additional Books" (pages 104–105), record key images from the stories in the appropriate insect body parts. Be sure to label each insect with the title of the story.

Math Connections

Insects Have Six Legs

One characteristic of insects is that they have six legs. Focus on counting and writing numbers from one to six. Extend this lesson by introducing skip counting.

Skills: counting, number identification, number writing, quantity of six, counting by twos and threes

Materials:

- pictures of insects with legs clearly visible
- Insects Have Six Legs (page 113)
- scissors
- markers and crayons
- glue
- numbers one through six written so they are clearly visible to students

Teacher Preparation:

1. Make a copy for each student of Insects Have Six Legs

Procedure:

1. Display pictures or photos of insects from Interesting Insects on pages 112–113, magazines, books, etc.
2. If the Science Connections lesson (page 108) has already been taught, then ask students to review the general characteristics of insects: they have three body parts (head, thorax, abdomen), six legs, some have wings, etc.
3. If the Science Connection lesson has not been taught yet, ask students to look at the insects displayed and think about some things that they all have in common. Direct their attention to the number of legs.
4. Tell students that insects have six legs, as compared to other bugs, which may have more or less. Spiders, for example, have eight legs.
5. Distribute "Insects Have Six Legs." Have students cut out the insect legs.
6. Once students have cut the insect legs, count them out loud, as a group.
7. Review (or introduce) the fact that an insects legs are in pairs (meaning two together) attached to the thorax (the middle part of the insect).

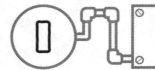

Math Connections (CONT.)

Insects Have Six Legs (CONT.)

8. Discuss that people's arms and legs come in pairs, also; one arm or leg is on one side of the body and the other arm or leg is on the other side of the body. Have students hold up their own pairs of arms and legs. Note: Use sensitivity in discussing typical arms and legs.

9. Direct students' attention to the written numbers 1-6. Have them write these numbers on the insect legs, and then put them in the following order: legs 1 and 2 together, legs 3 and 4 together, legs 5 and 6 together.

10. Have students glue the pairs of legs onto the thorax of the insect. Legs 1 and 2 should be first, with 1 on the right side of the thorax and 2 on the left, then legs 3 and 4, and finally, legs 5 and 6.

Extension:

After the legs are glued on, introduce the concept of skip counting. Have students count the legs on the right side: 2, 4, 6.

Science Connections

It's an Insect, Not a Bug!

Insects share specific characteristics that are not shared by all bugs. All insects have:

- three body parts—a head, thorax, and abdomen
- six jointed legs
- two antennae on top of their heads to sense the world around them
- an exoskeleton (outside skeleton)
- many insects have two pairs of wings.

Make a chart with insect characteristics labeled and pictured across the top row. Write names and add pictures of familiar bugs in the first column. If a bug has a particular characteristic, write *yes* or draw a happy face in the corresponding grid. If it does not have a characteristic, write *no* or draw a sad face in the corresponding grid. If a bug does not have the above four characteristics, then it is not an insect! Spiders are not insects because they have eight legs. But, caterpillars are insects—they're just not quite finished growing up.

For more information about insects, consult books about insects, such as *Amazing Bugs* by Miranda MacQuitty (DK Publishing, 1996) or the Internet. The University of Kentucky's Entomology Department has a resourceful Web site with links for pages just for teachers and kids at *http://www.uky.edu/Agriculture/Entomology/enthp.htm*

Social Studies Connections

Occupation: Entomologist

Scientists who study insects and other bugs are called *entomologists*. Invite an entomologist to come to the classroom as guest speaker. He or she can discuss insects that are helpful and those that are harmful, how insects, people and plants need each other to live happily and healthily, and what types of insects might be living around the community.

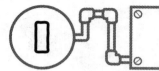 
Art Connections

Insect Creations

Have students apply their knowledge about insects to create their own buggy version.

Materials:

- 3 toilet paper or paper towel rolls
- single hole punch
- chenille stems (cut into two to three inch pieces)
- tissue paper
- wiggly eyes
- markers
- crayons

Teacher Preparation:

1. Prior to this art activity, spend time discussing the characteristics of insects.
2. Cut the toilet paper and paper towel rolls into various sizes so they can be used for head, thorax and abdomen.

Procedure:

1. Review the body parts of all insects (6 legs, 3 body parts), antennae, wings (for most insects).
2. Have students select the paper rolls that they will use for the head, thorax, and abdomen.
3. Punch holes in the paper rolls so they can be tied together. Use chenille stem pieces to tie the rolls together.
4. Have students glue wiggly eyes to the head.
5. Have students who wish to add wings make them out of tissue paper and glue them onto the top of the thorax.
6. Make two holes in the head and fasten the pipe cleaners for antennae.
7. Have students glue six chenille stem pieces onto the thorax for legs.

Follow-up:

Students can create names for their insect and write stories about them.

Insects

Music, Movement, Rhythm, and Rhyme

Ant March

Teach students the following ditty, then go on a march.

The Ants Go Marching

The ants go marching one by one, hurrah, hurrah

The ants go marching one by one, hurrah, hurrah

The ants go marching one by one,

The little one stops to suck his thumb

And they all go marching down to the ground

To get out of the rain, BOOM! BOOM! BOOM!

For the following verses, repeat the first two and last two lines.

The ants go marching two by two,

The little one stops to tie his shoe

The ants go marching three by three,

The little one stops to climb a tree

The ants go marching four by four,

The little one stops to shut the door

The ants go marching five by five,

The little one stops to take a dive

The ants go marching six by six,

The little one stops to pick up sticks

The ants go marching seven by seven,

The little one stops to pray to heaven

The ants go marching eight by eight,

The little one stops to shut the gate

The ants go marching nine by nine,

The little one stops to check the time

The ants go marching ten by ten,

The little one stops to say, "The end!"

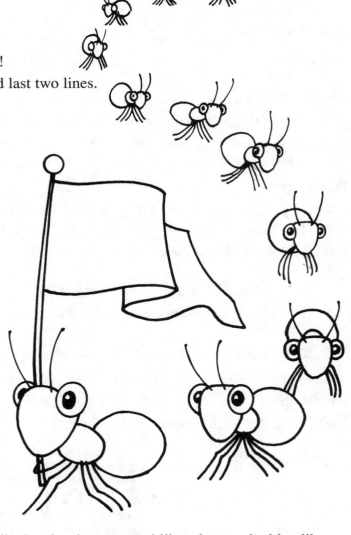

Buzzing Around

Act like insects: fly like butterflies, skittle along like beetles, buzz around like a bee, and whine like a mosquito. Play insect charades and have students try to guess what insects are being acted out.

Music, Movement, Rhythm, and Rhyme (CONT.)

Bug Hunt

Take a nature walk, and look for insects. At the same time, discuss insect habitats, and emphasize the importance of not disturbing animals or insects in the own space. Have students take pencils and paper and draw insects that they see. Upon returning to the classroom, discuss students' observations during the nature walk.

Centers

Set up centers to encourage students to explore the theme further during a free choice period, or assign small groups to parent-guided centers while you work with other students.

Math Center

Skills: sorting, categorizing

It's a Buggy World

Have students sort through pictures of bugs (insects, worms, spiders, etc) from nature magazines and other sources and categorize them according to type, size, number of legs, and other characteristics.

Snacks

Be sure to check with parents about allergies before serving students any food.

Build an Insect

Have students build their own insect snacks using healthy vegetables and a sweet treat.

Ingredients (per student):
- one celery stick
- filling, such as cream cheese or peanut butter
- six carrot sticks
- two small licorice sticks
- two raisins

Directions:
1. The celery sticks are the body.
2. The carrot sticks are the legs.
3. The licorice sticks are the antennae.
4. The raisins are the eyes.

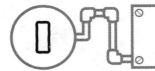
Interesting Insects

Directions: Copy and cut out. Use with the Phonemic Awareness activity on page 105.

bee

fly

ant

wasp

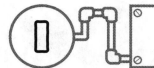 

Interesting Insects (CONT.)

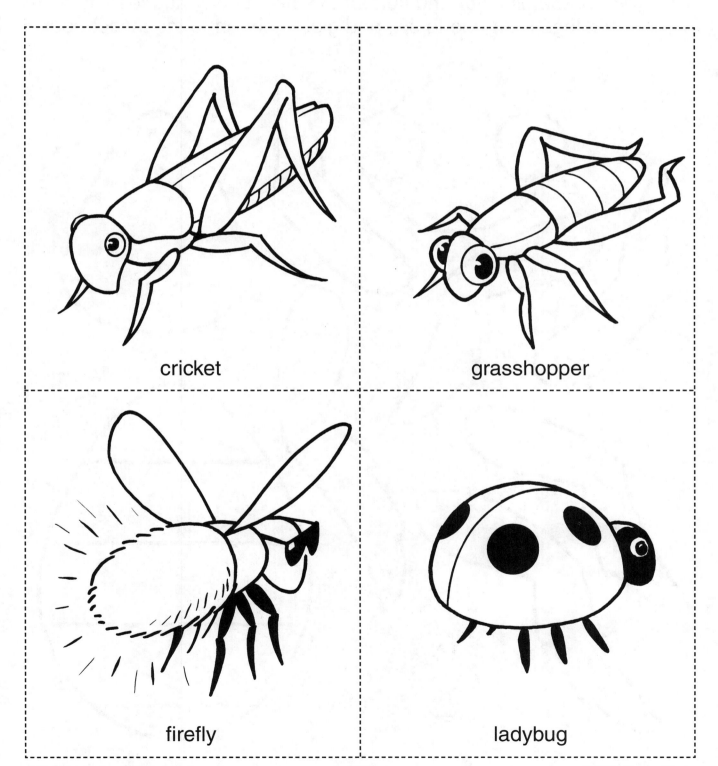

cricket

grasshopper

firefly

ladybug

Insects Have Six Legs

Directions: Use this with the Math Connections activity on pages 107–108. Students color and cut out the insect body and legs, then number the legs from one to six, and glue them on to the insect body.

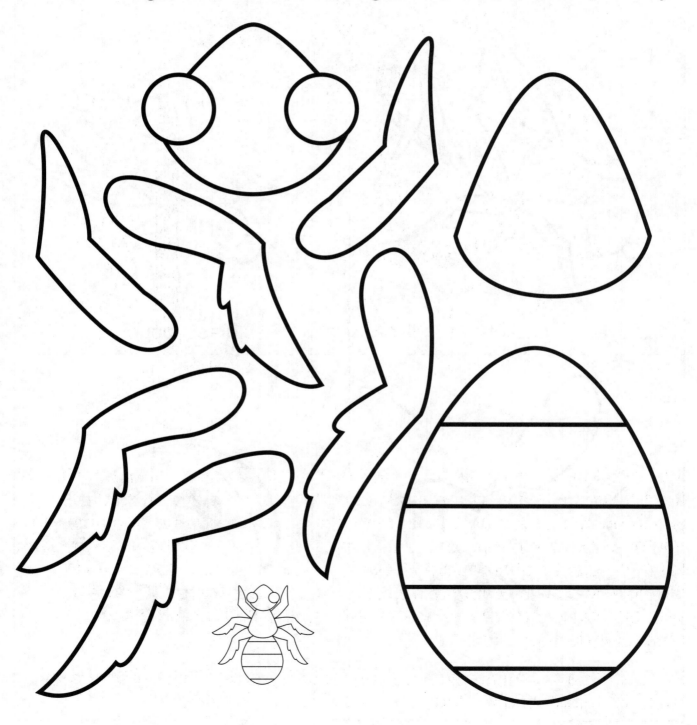

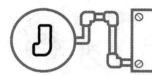 

Jack and the Beanstalk

Unit Overview

Many children are familiar with the tale of "Jack and the Beanstalk." In the traditional telling of the story, Jack embarks on an adventure in which he climbs a magical beanstalk and enters a world of giants. In this unit, explore other versions of the story. For example, look at Jack from the giant's perspective in *Giants Have Feelings, Too* by Alvin Granowsky (Steck-Vaughn, 1996), or read Mary Pope Osborne's version, *Kate and the Beanstalk* (Atheneum, 2000), and discuss character development.

Integrate math, writing, science, and social studies activities for a fun-filled, imaginative unit study.

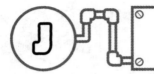

Jack and the Beanstalk

Language Arts Connections

Core Book

Granowsky, Alvin. *Giants Have Feelings, Too/Jack and the Beanstalk*. Steck-Vaughn, 1996.

Giants Have Feelings, Too offers two books in one. One side of the book is the traditional telling of "Jack and the Beanstalk." Flip the book over to read *Giants Have Feelings, Too*, in which the giant's wife tells her side of the story. According to her, not only is the giant innocent of intending to inflect harm, but it turns out that he's the victim!

Read-Aloud Activities

Before Reading

- Ask students if they have ever heard the story of "Jack and the Beanstalk" before.
- Read the title and the author's name, pointing at the words as you read.

During Reading

- As you read, make sure that each student can see the illustrations. Hold the book so that it is facing the students, and turn it slowly as you read.
- Be expressive. Your voice and facial expressions will draw students into the story. A note of caution: this tale can be frightening for some young children. Try to gauge student responses during reading. If any students appear to be uncomfortable, alleviate fears by saying, "Boy, this story sure makes me nervous. I'm glad Jack is okay in the end."

After Reading

- Allow time for responses to the story.
- Ask students what part of the story they liked the best.
- Set the stage for the other side of the book *Giants Have Feelings, Too*. If there is time, read that version immediately after "Jack and the Beanstalk." If that version is to be read on another day, set the stage by telling students that you will be reading another story about that may make them think differently about his adventure.

Additional Books

Stock your class library with books that include a character named Jack. Students will enjoy looking at the illustrations and "reading" them to each other. When you read a story to your class, record yourself on tape. Then put the tape and the book in a literacy center so that your students can listen to it time and time again.

Osborn, Mary Pope. *Kate and the Beanstalk*. Atheneum Books for Young Readers, 2000.

Scieszka, Jon. *The Stinky Cheese Man and Other Fairly Stupid Tales*. Viking, 1992.

Tabeck, Sims. *This is the House that Jack Built*. G.P. Putnam's Sons, 2002.

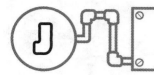

Jack and the Beanstalk

Language Arts Connections (CONT.)

Letter-Sound Introduction

Emphasize the /j/ in the word jack slowly and deliberately. (Remind students that "Jack" is a name and a "jack" is an object used in a game.) Ask students what beginning sound they hear in *jack*. Ask students if they know what letter makes that beginning sound of /j/. Tell students that the letter **j** makes the sound /j/.

Phonemic Awareness

Skill: Hearing and identifying similar word patterns

Recite nursery rhymes that contain the name Jack (see Music, Movement, Rhythm and Rhyme on page 122). Have students identify the rhyming words that they heard in the rhymes.

Letter Formation

After reading *Giants Have Feelings, Too* and introducing the letter-sound association, write the letters **J** and **j** so that all students can see them. Reinforce the association between the letter's formations and its sound by drawing the **J** and **j** into the shape of a beanstalk that Jack is climbing.

These activities will help to reinforce letter formation for students of all learning styles.

- Provide an assortment of jelly beans, glue, and construction paper. Write the letter **J** on the construction paper. Students glue the jelly beans onto the construction paper in the shape of letters. They can then draw a picture of Jack climbing up the beanstalk **J**.
- Encourage students to discover how to form **J** and **j** shapes using their bodies.
- Provide jam and jelly. Students can finger paint the letters **J** and **j** with jam and jelly. Just make sure to provide lots of towels or wipes for cleaning up.

Character Development

Traditionally, the tale of the magic beanstalk centers around Jack, an adventurous (some would say mischievous) boy who embarks on a grand adventure. Mary Pope Osborne has modified the story by changing the main character to a girl, Kate (see "Additional Books," page 116). In *Kate and the Beanstalk*, Kate is a heroine who regains her father's castle in her bid to defeat the giant.

Compare the characters of Jack and Kate. On a piece of butcher paper, write the characters' names, or draw their pictures to distinguish between them. Have students brainstorm character traits. Write these descriptions under each name, and compare the similarities and differences between the characters.

Jack and the Beanstalk

Language Arts Connections (CONT.)

The Hen's Story

In *Giants Have Feelings, Too* the giant tells his side of the story. Continue exploring different points of view in a sequel. Write a class story, this time from the point of view of the hen that lays the golden eggs.

Note: This lesson should be conducted over four days: create a brainstorm and story map on the first day; write the story draft on the second day; edit the draft on the third day; and write a final draft and illustrate on the fourth day.

Skills: Writing Process: brainstorming ideas, drafting and revising story; point of view

Materials:

- butcher paper
- large pieces of story writing paper or white construction paper
- markers
- crayons

Teacher Preparation:

On the first two days, display a large piece of butcher paper so that all students can see it.

Day One Procedure—Brainstorming:

1. Review both stories told in the book *Giants Have Feelings, Too*, and discuss how the book told the story from Jack's and the giant's side.

2. Ask students if they have ever thought about what happened after Jack escaped with the hen. Tell them that they now will have a chance to write a sequel (the next part) to the story from the hen's side.

3. Explain that before writing a story, a writer usually makes a plan. Before writing the hen's tale, the students will plan the story.

4. Write "Story Ideas," saying the sounds of the words as you write the letters, on one sheet of butcher paper.

5. Ask for ideas about what the story should be about. Provide prompts, such as,

   a. Who will be in the story?

   b. Where will this story happen?

   c. What will happen in the beginning of this story?

   d. Will there be any things that go wrong in the story?

   e. How will everything turn out?

6. Record the students' ideas. You may need to limit the ideas to two or three ideas per category.

7. Tell the students to think about how they will put these ideas together to tell a story.

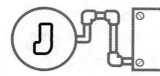

Jack and the Beanstalk

Language Arts Connections (CONT.)

The Hen's Story (CONT.)

Day Two Procedure—Draft:

1. Review the ideas that the class wanted to include in the story. Tell students that yesterday they planned what they would write, and today they will begin writing. Say that good writers sometimes write and rewrite a story many times before they feel it is ready. This method of writing many times is called drafting and each different version of the story is a *draft*. A draft is a place to write the story and not worry about things that can be fixed later, such as spelling and punctuation.

3. Display the second sheet of butcher paper and write "Story Draft," saying the words as you write them.

4. Guide the students to write the story using their brainstormed ideas.

   Suggestion: Keep the story short and simple.

5. Model the process of story writing by modeling your thinking aloud. For example, you could say,

   a. "What should we write first? We need a beginning to the story. Can anyone think of how we can start it off?"

   b. "What happens first? I need to look at the ideas that you thought of yesterday."

   c. "Then what happens? Let's look at our ideas."

   d. "Did the characters in the story have any problems or did anything go wrong? How should we write that?"

6. Continue with these questions, turning the answers into sentences in the story, until the story has been written.

Day Three Procedure—Editing:

1. Begin the editing phase of the writing process. Reread the story, and ask the students if they have any changes.

2. Model the editing process by crossing out words or sentences and writing in revisions.

Day Four Procedure—Final Draft:

1. Tape pieces of story writing paper or white construction paper on the chalkboard.

2. Reread the story draft and review revisions.

3. Ask if there are any more changes that should be made.

4. Determine how to write the story onto the story sheets.

5. Write the final version of the story on the story sheets. As you write, ask for student input regarding spacing, capital letters and punctuation.

6. Leave ample room for illustrations.

7. Have the class decide on the title.

8. Pass out the pages to groups or pairs of students to illustrate. Have one group illustrate the book cover.

9. Once all pages have been illustrated, assemble into a book by stapling the pages together. Put the completed book in the classroom library.

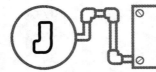

Jack and the Beanstalk

Math Connections

The Beanstalk

Plant a bean (see "Science Connections," page 121) and measure the growing plant. Prepare a chart (see a sample on page) to track its rate of growth.

Skills: measurement and using line graphs

Materials:

- "Beanstalk Growth Chart" (page 124)
- construction paper
- bean plant (from "Science Connections," page 121)

Teacher Preparation:

1. Make a copy of "The Beanstalk Growth Chart" and paste it onto construction paper.

Procedure:

1. After planting the bean as directed in the "Science Connections" lesson, ask students how tall they think the bean plant will grow.
2. Record the students' predictions, and tell students that in a couple of weeks, they can check the predictions to see how close they were.
3. Show students the chart, and tell them that it will help with tracking the plant's growth.
4. Point out the features of the chart, including the days and the number of inches and centimeters.
5. Measure the plant every few days, and mark the growth on the chart accordingly.

The Golden Eggs

In the traditional story of "Jack and the Beanstalk," the hen continued to lay her golden eggs while Jack and his mother lived happily ever after. With this activity, students practice identifying and matching numbers while the hen lays her golden eggs.

Skills: number identification

Materials:

- "The Golden Eggs" (pages 125–126)
- "Hen House Counting" from "F—Farm" (page 78)

Teacher Preparation:

1. Make a copy of "The Golden Eggs" and the hen and nest from "Hen House Counting" for each pair of students.

Procedure:

1. Students cut out the eggs and hen.
2. Students lay the eggs on the table, number or dot side down, in two groups (eggs with numbers and eggs with dots).
3. Students turn over two eggs at a time, one from each group. If the number of dots on one egg matches the number on the other, the matched pair goes into the hen's nest.
4. The game is over when all the eggs are in the nest.

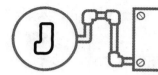 

Jack and the Beanstalk

Science Connections

Plant a Bean

Jack's beanstalk grew very tall very fast. See just how quickly a real bean plant will grow with this incredibly easy science lesson.

Materials:

- 3-4 dry beans (pinto or lima beans work well)
- soil
- clear jar
- water

Teacher Preparation:

1. Gather materials.

Procedure:

1. Dampen the soil well, but not so that it is overly wet.
2. Insert the beans into the soil so that they are next to the glass.
3. Sit back and observe over the coming days and weeks. You'll be able to see the bean seed expand and then send out roots.
4. Don't forget to keep the soil moist!

Extension:

1. Follow-up with "The Beanstalk" math lesson on page 120.

Social Studies Connections

In the story *Giants Have Feelings, Too,* the giant gets an opportunity to tell his side of the story. Every story has as many sides as there are participants, or characters. Discuss with your students how the giant feels and how their feelings toward the giant may have changed after hearing his side.

Art Connections

Bean Picture

Use different sizes, colors, and shapes of beans to create pictures.

Materials:

- assortment of coloring pages
- assortment of dried beans
  (black beans, pinto beans, kidney beans, peas, etc.)
- glue
- construction paper

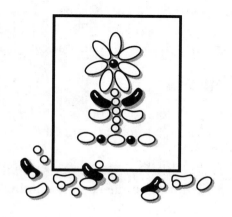

Procedure:

1. Students select coloring pages that they want to use.
2. Students glue beans onto coloring pages, using different beans as the different colors.
3. Allow to dry thoroughly.

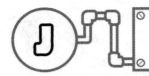

Jack and the Beanstalk

Music, Movement, Rhythm and Rhyme

Little Jack Horner

Little Jack Horner
Sat in a corner,
Eating his Christmas pie;
He put in his thumb,
And pulled out a plum
And said, "What a good boy am I!"

Jack Be Nimble

Jack be nimble,
Jack be quick,
Jack, jump over the candlestick.

Jack and Jill

Jack and Jill went up the hill,
To fetch a pail of water.
Jack fell down
And broke his crown,
And Jill came tumbling after.

Climb the Beanstalk

Imagine climbing a beanstalk! Jack must have been a strong boy! If you have appropriate playground equipment, let the students climb it as if they were Jack. Use caution, and reinforce safety rules.

Jack Be Nimble

Recite the nursery rhyme "Jack Be Nimble," above. Assign two students to hold an object, such as a rope, between them. Or place a soft object, such as a pillow, on the floor. One at a time, each student jumps over the object. The students holding the rope raise it a little higher once each student has had a turn. If a pillow is used, stack it on another pillow. When a student touches the object, he or she is out.

Centers

Set up centers to encourage students to explore the theme further during a free choice period, or assign small groups to parent-guided centers while you work with other students.

Math Center

Skills: sorting, sequencing, counting,

The Bean Bags

Set out an assortment of beans. Have students sort by color, size, or shape into small bags.

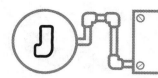 

Jack and the Beanstalk

Snacks

Be sure to check with parents about allergies before serving students any food.

Bean and Vegetable Soup

Make bean soup after reading the "Jack and Beanstalk" stories suggested in this unit. Serve on a cool day with a roll for a warm and delicious meal. This recipe yields about 8 cups.

Ingredients:

- 1 ½ cups dried beans (navy, kidney, or marrow beans)
- 5 cups water for soaking beans
- 1 ham bone
- 8 cups water
- 1 bay leaf
- 2 medium carrots, sliced
- 1 medium onion, diced
- 2 medium celery stalks, sliced
- 1 large potato, peeled and diced
- 1 14 oz can diced tomatoes
- * optional: spices such as salt, pepper, oregano, garlic

Directions:

1. Wash and rinse beans thoroughly.
2. Soak beans overnight in 5 cups of water.
3. Rinse beans and discard soaking water.
4. Bring 8 cups of water to a boil. Add ham bone and beans. Cook until the beans are soft, about 2½ hours.
5. Skim fat as the soup boils.
6. Remove ham bone and dice the meat. Return the meat to the soup pot.
7. Add vegetables and spices.
8. Add additional liquid as needed.
9. Cook for an additional ½ hours, until the vegetables are soft.
10. Allow to cool, and then serve.

Alternative Cooking Methods:

Use a crock pot instead of a stove to cook this soup. Soak the beans as directed. Put the beans, water and ham bone in the crock pot. Cook until the beans are tender. Add the vegetables and spices, and cook until tender.

Use canned beans instead of dry to cut down on cooking time. Put beans in boiling water, add vegetables and remaining ingredients. Cook until vegetables are tender.

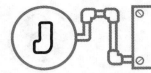

Jack and the Beanstalk

The Beanstalk Chart

(Use with "The Beanstalk" math lesson in this unit.)

7"														
6½"														
6"														
5½"														
5"														
4½"														
4"														
3½"														
3"														
2½"														
2"														
1½"														
1"														
½"														
# inches	1	2	3	4	5	6	7	8	9	10	11	12	13	14

Number of Days

14 cm														
13 cm														
12 cm														
11 cm														
10 cm														
9 cm														
8 cm														
7 cm														
6 cm														
5 cm														
4 cm														
3 cm														
2 cm														
1 cm														
# centimeters	1	2	3	4	5	6	7	8	9	10	11	12	13	14

Number of Days

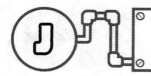

Jack and the Beanstalk

The Golden Eggs, Set One

Directions: Color and cut the eggs. Use with "The Golden Eggs" math lesson on page 119.

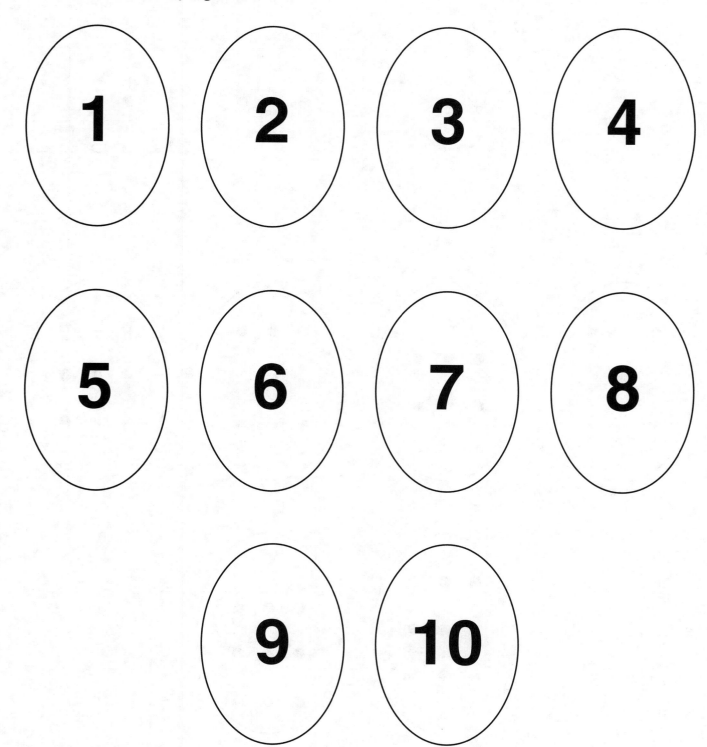

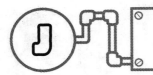

Jack and the Beanstalk

The Golden Eggs, Set Two

Directions: Color and cut the eggs. Use with "The Golden Eggs" math lesson on page 120.

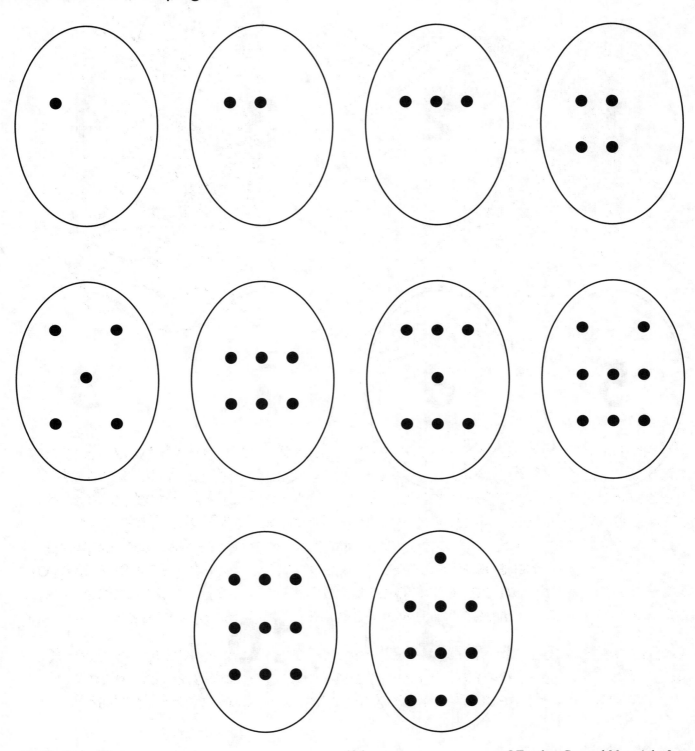

Kings

Unit Overview

Enter the world of kings and queens, and the land of fantasy. Explore the /*k*/ sound through stories about kings, queens, and the land of nursery rhymes and fairy tales. Begin by reading *King Bidgood's in the Bathtub*, written by Audrey Wood (Harcourt, 1985). Play with words and language, develop reading and writing skills, and explore math, science and social studies connections. Finally, select a day on which everyone can be a "King or Queen for a Day" and parade around the school wearing jewel-adorned crowns and capes.

Continue the theme with "Q—Queens," (or consider studying both K and Q at the same time). Extend into a longer folklore unit with "N—Nursery Rhymes," "P—Pigs," and "J—Jack in the Beanstalk."

 **Kings**

Language Arts Connections

Core Book

Wood, Audrey. *King Bidgood's in the Bathtub.* Harcourt, 1985.

King Bidgood is in the bathtub, and he refuses to get out. When the knight, the queen, and even the court try to entice him out, he simply invites them in! No one knows what to do, until a page comes up with the solution. This book received a Caldedcott Honor Medal for its elaborate illustrations.

Read-Aloud Activities

Prior to Reading

- Read the title and the author's and illustrator's names, pointing to the words as you read. Remind students that they may have read other books by the author and illustrator team of Audrey and Don Wood, such as *The Little Mouse, the Big Hungry Bear and the Red Ripe Strawberry* or *Piggies.*

During Reading

- As you read, make sure that each student can see the illustrations, which are hilarious. Allow plenty of time for the students to look at them. Mention that this book was selected as a Caldecott Honor Book for its pictures.

After Reading

- Turn back to some of the illustrations and look at the facial expressions of the characters in the story. Ask students what they think the characters were thinking as they sat in the tub with the king.
- Follow up with the oral language activity in which students discuss what they would have said to try to get the king out of the water.

Additional Books

Stock your class library with books about kings. Students will enjoy looking at the illustrations and "reading" them to each other. When you read a story to your class, record yourself on tape. Then put the tape and the book in a literacy center so that your students can listen to it time and time again.

Denis-Huot, Christine. *The Lion: King of the Beasts.* Charlesbridge Publishing, 2000.

Dr. Seuss. *Bartholomew and the Oobleck.* Random House, 1970.

Dr. Seuss. *The 500 Hats of Bartholomew Cubbins.* Random House, 1989.

Dr. Seuss. *The King's Stilts.* Random House, 1998.

Dunn, Carolyn. *A Pie Went By.* Harper Collins Publishers, 2000.

McKay, Sindy (adaption), Anderson, Hans Christian. *The Emperor's New Clothes.* Treasure Bay, Inc., 1997.

Pfister, Marcur. *How Leo Learned to Be King.* North South Books, 1998.

Letter-Sound Introduction

Say the word *king* slowly and deliberately, emphasizing the sound /k/. Ask students what beginning sound they hear in *king*. Tell students that the letter **k** makes the sound /k/. Remind students that the /k/ sound is also made by the letter **c**, as in *cat*.

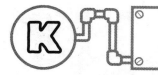

Kings

Language Arts Connections (CONT.)

Phonemic Awareness

Skill: Hearing and identifying similar word patterns.

Prior to the activity, read one of the rhymes about kings on page 132. Identify several pairs of words, some that rhyme and some that do not rhyme. Recite the rhyme to the class, and then say the word pairs to the students. Ask the students to indicate to you whether the words are a rhyming pair. If they do rhyme, they show thumbs up, if they don't rhyme, they show thumbs down.

Letter Formation

After reading *King Bidgood's in the Bathtub* and introducing the letter-sound association, reinforce the association between the letter's formations and its sound by drawing the **K** and **k** into the shape of a crown on a king's head.

These activities will help to reinforce letter formation for students of all learning styles.

- Emphasize the /k/ sound at the end of *stick*. Send students outside to look for small sticks. (Be sure to discuss appropriate behavior when carrying and gathering sticks—no poking or running with them.) Students glue their sticks onto construction paper into the forms of **K** and **k**.
- Provide magazines with pictures of animals, nature scenes, and "kids." Students can cut out pictures of things that begin with **k** and glue them into a collage or into a **k** shape. (Use this opportunity to discuss that **k** and **c** both make a /k/ sound.)
- Take the entire class outside to the playground. Organize the "kids" into a giant **K**.

King Bidgood's in the Bathtub Class Book

In the core book, everyone tries to come up with an activity that would interest King Bidgood enough to get him out of the tub. In this activity, students brainstorm ways of enticing the king to get out of the tub.

Skills: brainstorming, oral language, writing

Materials:

- sheets of large art paper
- crayons and markers

Procedure:

1. After reading *King Bidgood's in the Bathtub*, brainstorm activities that would be hard to do in the bathtub and that might entice the king.
2. Have each student choose one event to describe orally. On sheets of art paper, have students draw pictures of the events that they choose.
4. On the top of page, write "I do," said (insert the student's name). "Get out to _____, King Bidgood." Have the students fill in the blanks using their developing writing skills, or fill in the words that the students dictate.
5. Create a book cover and a title page. On the title page, write, "King Bidgood's in the bathtub and he won't get out! Who knows what to do?"

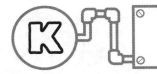

Math Connections

Four and Twenty Blackbirds

Use the traditional nursery rhyme "Sing a Song of Sixpence" to practice number identification skills and counting from 1–24. Consider doing this activity at a math center.

Skills: number identification, counting to 24, sequencing numbers from 1–24

Materials:
- Four and Twenty Blackbirds (page 134)
- Four and Twenty Blackbirds Pie (page 135)
- optional: laminate or clear contact paper
- Velcro squares
- flannel board

Teacher Preparation:
1. Make a display copy of "Four and Twenty Blackbirds."
   a. Make six copies of "Four and Twenty Blackbirds" for a total of 24 birds. Number the birds from 1 to 24.
   b. Make two copies of the pie, one for the front and one for the back. Cut out and staple the bottom and sides together so that the top remains open.
   c. Affix Velcro squares to the back of each blackbird and the pie. The Velcro will hold the objects to the flannel board.
   d. Put the blackbirds into the top opening of the pie.
2. Optional: Make copies of the blackbirds and pies for the students.

Procedure:
1. Recite the nursery rhyme, "Sing a Song of Sixpence," located on page 132.
2. Ask students what "four and twenty blackbirds" means. Tell them that it means 24 blackbirds.
3. Begin pulling blackbirds out of the pie. Have the students orally count them as you put them on the flannel board.
4. Have the students put them in numerical order on the flannel board.

Extensions:
1. Make copies of the "Four and Twenty Blackbirds" sheet for a free choice center activity, or make individual copies for students. Suggestion: Have parent volunteers cut out the blackbirds and cut out and staple the pies. The blackbirds can be put into the pies in random order for each student.
2. Have the students glue the birds in numerical order on sheets of blank paper. The pie can be glued under the blackbirds, as if they are flying out of it.
3. For more advanced students, make up story problems with the birds. For example, "Two birds flew away. How many were left?"

Kings

Science and Social Studies Connections

Lion: The King of the Jungle

The lion has been called "the 'king' of the jungle." As an introduction to this lesson, read Marcus Pfister's *How Leo Learned to be King* (North South Books, 1998) and then study this African mammal.

Compose a "KWL" chart with the questions, "What Do We Already **Know**?" "What Do We **Want** to Know?" and "What Did We **Learn**?" written in three large columns on a sheet of butcher paper. Have students brainstorm things that they already know about lions and record these ideas in the "What Do We Already Know?" column. Then have them brainstorm things that they would like to discover about lions, and record them in the "What Do We Want to Know?" column.

Provide resources about lions, such as *The Lion: King of the Beasts* by Christine Denis-Huot (Charlesbridge Publishing, 2000). Assist students with researching the answers to their questions about lions. Record these answers in the "What Did We Learn?" column.

Lions once lived in many places throughout the world, but today they are found only in small areas of Africa and in a very small section of India. Locate Africa and India on a world map or a globe.

Social Studies Connections

In many countries, kings and queens continue to govern. Discuss the head of government in your country, and compare it with a monarchy. Is the head of your country voted in or did he or she inherit the position? Identify existing monarchies, such as Great Britain, on a world map.

Art Connections

"King (or Queen) for a Day" Crown

Select a day on which everyone can be a "King or Queen for a Day." Students will design and make their own crowns, adorn them with "jewels," and then march in procession around the school or classroom as kings and queens. If you are doing the "Q—Queen" unit at the same time as "K—Kings," then make the "Queen or King for a Day" cape to wear with the crown.

Materials

- copy of crown template (page 134)
- construction paper
- faux plastic jewels (available from most craft supply stores)
- glitter
- crayons and markers
- scissors
- staplers and staples
- glue

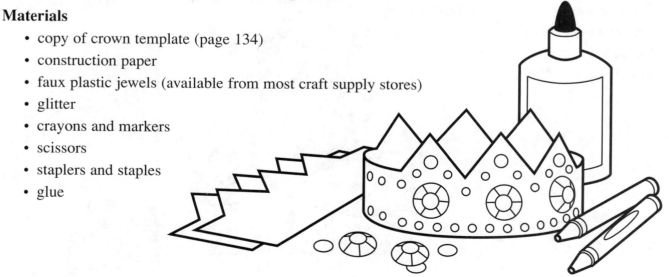

Kings

Art Connections (CONT.)

"King or Queen for a Day" Crown (CONT.)

Teacher Preparation:

1. Copy the crown template onto white paper. Cut out, and then copy again onto several pieces of heavy card stock. Cut out these templates for student use.

2. Arrange for a parent volunteer or aide to assist.

Procedure:

1. Students trace crown template onto construction paper, and then cut out crown shapes. (Teachers or parent volunteer assist students as needed.)

3. Teachers or parents wrap crown around students' heads, hold size with fingers, and staple the two crown pieces together.

4. Students decorate crowns with art materials, such as faux plastic jewels and glitter.

5. Allow to dry.

Music, Movement, Rhythm, and Rhyme

Sing a Song of Sixpence

Sing a song of sixpence,
A pocket full of rye;
Four and twenty blackbirds,
Baked in a pie.
When the pie was opened,
The pie began to sing,
Was that not a dainty dish
To set before the king?

The king was in his counting house,
Counting all his money;
The queen was in the parlor,
Eating bread and honey.
The maid was in the garden,
Hanging out the clothes,
Along came a blackbird,
And tweaked her on the nose.

Old King Cole

Old King Cole was a merry old soul,
An a merry old soul was he;
He called for his pipe,
And he called for his bowl,
And he called for his fiddlers three.
Each fiddler he had a fiddle,
And the fiddlers went tweedle-dee;
Oh, there' non so rare as can compare
With King Cole and his fiddlers three.

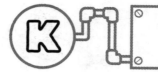 

Kings

Music, Movement, Rhythm, and Rhyme *(CONT.)*

The King/Queen Says...

Modify the traditional game "Simon Says" to "The King (Or Queen) Says."

Appoint one student to be a king or queen. That student says, "The king (or queen) says . . . touch your toes." Students touch their toes. If the king or queen does not preface the phrase and simply says, "Touch your toes," then the students should not imitate the action. Students are "out" if they do imitate the action. The game continues until one student remains. That student is the next king or queen.

Centers

Set up centers to encourage students to explore the theme further during a free choice period, or assign small groups to parent-guided centers while you work with other students.

Math Center

Skills: money, counting

The King's Treasure Chest

In many folk stories, kings have chests filled with gold coins and jewels. Students practice counting and identifying money in this center, with a "treasure chest" filled with play coins and faux jewelry.

Snacks

Be sure to check with parents about allergies before serving students any food.

Mini Fruit Pies

Four and twenty blackbirds baked in a pie might not be such a fitting dish to set before a child; make fruit-filled pies instead!

Ingredients:

- ready-made pie crust
- ready-made fruit pie filling (cherry, blueberry, apple)

Directions:

1. Cut the pie crust into top and bottom crusts.
2. You can use muffin tins to hold the crusts and bake the pies. If you choose to use muffins tins, be sure to cut the top crust so that it is smaller than the bottom.
3. Scoop fruit pie filling onto the bottom crust.
4. Add top crust. Pinch top and bottom crusts closed.
5. Prick top crust with fork.
6. Bake in toaster oven for 15 minutes or until pie crusts are browned.
7. Cool and serve.

Crown Template

Directions: Use with Art Connections project, "King or Queen for a Day," page 130.

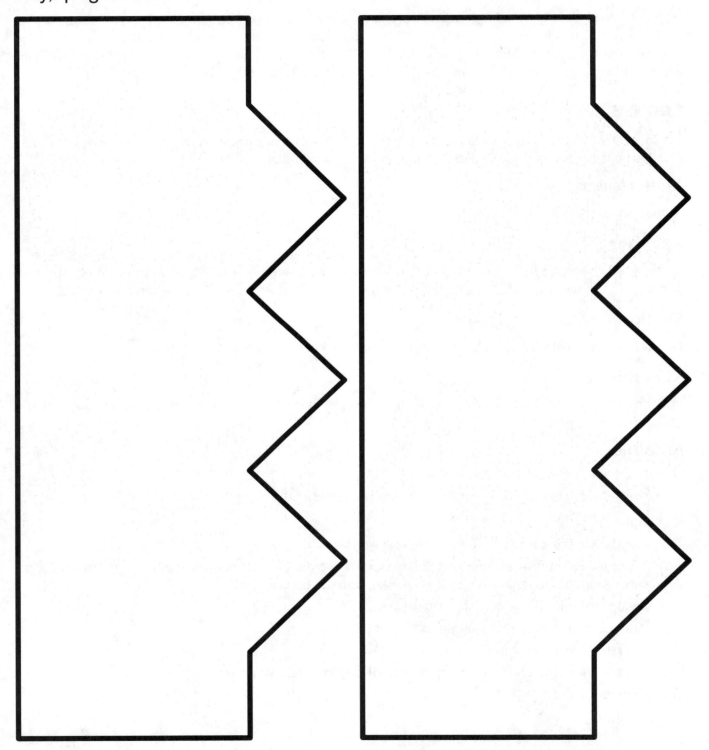

Four and Twenty Blackbirds

Directions: Use with the Math Connection lesson on page 130. Make six copies (for a total of twenty-four birds). Write numbers 1–24 on the birds.

Four and Twenty Blackbirds Pie

Directions: Use with page 135 for the Math Connection lesson on page 130. Make two copies for each student.

Leaves

Unit Overview

Fall evokes images of changing colors, stomping through piles of fallen leaves, and sipping hot apple cider on a cold night. Welcome fall into your classroom by studying "L—Leaves"—collect leaves for counting and sorting, create leaf pictures, share stories about seasonal activities, and taste edible leaves.

Use this unit after "A—Apples" and "V—Vegetables" as a part of an extended study of fruits and vegetables, plants, and seasons. Then study colors with "Y—Yellow."

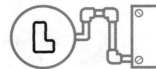 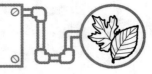

Leaves

Language Arts Connections

Core Book

Hall, Zoe. *Fall Leaves Fall!* Scholastic Press, 2000.

Fall is coming! Its time to catch falling leaves, stomp on crunchy piles, and collect as many different kinds of leaves as possible. Leaves of all colors, sizes and shapes are beautifully illustrated in *Fall Leaves Fall!* There is a simple explanation of how leaves grow at the end of the story.

Read-Aloud Activities

Prior to Reading

- Introduce this book by talking about the fall season. For example, say "In the fall, leaves are changing colors, the weather is getting colder, and everyone is getting ready for winter. This is a story about two children who are excited it is fall."
- Read the title and author's name, pointing to the words as you read.
- Point out the illustrations on the front and back covers. Ask students to predict what might happen in the story based on the illustrations.

During Reading

- As you read, make sure that each student can see the illustrations. Hold the book so that it is facing the students, and turn it slowly as you read.
- Be expressive. Your voice and facial expressions will draw students into the story.

After Reading

- Allow time for students to respond. This story may remind them about playing in the leaves with a sibling, or jumping in leaf piles. Wait a few moments so they can think about what they would like to say.
- If there is not enough time for all students to share, let them know that there will be time during the day for them to write or dictate stories. Or, invite students to share their stories with a partner. Circulate so you can hear their responses.
- Respond to the story yourself with a comment on how this story made you feel, or share a memory from your childhood about fall celebrations.

Additional Books

Stock your class library with books about leaves. Students will enjoy looking at the illustrations and "reading" them to each other. When you read a story to your class, record yourself on tape. Then put the tape and the book in a literacy center so that your students can listen to it time and time again.

Ehlert, Lois. *Red Leaf, Yellow Leaf.* Harcourt Brace Jovanovich, Publishers, 1991.

Marzollo, Jean. *I Am a Leaf.* Scholastic, Inc., 1998.

Robbins, Ken. *Autumn Leaves.* Scholastic, Inc., 1998.

Sohi, Marteza E. *Look What I Did With a Leaf.* Walker and Company, 1993.

Leaves

Language Arts Connections (CONT.)

Letter-Sound Introduction

What is first sound of the word *leaves*? Say *leaves* slowly and deliberately, emphasizing the /*l*/ sound. Tell students that the letter **L** says the sound /*l*/.

Phonemic Awareness

Skill: phoneme blending

Make several copies of the leaves on page 146. Cut them out, and cut each leaf in half. Write beginning **L** words on the leaves, with the **L** on the first half, and the rest of the word on the second half. Do the same with *laugh, like, love, little, long,* etc.

Tell students that you need help putting the leaves back together again. Right now the leaves are split in half because the first sound is separated from the other sounds. If they blend the sounds together into a word, you can put the leaves back together.

Hold up the two halves of each leaf, one in each hand, arms held wide. Students say each word, segmenting the first phoneme (/*l*/). Draw your hands closer together. Students shorten the segmented sound as your hands get closer together. When your hands come together, students say leaf. Continue with the other **L** words.

Letter Formation

After reading *Fall Leaves Fall* by Zoe Hall, and after introducing the letter-sound association, write the letters **L** and **l** so that all the students can see them. Reinforce the association between the letter's formations and its sound by drawing the **L** and **l** into the shape of a leaf.

These activities will help to reinforce letter formation for students of all learning styles.

- Put magnetic letters with similar shapes (**I, i, J, j, L, l, T, t**) into a paper bag stapled shut or a closed box with a hole in its side. Students reach in and feel each letter. They say its name, its sound, and then pull it out of the box or bag to check their answer.

- Guide students in warming up their fingers, hands, and arms by "air writing" vertical lines and right angles.

- Have your students use **L** objects (such as leaves or letters) to form the shapes of the letters **L** and **l**.

- Slice lemons in half for the students to use as paint stamps to form the shapes of the letters **L** and **l**.

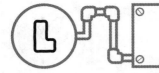

Leaves

Language Arts Connections *(CONT.)*

My Favorite Season Book

Use *Fall Leaves Fall!* by Zoe Hall to encourage your students to share their fondest memories about leaves, the changing seasons, or their favorite seasonal activities. Do this as a center activity with small groups of students.

Materials:
- "Leaf Book Template" (page 145)
- paper cut slightly smaller than the "Leaf Book Template"
- pencils
- crayons and markers
- construction paper

Teacher Preparation:
1. Make a copy of the book cover template and cut it out. Trace the shape onto a file folder or heavy weight paper. Cut that out.
2. Determine whether you will work with individual students or small groups as you record their dictations.
3. Arrange for assistance with the rest of your class while you record dictations.

Procedure:
1. After reading *Fall Leaves Fall!*, tell students what you love about your favorite season.
2. When your students begin to share their stories, tell them that you are eager to hear them all. Encourage students to share their stories quietly with partners, or to illustrate a story idea while they are waiting for their turn to dictate.
3. Invite each student to tell you his or her story. Record their words. If the students need guidance, provide them with sentence starters, such as:
    - "My favorite season is _____."
    - "In the _____, I love to _____."
    - "I also like to _____."
    - "_____ is my favorite season because _____."
4. Return the story to the student so he or she can illustrate it.
5. If students would like to use the leaf template, have them trace the template onto two pieces of construction paper. Assist with cutting them out, if necessary. They can also make their own book covers according to the season they wrote about. For example, they could make snowmen for winter stories.
6. Supervise students with assembling covers and story pages, and then assist with stapling.

Follow-up Activity:

Invite your students to "read" their stories to each other.

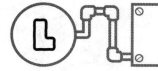 

Leaves

Math Connections

All Kinds of Leaves

Take your class outside for a leaf hunt (see page 144). Then use those leaves in a math lesson. How many different kinds of leaves did they find? Sort and categorize them!

Skills: estimating, counting, sorting, charting

Materials:

- leaves
- butcher paper or chalk board to draw chart
- markers or chalk
- trays, bags or bowls to hold the different categories of leaves
- optional: "All Kinds of Leaves" (page 146) copied onto green, yellow, red and brown paper

Teacher Preparation:

1. Dump a pile of leaves on a sheet of butcher paper on the floor or on a table where all the students can see them.

2. If you will be teaching this lesson to the entire class, you might want to break the class into small groups, and set up sorting centers.

3. Decide whether you will have your students identify the categories, or if you will designate categories of leaves (color, shape, size, etc.).

4. If you will designate the categories, draw symbols on the outside of the bags or whatever container you use to hold the groups of leaves.

5. Note: If taking your class outside for a leaf hunt is not an option, make copies of "All Kinds of Leaves" sheet onto green, yellow, red, and brown paper. Cut out each leaf.

Procedure:

1. Direct your students' attention to the pile of leaves, and ask them to help you sort them into groups to be used for different class activities.

2. Ask for ideas of different ways that the leaves could be sorted.

3. If you have chosen to designate the categories for sorting, tell the students how you plan to have them organize the leaves into groups.

4. If you have chosen to have your students determine how to sort the leaves, assist them with making a final decision (color, shape, or size).

5. Set out the bags or containers to hold the different groups. Draw a symbol (square of color, leaf shape, or size) on the outside of the container. Explain that these containers will hold the different groups of leaves.

6. Ask the students to predict which category will have the most leaves.

7. Have the students sort the pile(s) of leaves into categories. Circulate and assist as needed.

8. Once all the leaves have been sorted, ask your students which category had the most leaves.

9. Count the leaves and chart the results on the board or on a sheet of butcher paper.

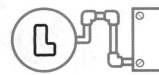

Leaves

Science Connections

What Leaves Do We Eat?

Ask your students if any of them have ever eaten a leaf. For those that respond that they have, ask if they know what type of leaf it was. Explain that many people eat leaves everyday. Provide samples of the types of leaves that we eat, such as lettuce, cabbage, endive, spinach, etc. Invite your students to taste the different types of leaves, and take a vote on which leaf taste the best.

This would be a great opportunity to remind your students to be careful about eating any foods that they might find in their gardens or around their homes. Some plants will make us sick if we eat them, and all children should check with a parent or guardian before eating something from outside.

What Kinds of Leaves?

Your students can identify the types of leaves they find with a bit of research. Have leaf books on hand, such as *Fall Leaves Fall!* by Zoe Hall and *Autumn Leaves* by Ken Robbins (Scholastic, Inc., 1998). (Also see "Additional Books" on page 138). With your students, look through the books, and try to match up the leaves they have found with those identified in the books.

Social Studies Connections

Using Leaves

Leaves are used around the world for many different purposes. Find pictures on the Internet and in books and magazines of leaves used in different ways. Either do this ahead of time, or as a class activity. You may find leaves used as thatching on huts, as clothing on a tropical island (hula skirts), or as food. Post these pictures on butcher paper, and discuss them with the class. Pose the question, "In what other ways can leaves be used?" Record student answers on the butcher paper with illustrations.

Art Connections

Leaf Rubbings

Materials:

- red, yellow, brown, and green crayons
- thin art paper or squares of white butcher paper
- heavy construction paper, torn into long strips of varying widths
- leaves

Teacher Preparation:

1. Assemble materials

Procedure:

1. Students place strips of heavy construction paper under the art paper.
2. Using the side of the crayon, students rub over the construction paper, forming the image of the tree trunk.
3. Students place leaves under art paper, and then rub crayons over the leaves.
4. Encourage students to use a variety of colors when rubbing the leaves.

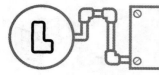 **Leaves**

Art Connections (CONT.)

Leaf Pictures

Take your students on a leaf hunt (see page 143). They students can make pictures using their leaves, just like the children in *Fall Leaves Fall!* An additional resource is *Look What I Did with a Leaf* by Morteza E. Sohi (Walker and Company, 1993.)

Materials:

- leaves of all different shapes, sizes, and colors.
- glue and rubber cement.
- heavy construction paper, cardstock, or cardboard
- crayons and markers

Teacher Preparation:

1. Assemble materials. Optional: Create a sample leaf picture.

Procedure:

1. Show students the pictures of the leaf pictures that the characters created in *Fall Leaves Fall!*
2. Tell them that they will be able to create their own leaf pictures using the leaves collected during the leaf hunt.
3. If you choose, create a demonstration picture prior to having the students make theirs. Show samples from *Look What I Did with a Leaf.*
4. Assist students with creating their own leaf pictures. Suggest that they experiment a little before gluing the leaves into their final position.
5. Select leaves, position, and glue.
6. Students can use crayons and markers to further illustrate their leaf pictures.

Music, Movement, Rhythm, and Rhyme

The Leaves Are Green

The leaves are green
The nuts are brown,
They hang so high
They will not come down.
Leave them alone
Till frosty weather,
Then they will all
Come down together.

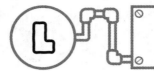 

Leaves

Music, Movement, Rhythm, and Rhyme (CONT.)

Leaf Hunt

Take your students on a leaf hunt. Draw pictures on one half of an 8.5" x 11" piece of paper of leaves that students will find around the school grounds or along a pre-selected walking route. Attach copies of the picture to the outside of small brown lunch bags. Equip each child with a leaf collecting bag, and accompany the class on a leaf hunting expedition. Or, just tell your students to find as many different kinds, colors, sizes and shapes of leaves as they can. Use the leaves in the math lesson and the art project, or just invite your students to take them home and share them with their families.

Centers

Set up centers to encourage students to explore the theme further during a free choice period, or assign small groups to parent-guided centers while you work with other students.

Sensory Center

Skills: sensory awareness, vocabulary building

Leaf Piles

Dump a pile of leaves into a large open container. Students crush and crunch leaves with their hands, and then describe the how the leaves feel. Older students can write or dictate describing words on a sheet of butcher paper above the leaves.

Snacks

Be sure to check with parents about any allergies before serving students any food.

Raw Leaf Vegetables

Provide an assortment of edible raw leaves, such as spinach, lettuces, and cabbages. Have students taste leaves, vote on favorite type of leaf, and then make a large salad for snack time.

Ingredients:

- assorted edible leaves
- carrots
- cucumbers
- celery
- tomatoes
- salad dressing

Procedure:

1. Have the students wash the vegetables.
2. Have the student tear the leaves in to bite sized pieces.
3. After an adult has sliced the vegetables, have the students add them to the leaves.
4. Add salad dressing.

Leaf Booklet Template

Directions: Use with the "My Favorite Season" activity on page 140.

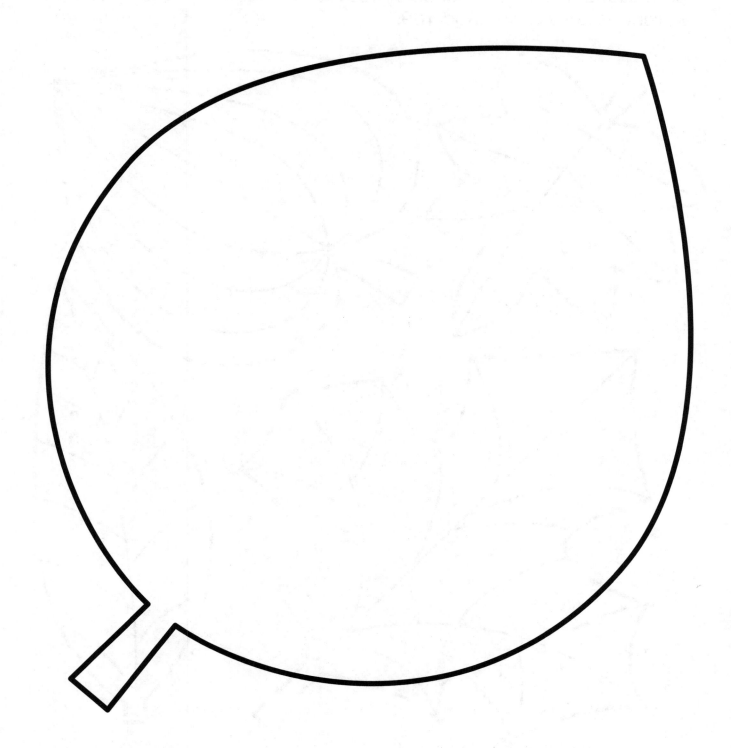

All Kinds of Leaves

Directions: Copy and cut out the leaves. Use with the Math Connections activity, "All Kinds of Leaves" on page 141 and Phonemic Awareness activity on page 139.

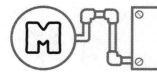 

Overview

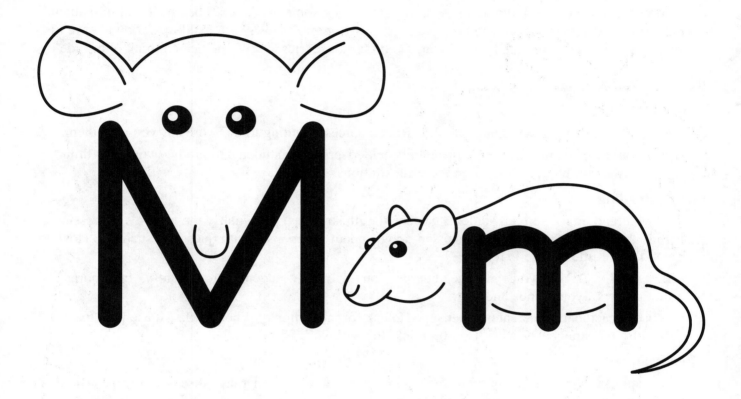

Introduce the letter **M** with a mouse unit. Begin by reading aloud *The Little Mouse, the Red Ripe Strawberry, and the Big Hungry Bear* by Don and Audrey Wood (Child's Play, 1984). Use the traditional nursery rhyme, "Hickory Dickory Dock" in the math lesson, make mouse masks, and make a class book.

Consider using this unit when studying other "Creatures, Creepers and Crawlers" such as "S—Snakes and Salamanders," "I—Insects," "C—Caterpillars," and "B—Butterflies."

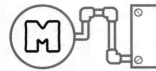 **Mouse**

Language Arts Connections

Core Book

Wood, Don and Audrey. *The Little Mouse, the Red Ripe Strawberry, and the Big Hungry Bear*. Child's Play, 1984.

Little Mouse is all set to pick that red ripe strawberry, when someone (a fox?) begins to tell him about the big hungry bear who can sniff red ripe strawberries from miles away. In his desperation to save his red ripe strawberry from the big hungry bear, the little mouse tries everything he can think of to hide it.

Read-Aloud Activities

Prior to Reading

- Read the title, the author's, and the illustrator's names, pointing to the words as you read them.
- Point out the illustrations on the front and back covers. Ask students to predict what they think the story might be about based on these illustrations.

During Reading

- As you read, make sure all students can see the illustrations, particularly the mouse's expressions. Talk about these facial expressions, and draw students' responses with questions such as, "How do you think Little Mouse is feeling?"
- Be expressive. Your voice and facial expressions will draw students into the story. Incorporate motions with your hands and feet.
- Pause occasionally to create suspense, or to ask for predictions. When Little Mouse tries to disguise the strawberry, ask, "Do you think this will work?"

After Reading

- Ask students for ideas about who was talking to the mouse. Generate a discussion about who this character was, and what it was trying to do.

Additional Books

Stock your class library with books about mice. Students will enjoy looking at the illustrations and "reading" them to each other. When you read a story to your class, record yourself on tape. Then put the tape and the book in a literacy center so that your students can listen to it time and time again.

Aylesworth, Jim. *The Completed Hickory Dickory Dock*. Atheneum, 1990.

Hendry, Diana. *The Very Noisy Night*. Scholastic, Inc., 1999.

Henkes, Kevin. *Wemberly Worried*. Greenwillow, 2000.

Kraus, Robert. *Whose Mouse Are You?* Simon and Schuster, 1970.

Lionni, Leo. *Frederick*. Alfred A. Knopf, 1990.

Nivola, Claire. *The Forest*. Frances Foster Books, 2002.

Numeroff, Laura Joffe. *If You Give a Mouse a Cookie*. HarperCollins Publishers, 1985.

Ryan, Pam Munoz. *Mice and Beans*. Scholastic, 2001.

Walsh, Ellen Stoll. *Mouse Paint*. Harcourt Brace and Company, 1989.

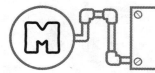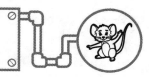
Language Arts Connections (CONT.)

Letter-Sound Introduction

What is first sound of the word mouse? Say mouse slowly and deliberately, emphasizing the /m/ sound. Tell students that the letter **m** makes the sound /m/. (Be careful to say, /m/ not "muh")

Phonemic Awareness

Skill: sequence of sounds—identifying where /m/ is heard in a word

'Marbl-eous" M Words: Set out three clear jars and a bag full of marbles. Put a sheet of paper in front of each jar. Label the first sheet, "beginning," the second, "middle" and the third, "ending."

Tell students to brainstorm words that have the sound /m/. One at a time, have students say their m words. For each word, ask the students where they hear the /m/. Is it in the beginning, middle, or end of the word? If it is the beginning of the word, the student who said the word drops a marble into the first jar. If the /m/ is in the middle of the word, the student drops a marble into the middle jar. If it is at the end of the word, the student drops a marble in the last jar. Write each word on the sheet for that jar.

At the end of the activity, count the marbles in each jar to determine where /m/ was heard most often—at the beginning, middle or ending of words. Keep the jars out, and invite students to add to the lists of words, dropping marbles in the appropriate jars, throughout the "M Mouse" unit.

Letter Formation

After reading *The Little Mouse, The Red Ripe Strawberry, and the Big, Hungry Bear* and introducing the letter-sound association, write the letters **M** and **m** so that all the students can see them. Reinforce the association between the letter formations and its sound by drawing the **M** and **m** into a picture of a big and little mouse.

These activities will help to reinforce letter formation for students of all learning styles.

- Tell students to think of **M** as two mountains and **m** as two hills.
- Put magnetic letters with similar shapes (**M, N, V, W, Y, Z, m, n, h, u, v, w,**) into a paper bag stapled shut or a closed box with a hole in its side. Students reach in and feel each letter. They say its name, its sound, and then pull it out of the box to check their answer.
- Have students hunt for shapes in the environment that resemble the letter shapes **M** and **m**. They can draw pictures of the objects that they find.
- Have students brainstorm objects in the classroom that begin with the /m/ sound: marbles, M & M candies, magazines. Students use those objects to form the letters **M** and **m** (in many different sizes, according to the items used).

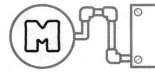 
Language Arts Connections (*CONT.*)

The Little Mouse and The Red Ripe Strawberry Class Book

The sly trickster in *The Little Mouse, The Red Ripe Strawberry, and the Big, Hungry Bear* managed to convince little mouse that the only way to save that red ripe strawberry was to eat it up!

Skills: writing, comprehension, problem solving

Materials:

- paper
- pencils
- optional: Mouse Face Mask (page 156)

Teacher Preparation:

1. The Mouse Face Mask can be used as a book cover template for this activity. Make a copy of the mask template. Draw in the mouse's ears. Use this as a cover for the book.

Procedure:

1. After reading *The Little Mouse, The Red Ripe Strawberry*, and *The Big, Hungry Bear*, ask students to recall the ways in which Little Mouse tried to save that strawberry from the bear.
2. Have students brainstorm other ways in which Little Mouse could have hidden the strawberry.
3. Write student ideas as they dictate them, or have students write their own ideas by sounding out the words.
4. Have students illustrate their ideas.
5. Display student ideas in the classroom, and then assemble into a class booklet, using the mouse face as a book cover.
6. Put the book in the class library so students can read it over and over again.

Math Connections

The Mouse Ran Up the Clock

Use the traditional nursery rhyme, "Hickory Dickory Dock," to teach concepts about clocks and telling time.

Skills: number identification, rhythm and rhyme, reading clocks

Materials:

- Hickory Dickory Dock Clock (page 153) copied onto heavy paper
- Hickory Dickory Dock Animals (pages 158–160)
- brass-plated paper fasteners (one per clock)
- an actual clock

Teacher Preparation:

1. Make one copy each of the clock and the animals.
3. Cut out the clock hands and attach them to the clock. Place the hands at 12.
4. Color and cut out the animal figures.

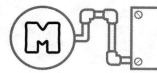 

Mouse

Math Connections (CONT.)

The Mouse Ran Up the Clock (CONT.)

Procedure:

1. Recite the poem "Hickory Dickory Dock" on page 153, using the clock and the animals.

2. For example, for "one," recite:

   Hickory Dickory Dock,

   The mouse ran up the clock. (Run the mouse up the clock.)

   The clock struck one, (Move the little hand to one)

   The mouse ran down, (Run the mouse down the clock.)

   Hickory Dickory Dock,

3. Continue with the rhyme, using the animals and clock to act out the stanzas.

4. Show a real clock to the students, and compare the play clock with the real one. Discuss how the hands of the real clock move: the big one moves fast and the small one moves slowly.

Follow-up:

Have students make their own clocks with which to practice.

Science and Social Studies Connections

The Health and Safety of Mice and Men

Like all animals, mice have special needs. Discover the special needs of mice, and reinforce the home-school connection by instructing students to look for information about mice with their parents or caregivers. (They could search on the Internet, go to the library and check out books about mice, or visit a local pet store or veterinarian.) Ask parents to write findings using simple words and phrases, or have their children draw pictures to illustrate the information. Students can share this information with each other in class. Assemble the written materials in a class book about mice.

Adopt a classroom mouse to care for. Students should share in the responsibility of taking care of the mouse. Prepare a chart listing daily mouse "jobs" such as checking its water and food, and "Ways to Keep Our Mouse Healthy." Be sure to check with students' parents for any animal allergies before adopting a classroom pet.

Discuss the importance of never touching a wild animal, even something as small as a mouse. Some wild animals carry diseases that would make people very sick. When an animal is frightened, it will often bite in order to protect itself. Brainstorm things that students could do if they ever encountered a mouse.

 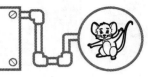

Art Connections

Mouse Mask

Make a mouse mask using the mouse face template on page 156, a number 2 cone shaped coffee filter, chenille stems, and buttons or cotton balls. Students wear their mouse masks while reciting "Hickory, Dickory Dock" on page 153.

Materials:

- Mouse Face Mask template (page 156)
- one #2 cone-shaped coffee filter for each student
- one thin cardboard sheet (minimum size 8" x 10") for each student
- scissors
- markers
- glue
- grey paint and paintbrushes
- chenille stems
- black buttons or cotton balls painted black

Teacher Preparation:

1. Make a copy of the Mouse Face Mask.
2. Cut out the mouse face, and trace the pattern onto several pieces of cardboard. Students will use these as templates to make their own masks. Each small group should have a minimum of two templates.
3. Optional: If students' scissor-using skills are not well developed, pre-cut the following materials:
   a. Copy the template onto a thin cardboard sheet and cut out a mouse face mask for each student.
   b. Cut the coffee filters along the creases. Each half of the coffee filter will make one mouse ear.

Procedure:

Note: Skip Steps 1–3 if you prepared the mouse masks for the students.

1. Distribute mouse face mask templates (two per small group), cardboard sheets (one per student), markers and scissors. Instruct students to trace the template onto the cardboard sheets, and then cut out the mask face. Assist as needed.
2. Assist students with cutting eye holes as indicated on the mouse face mask. Be sure the masks are labeled on the back with students' names.
3. Distribute coffee filters, one per student, and the glue. Instruct students to cut each filter in half by holding the coffee filters open, and cutting the creases. Assist as needed.
4. Instruct students to glue the coffee filter halves onto the mouse face as ears. Assist as needed.
5. Distribute paint and paint brushes. Instruct students to paint mouse faces and ears.
6. Allow to dry thoroughly.
7. Once the masks are dry, glue on chenille stems as whiskers and buttons or cotton balls as noses. Allow to dry thoroughly.

Music, Movement, Rhythm and Rhyme

Hickory, Dickory Dock

Hickory, Dickory Dock,
The mouse ran up the clock.
The clock struck one,
The mouse ran down!
Hickory, Dickory Dock!

Hickory, Dickory Dock,
The bird looked at the clock,
The clock struck two,
Away she flew,
Hickory, Dickory Dock!

Hickory, Dickory Dock,
The dog barked at the clock,
The clock struck three,
Fiddle-de-dee,
Hickory, Dickory Dock!

Hickory, Dickory Dock,
The bear slept by the clock,
The clock struck four,
The bear ran out the door.
Hickory, Dickory Dock!

Hickory, Dickory Dock,
The bee buzzed round the clock,
The clock struck five,
She went to her hive,
Hickory, Dickory Dock!

Hickory, Dickory Dock,
The hen pecked at the clock,
The clock struck six,
Oh, fiddle-sticks,
Hickory, Dickory Dock!

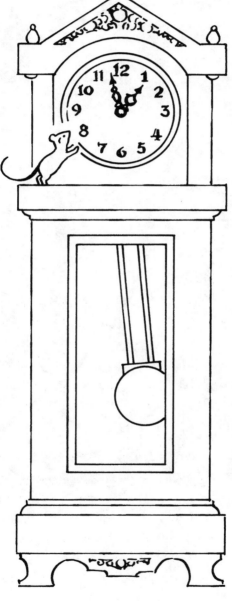

Hickory, Dickory Dock,
The cat ran round the clock,
The clock struck seven,
She wanted to get'em,
Hickory, Dickory Dock!

Hickory, Dickory Dock,
The horse jumped over the clock,
The clock struck eight,
He ate some cake,
Hickory, Dickory Dock!

Hickory, Dickory Dock,
The cow danced on the clock,
The clock struck nine,
She felt so fine,
Hickory, Dickory Dock!

Hickory, Dickory Dock,
The pig oinked at the clock,
The clock struck ten,
She did it again,
Hickory, Dickory Dock!

Hickory, Dickory Dock,
The duck quacked at the clock,
The clock struck eleven,
The duck said "oh heavens!"
Hickory, Dickory Dock!

Hickory, Dickory Dock,
The mouse ran up the clock,
The clock struck noon,
He's here too soon!
Hickory, Dickory Dock!

Mouse Race

Make "mice" out of empty walnut shell halves. Glue wiggly eyes, small black beads as noses, small felt ears, and chenille stems as tails onto the nutshells. Once the mice are made, students place a marble in the walnut shell hollows of their mice, and then push the mouse along the track on page 154.

Mouse

Mouse Race

Directions: Use with mice students made following directions on page 153.

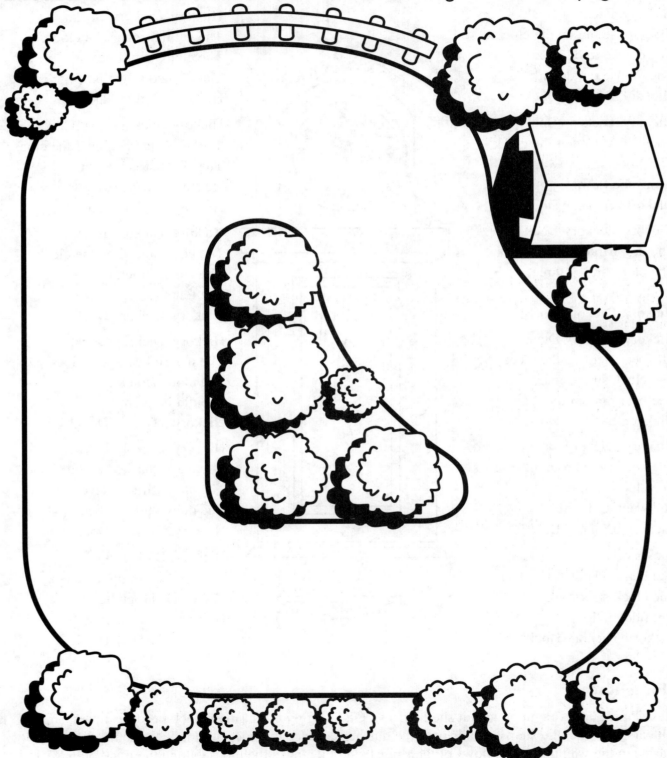

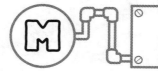 # Mouse

Centers

Set up centers to encourage students to explore the theme further during a free choice period, or assign small groups to parent-guided centers while you work with other students.

Math Center

Skills: problem solving

Mouse House

Mice make their homes by using things that they find. Set out a variety of materials: tissue boxes, toilet paper rolls, cereal boxes, yarn, buttons, etc., and challenge students to create mouse houses. Students should think not only about the exterior of the house, but the interior, as well. Ask questions such as, "What will the mouse sleep on?"

Snacks

Be sure to check with parents about allergies before serving students any food.

Strawberry Pie

The Little Mouse certainly loved red, ripe strawberries. When strawberries are in season, eat them fresh, or make the following mini strawberry pies. The following recipe yields 18 mini pies.

Ingredients:

- 3 cups sugar (with sweet strawberries, reduce to 1½ cups)
- 9 cups strawberries (3 cups mashed and 6 cups sliced)
- 9 tablespoons cornstarch
- 4 drops red food coloring
- 18 mini graham cracker pie crusts
- whipped cream

Directions:

With students, in small groups:

1. Wash and hull the strawberries.
2. Mash 3 cups and slice the remaining 6 cups. Set aside in separate containers.
3. Add enough water to the mashed strawberries to make 4 cups.
4. In a saucepan, combine the sugar, mashed berries/water mixture, cornstarch and food coloring.
5. Cook over medium heat until thick. Stir in the sliced strawberries.
6. Pour into the mini pie shells.
7. Chill
8. Top with whipped cream

Cheese Snacks

Mice love cheese! Have the students sample different types of cheeses, and then vote for their favorite types in a class poll. Record the results of the poll on a chart or bar graph.

Mouse Face Mask

Directions: Copy onto white paper. Cut out and trace pattern onto thin cardboard sheet. Cut apart and attach halves of a #2 cone-shaped coffee filter as ears. Paint gray, and allow it to dry. Glue on chenille stems as whiskers.

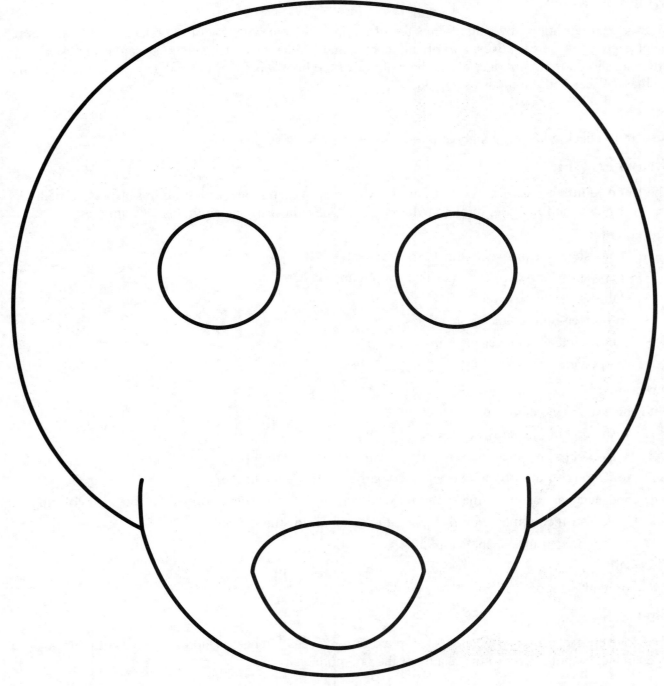

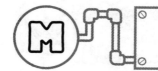 # Mouse

Hickory Dickory Dock Clock

Directions: Cut out the clock and hands. Fasten the hands onto the clock with a brass-plated fastener through the hole in the center of the clock. Use the clock and animals (on page 158–160) to recite the nursery rhyme, "Hickory, Dickory Dock" as directed in the Math Connection activity on pages 150–151.

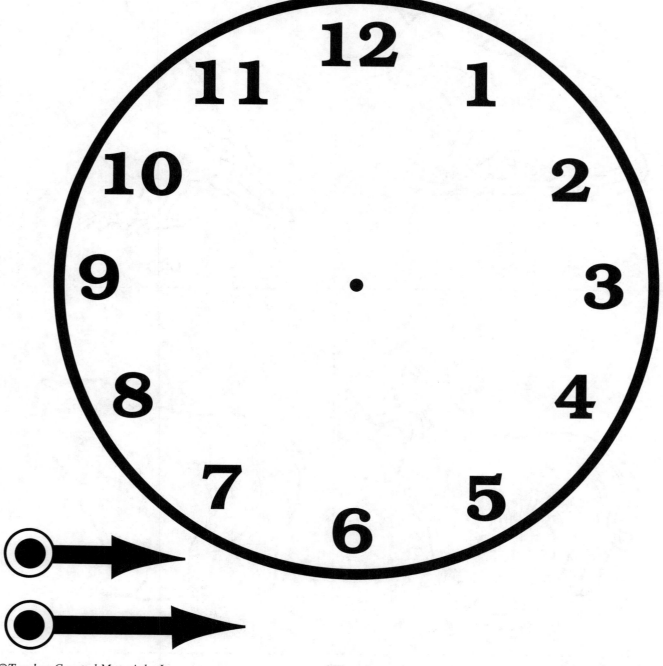

 # Mouse

Hickory Dickory Dock Animals

mouse

bird

dog

bear

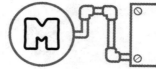 
Hickory Dickory Dock Animals (CONT.)

bee

cat

hen

horse

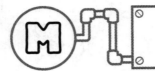 
Hickory Dickory Dock Animals *(CONT.)*

cow

pig

duck

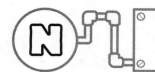

Overview

Nursery rhymes are an ideal tool for teaching early literacy skills to young children. Introduce the letter **N** to students with a study of nursery rhymes. Create a language-rich environment that promotes early literacy skills while also integrating math, science, social studies, art and movement.

If you choose to expand on this theme, follow-up with familiar fairy tales in "J—Jack and the Beanstalk" and "P—Pigs."

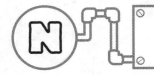 

Nursery Rhymes

Language Arts Connections

Core Book

Stevens, Janet and Stevens Crummel, Susan. *And the Dish Ran Away with the Spoon*. Harcourt, Inc., 2001.

The rhyme "Hey Diddle, Diddle" has ended, but the dish and the spoon have yet to return! Join the cat, the dog and the cow as they search through the land of nursery rhymes for the runaway dish and the spoon.

Read-Aloud Activities

Prior to Reading

- Read the title and the author's name, pointing at the words as you read. Remind students of the nursery rhyme "Hey Diddle Diddle."
- Point out the illustrations on the front and back covers. Look at some of the illustrations inside the book.
- Ask students to predict what they think the story might be about based on the title and cover illustrations.

During Reading

- As you read, make sure that each student can see the illustrations and the characters from all the different nursery rhymes. Discuss which nursery rhymes and folk tales the students recognize throughout the story.
- Be expressive. Adopt different voices for the different characters.

After Reading

- Ask students to recall the nursery rhymes they saw in this story.

Additional Books

Stock your class library with books with and about nursery rhymes. Students will enjoy looking at the illustrations and "reading" them to each other. When you read a story to your class, record yourself on tape. Then put the tape and the book in a literacy center so that your students can listen to it time and time again.

Ahlberg, Janet and Allan. *Each Peach Pear Plum*. Viking-Penguin, 1978.

Cabrera, Jane. *Old Mother Hubbard*. Holiday House, 2001.

Green, Alison. *The Macmillan Treasury of Nursery Rhymes and Poems*.
    Macmillan Children's Books, 1998.

Hooper, Caroline. *The Usborne Nursery Rhyme Songbook*. EDC Publishing, 1996.

Loomans, Diane; Loomans, Julia; Kolberg, Karen. *Positively Mother Goose*. H J Kremer Inc., 1991.

McKellar, Shona. *Counting Rhymes*. Dorling Kindersley, 1993.

Miranda, Anne. *To Market, To Market*. Voyager Books, 2001.

Opie, Iona (editor). *My Very First Mother Goose*. Candlewick Press, 1996.

Rankin, Laura. *Merl and Jasper's Supper Caper*. Alfred A. Knopf, 1997.

Scieszka, Jon. *The Stinky Cheese Man and Other Fairly Stupid Tales*. Viking, 1992.

Tabeck, Sims. *This is the House that Jack Built*. G.P. Putnam's Sons, 2002.

Trapani, Iza. *I'm a Little Teapot*. Whispering Coyote Press, 1996.

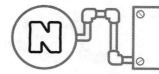

Language Arts Connections (CONT.)

Letter-Sound Introduction

Say the word *nursery* slowly and deliberately, emphasizing the sound /n/. Ask students what beginning sound they hear in *nursery*. Tell students that the letter **n** makes the sound /n/.

Phonemic Awareness

Skill: identifying similar word patterns

Rhyme Time

Create a collection of word groups from nursery rhymes used in this unit.

Cut strips of construction paper or poster board. After reciting or reading a nursery rhyme, have students identify and write down the words that rhymed. Post these in word groups on a wall titled "Rhyme Time." To reinforce the language visually, draw a symbol or picture on the card next to the word.

Letter Formation

After reading *And the Dish Ran Away with the Spoon* and introducing the letter-sound association, reinforce the association between the letter's formations and its sound by drawing the **N** and **n** into the shape of scenes from a nursery rhyme. For example, **N** could be drawn in the shape of the "Old Woman Who Lived in a Shoe" and **n** could be the wall on which Humpty Dumpty is sitting.

These activities will help to reinforce letter formation for students of all learning styles.

- Put plastic letter shapes (such as the refrigerator letter magnets) into a paper bag stapled shut or a closed box with a hole in its side. Students put their hand in the hole and identify each letter that they feel. They check themselves by pulling the letter out of the box or bag.

- Provide a variety of different shapes: lines, circles, ovals, rectangles, and squares. Which shapes can be used to form the letters **N** and **n**?

- Draw the letters **N** and **n** onto 2 foot lengths of butcher paper. Students draw images or glue on pictures of objects that begin with the sound /n/.

- Cue auditory learners by verbally walking them through the letter formation. For example, say, "To make the letter **N** we draw a line up, and then slide down in the valley, and then another line back up."

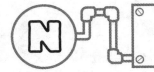

Nursery Rhymes

Language Arts Connections (CONT.)

Nursery Rhyme Scramble

Students unscramble the phrases of familiar nursery rhymes and put them back in order with the help of picture cues. Use this activity at a guided literacy center with small groups of students. (This activity requires prior knowledge of familiar nursery rhymes, and may necessitate teaching of those rhymes.)

Skills: comprehension, sequencing

Materials:

- Nursery Rhymes (pages 169–172)
- scissors
- glue sticks
- paper

Teacher Preparation:

1. Make enough copies of "Nursery Rhymes" so that each student has at least one rhyme.
2. Cut the nursery rhymes into mini-book pages.
3. Shuffle the mini-book pages so the sentences are out of order. Paperclip each group.

Procedure:

1. Distribute sets of nursery rhymes to students. Explain that they each have the sentences of a nursery rhyme, but the sentences have been mixed up. The pictures with each sentence will help them to figure out what the sentence says.
2. Review the nursery rhymes "Jack and Jill," "Hey Diddle, Diddle," "Humpty Dumpty," and "Little Bo Peep."
3. Ask students to try to identify which nursery rhyme they have based on the pictures. Beginning readers could attempt to identify words within each phrase.
4. Instruct students to look at the pictures next to each sentence and to try to determine what the sentence says, based on the picture.
5. Have the students sort sentences into correct sequence or staple into mini-books.

Math Connections

Counting Rhymes

Take a few minutes daily to recite counting rhymes, and provide students with opportunities to practice counting skills.

Skills: counting, number identification

Materials:

- counting rhymes from "Music, Movement, Rhythm, and Rhyme" (page 166)
- flannel numbers on felt board or magnetic numbers on magnetic board

Procedure:

1. Recite counting rhymes and teach them to students.
2. As students recite counting rhymes, put numbers on felt or magnetic boards as each number is called out.

Nursery Rhymes

Science Connections

Poems and Rhymes about Weather

There are many nursery rhymes and songs about the weather and seasons. Recite and teach these rhymes to your students during lessons about the weather.

March Winds

March winds and April showers bring forth May flowers.

Calm in June

Calm weather in June sets corn in tune.

Winter

Cold and raw the north wind doth blow,

Bleak in the morning early.

All the hills are covered with snow,

And winter's now come fairly.

Rain on the Green Grass

Rain on green grass,

And rain on the tree;

Rain on the house top,

But not on me!

Social Studies Connections

Family Favorites

Reinforce the home-school connection. Ask parents to share their favorite nursery rhymes—perhaps those they remember best from their own childhood—with their children. Encourage parents to recite nursery rhymes on a regular basis with their children to continue to build foundations for reading skills.

Art Connections

Nursery Rhyme Stick Puppets

Provide students with their own pictures of characters from familiar nursery rhymes. Students will use them to create stick puppets with which to act out their favorite rhymes. Do this activity at a guided art center.

Materials:

- Nursery Rhyme Characters (pages 173–179)
- craft sticks
- crayons and markers
- scissors
- glue sticks

Teacher Preparation:

1. Make copies of Nursery Rhymes Characters for each group.

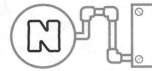

Nursery Rhymes

Art Connections (CONT.)

Nursery Rhyme Stick Puppets (CONT.)

Procedure:

1. Have the students choose nursery rhyme characters that they want to make into puppets.
2. Have the student color and cut out the characters. Assist as needed.
3. Have the students glue the characters onto craft sticks.
4. Have the students recite nursery rhymes using their characters.

Alternative:

Instead of making stick puppets, laminate the nursery rhyme characters and put a Velcro tab on the back of each. Students can use the characters with felt or flannel boards to recite nursery rhymes in a free choice center.

Music, Movement, Rhythm, and Rhyme

One, Two, Buckle My Shoe (Traditional)

One, two, buckle my shoe.

Three, four, shut the door.

Five, six pick up sticks.

Seven, eight, lay them straight.

Nine, ten, a big fat hen.

Eleven, twelve, dig and delve;

Thirteen, fourteen, maids a-courting.

Fifteen, sixteen, maids in the kitchen.

Seventeen, eighteen, maids a-waiting.

Nineteen, twenty, my plate's empty.

One, Two, Three (Traditional)

One, two, three, four, five,

Once I caught a fish alive.

Six, seven, eight, nine, ten,

Because it bit my finger so.

Which finger did it bite?

The little one upon the right.

Going to St. Ives (Traditional)

As I was going to St. Ives,

I met a man with seven wives.

Every wife had seven sacks.

Every sack had seven cats.

Every cat had seven kits.

Kits, cat, sacks, and wives.

How many were going to St. Ives? (one)

Fingerplays and Nursery Rhymes

Sing and play along with nursery rhymes that incorporate movements and rhythm. Recite some of these familiar nursery rhymes, or play a cassette tape with nursery rhymes and songs that encourage movement. *Wee Sing© Children's Songs and Fingerplays*, by Pamela Conn Beall and Susan Hagen Nipp (Price Sloan Stern, 1979) is a tape and book set with illustrations and detailed instructions for finger plays.

Music, Movement, Rhythm and Rhyme (CONT.)

Here We Go Round the Mulberry Bush (Traditional)

Four or five students join hands so that they form and circle, and chant or sing this rhyme as they go around and around a small object representing the bush.

Here we go round the mulberry bush,

The mulberry bush,

The mulberry bush,

Here we go round the mulberry bush,

So early in the morning.

Eensy, Weensy Spider

Student use their fingers and hands to create the spider, rain, and sunshine as they sing or recite this familiar rhyme. Vary this song with lyrics such as "great big spider," "tiny bitty spider," etc.

The eensy, weensy spider
Climbed up the water spout.
  (opposite ring fingers and thumbs touch and
  rotate creating a climbing motion)
Down came the rain,
  (fingers wiggle in downward motion),
And washed the spider out.
  (hands sweep apart)
Out came the sun
  (hands join together in arch over head)
And dried up all the rain
  (body rocks back and forth under arched hands)
And the eensy, weensy spider
Climbed up the spout again
  (finger create climbing motion again)

Centers

Set up centers to encourage students to explore the theme further during a free choice period, or assign small groups to parent-guided centers while you work with other students.

Flannel Board Center

Skills: story retelling, rhythm and rhyme

Nursery Rhyme Characters Sets

Make a copy of the "Nursery Rhymes Characters" found at the end of this end of this unit. Copy, color, cut and laminate the characters from familiar nursery rhymes. Attach a Velcro square to the back of each, and use with a flannel board to retell the rhymes. Velcro will hold the figures onto a flannel board. Have students use these to retell the rhymes.

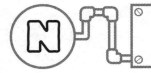 

Nursery Rhymes

Snacks

Be sure to check with parents about allergies before serving students any food.

Pease Porridge Hot

Pease porridge hot,

Pease porridge cold,

Pease porridge in the pot,

Nine days old.

Some like it hot,

Some like it cold,

Some like it in the pot,

Nine days old.

Porridge Hot

After reciting "Pease Porridge Hot," make some instant oatmeal as a mid-morning snack.

Ingredients:

- instant oatmeal
- hot water
- fresh and dried fruit chunks: apples slices, raisins
- chopped nuts
- brown sugar
- milk

Directions:

1. Mix oatmeal and water as directed.
2. Add fruit, nuts, sugar and milk to taste.
3. Allow to cool before serving.

Humpty Dumpty

Make scrambled eggs or hard boiled eggs after reciting "Humpty Dumpty":

Humpty Dumpty sat on a wall.

Humpty Dumpty had a great fall.

All the king's horses and all the king's men,

Couldn't put Humpty together again.

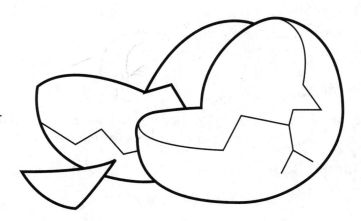

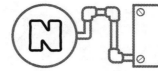 

Nursery Rhymes

Directions: Use this and the following three pages with Language Arts Connections Activity on page 163.

Jack and Jill

Jack and Jill went up the hill,

To fetch a pail of water,

Jack fell down and broke his crown

And Jill came tumbling after.

Nursery Rhymes (CONT.)

Hey Diddle Diddle

Hey, diddle, diddle,
the cat and the fiddle,

The cow jumped over the moon.

The little dog laughed
to see such fun

And the dish ran away
with the spoon.

Nursery Rhymes (CONT.)
Humpty Dumpty

Humpty Dumpty sat on a wall,

Humpty Dumpty had a great fall.

All the king's horses and
all the king's men,

Couldn't put Humpty
together again.

Nursery Rhymes (CONT.)

Little Bo Peep

Little Bo Peep has lost
her sheep

And can't tell where
to find them.

Leave them alone,
and they'll come

Wagging their tails
behind them.

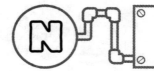

Nursery Rhyme Characters

Directions: Copy, color, cut and laminate these characters from familiar nursery rhymes. Attach a Velcro© square to the back of each, and use with a flannel board to retell the rhymes.

Humpty Dumpty

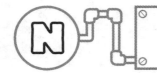 

Nursery Rhyme Characters (CONT.)

Humpty Dumpty (CONT.)

Mary Had a Little Lamb

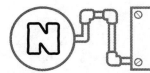

Nursery Rhymes

Nursery Rhyme Characters (CONT.)

Mary Had a Little Lamb (CONT.)

Nursery Rhyme Characters (CONT.)

Little Bo Peep

Jack and Jill

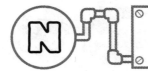 

Nursery Rhyme Characters (CONT.)
Eensy Weensy Spider

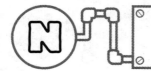

Nursery Rhyme Characters (CONT.)

Hey Diddle Diddle

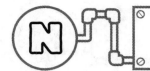

Nursery Rhyme Characters (CONT.)

Hey Diddle Diddle (CONT.)

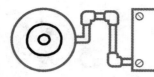

Octopi in the Ocean

Overview

Explore the sounds of **O** with an ocean unit. Begin with an ocean story and teach the letter/sound associations by drawing the shape of **O** into ocean illustrations during a retelling of the story. Integrate writing, math, and science with related activities. For a culminating project, your students can create their own ocean animals. Extend this unit by integrating the letter/sound studies for "W—Whales."

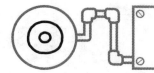

Octopi in the Ocean

Language Arts Connections

Core Book

Collicott, Sharleen. *Seeing Stars*. Dial Books for Young Readers, 1996.

Fuzzball isn't so sure he wants to leave the junkyard to accompany Motley's travels into space and escape from life in the junkyard. Reluctantly, he agrees to join Motley aboard their "junkbird" in a flight to the stars. What wonders they behold in "space." Soon, however, their junkbird encounters serious problems, and Fuzzball and Motley find themselves being rescued by some unexpected friends.

Read-Aloud Activities

Prior to Reading

- Before reading the story or showing the cover illustrations, tell students the title of the book, *Seeing Stars*. Ask students what they think the story might be about, based on the title alone. Then tell students to listen carefully to determine whether the story really is about "seeing stars."

During Reading

- As you read, make sure that each student can see the illustrations. The illustrations are a very important part of this story; the characters believe that they are in space, but the illustrations show that they are in the ocean. Ask questions such as, "Where do they think they are? Where are they really?"

After Reading

- Ask for student responses to the story. For example, have students find their favorite illustrations from the book, and discuss them with each other.
- Invite students to draw their own pictures about the duo's adventure.

Additional Books

Stock your class library with books about oceans and octopi. Students will enjoy looking at the illustrations and "reading" them to each other. When you read a story to your class, record yourself on tape. Then put the tape and the book in a literacy center so that your students can listen to it time and time again.

Cole, Joanna. *The Magic School Bus on the Ocean Floor*. Scholastic, 1994.
Frasier, Debra. *Out of the Ocean*. Harcourt, Inc., 1998.
Gay, Marie-Louise, *Stella, Star of the Sea*. Groundwood Books, 1999.
Kraus, Robert. *Herman the Helper*. Simon & Schuster, 1987.
Lambert, David. *The Kingfisher Young People's Book of Oceans*. Kingfisher Publications, 1997.
Lionni, Leo. *Swimmy*. Knopf, 1991.
Markes, Julie. *Good Thing You're Not an Octopus!* Harpercollins, 2001.
Morris, Rick. *Mysteries and Marvels of Ocean Life*. Usborne Publishing Ltd., 1983.
Most, Bernard. *My Very Own Octopus*. Harcourt Brace & Company, 1988.
Pallotta, Jerry. *The Ocean Alphabet Book*. Charlesbrdige Publishing, 1989.
Ryan, Pam Munoz. *Hello Ocean*. Tailwinds, 2001.
Toft, Kim Michelle. *Neptune's Nursery*. Charlesbridge Publishing, 1999.
Ward, Jennifer. *Somewhere in the Ocean*. Rising Moon, 2000.
Zuchora-Walske, Christine. *Giant Octopuses*. Lerner, 2000.

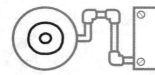

Octopi in the Ocean

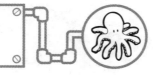

Language Arts Connections (*CONT.*)

Letter-Sound Introduction

Say *octopus* slowly and deliberately, emphasizing the /ŏ/ sound. Tell students that the letter **o** makes the sound /ŏ/. Next say *ocean*, and tell students that **o** also makes the /ō/. The long sound of **o** says its own name, like *ocean*. The letter **o** does not always say its sounds by itself. Sometimes other letters, like **a** and **e,** help.

Phonemic Awareness

Skill: identifying where **o** is heard in a word.

Fishing for O

After introducing the letter-sound association, have students brainstorm **o** words. In this activity, **o** words are defined as having /ō/ or /ŏ/ anywhere—beginning, middle or ending, for example, *ocean*, *octopus*, *on*, *boat*, *row*, *hop*, *blow*, etc. Write these words down on the copies of the fish cards on page 188.

The following day, prepare three "fishing nets" made out of paper bags. Line up the "nets" in a row. Clip a metal paper clip on each **O** word fish card, and drop the cards into an "ocean," such as a blue bucket. Make a fishing pole out of a stick, a piece of string and a small magnet. Tie the magnet onto the string, then tie the string onto the stick.

One at a time, have the students "fish" for word cards by dropping the magnet fishing pole into the bucket. When they "catch" a card, read it with them. Have them listen for where the /ō/ and /ŏ/ is heard—in the beginning, middle or at the end of the word. If it is heard in the beginning, they drop the fish card into the first net, into the second net for the middle, and into the third net for the ending.

Letter Formation

After reading *Seeing Stars* by Sharleen Collicott, and after introducing the letter-sound association, write the letters **O** and **o** so that all the students can see them. Reinforce the association between the letter formations and its sound by drawing the **O** and **o** into pictures of octopi swimming in the ocean.

These activities will help to reinforce letter formation for students of all learning styles.

- Prior to having each student practice writing the letter **o**. Have them move their arms in circle shapes, then their hands, then their fingers.

- Identify **o** shapes in the environment.

- Point out that when they say the long /ō/ sound (*o-cean*), their lips form an **o** shape.

- As a group, join hands and form a large circle. Individually, have the students figure out different ways to make the letter **o** using their bodies. Then have them form the letter **o** with one other student.

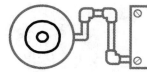 

Octopi in the Ocean

Language Arts Connections (CONT.)

A Fishy Tale

In this writing activity, students retell the story of Motley and Fuzzball from the perspective of one of the fish they encounter. This activity is best done over the course of the week. Take one day to brainstorm ideas, and then spend time each additional day writing pages of the story. Illustrating the pages will take a full day.

Skills: comprehension, point of view, brainstorming

Materials:

- butcher paper
- marker
- art paper
- crayons and markers
- a copy of *Seeing Stars*

Day One Procedure:

1. Review the story of Motley and Fuzzball's adventure.
2. Begin by talking about who the main characters of the story are, and how we learn about their adventure.
3. Introduce the concept of point of view by saying that we learn about what happens to Motley and Fuzzball because we can see everything that they can see, and more.
4. Ask, "What would happen if we were not in the bird ship, but instead we were one of the fish in the water? How would what we saw change?"
5. Brainstorm ideas with the students. Ask questions such as, "What do you think the fish were thinking?" Record student ideas on the butcher paper.

Days Two, Three, and Four Procedures:

1. Ask for suggestions for how to start the story. It could begin with a statement such as, "One day, I was swimming along, minding my own business, when suddenly a huge thing splashed in the water next to me."
2. Guide students through the process of turning the brainstormed ideas into sentences.
3. Write the sentences on art paper to be illustrated on the final day.

Day Five Procedure:

1. When the story is complete, have students brainstorm a title.
2. Pass the completed pages out to pairs or small groups of students to illustrate.
3. Have one group of students illustrate the book cover.
4. When all the pages have been illustrated, assemble the book.
5. Add the book to the class library so students can read it over and over again.

 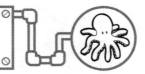

Octopi in the Ocean

Math Connections

The Eight-Armed Octopus

Use the eight arms of an octopus to focus on the number eight and to review number identification, writing and order. This activity is recommended for a math center with groups of four students.

Skills: counting, number identification, number writing, quantity of eight, (extension: adding, subtracting, concept of multiples of eight)

Materials:

- The Eight-Armed Octopus patterns (pages 189–190)
- book about octopi, such as *Giant Octopuses* by Christine Zuchora-Walske (Lerner, 2000)
- markers

Teacher Preparation:

1. Make one copy of the octopus body, and four copies of the octopus legs (for a total of eight legs), for each center.

Procedure:

1. Read one of the literature selections about octopi. Have students count the number of tentacles (legs) on an octopus pictured in the book.
2. Display the body of the octopus, and then tell the students that they will be adding the tentacles.
3. Review counting from one to eight.
4. Distribute markers, and have each student write two numbers (one to eight) on the tentacles (one number per tentacle).
5. Have students glue the tentacles onto the octopus body in numerical order.

Extension:

Introduce the concept of multiples to students who are able to count fluently to thirty-two. This is an activity for the entire class.

1. Divide the class into groups of four students each. Provide an octopus (with tentacles attached) to each group.
2. Count the total number of tentacles in the class, loudly emphasizing the multiples of 8.
3. Have the students clap as each group counts their last tentacle. For example, Group 1 claps when they get to number eight, Group 2 when they reach number 16, and so forth.
4. Write these multiples (8, 16, 24, 32) on the board.
   a. Ask the students why they think you wrote these numbers.
   b. Discuss how those are the numbers that were called as each group got to the end of counting the number of tentacles.
   c. Say that these are the numbers that we get when 8 is added to 8, then to another 8, etc. If students are ready, count as high as they can go by 8's.

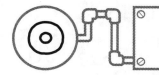

Octopi in the Ocean

Math Connections (CONT.)

The Eight-Armed Octopus (CONT.)

5. Ask questions such as, "How many tentacles were there all together when there were only two octopi?" "When another octopus joined them, how many tentacles were there then?"

6. Integrate other activities of counting in 8s throughout the day.

   a. For example, when the students line up for lunch, have them start counting off; when they get to the eighth person in line, have that student step forward or have everyone clap. Repeat with the sixteenth person, and twenty-fourth.

   b. Have the students pair up with another student. Challenge each pair to come up with a pattern that ends up with clapping on the eighth number. For example, touch a body part for each number: 1—left ear, 2—right ear, 3—left shoulder, 4—right shoulder, 5—left thigh, 6—right thigh, 7—spread hand in open gesture, 8—clap! Repeat for 9 to 16 and 17 to 24.

Science Connections

Water Habitats

After reading *Seeing Stars*, discuss the difficulties that Motley and Fuzzball began to experience when they were unable to breathe air. Ask why the fish seemed to be fine underwater. Then introduce the concept of the ocean as a habitat where some animals can live and others cannot. Provide photographs of different types of animals. Draw a picture of water with the words "ocean habitat" on one side of a chart and a picture of land and trees with the words "land habitats" on the other. Brainstorm with the students which animals they think could live in the ocean and which could not. Put the picture under the appropriate category on the chart.

Classroom Aquarium

Create a water habitat in an aquarium in the classroom. Discuss what the animals living in the aquarium will need to survive. Assign students to care for the habitat under supervision.

Make an Ocean

Make a portable ocean for each student. Pour equal amounts of vegetable oil and water into a small water bottle. Add blue food coloring. Screw the lid tightly onto the water bottle. Have students shake their ocean bottles and observe what happens. Add small plastic ocean animals, if desired.

Social Studies Connections

The Oceans of the World

Oceans cover over two-thirds of the earth's surface. Look at the oceans of the world with the students on a large world map or globe. Find the nearest ocean and discuss how far away that ocean is; for example, talk about how long it would take to drive there. Encourage questions and discussions prompted by the map or globe.

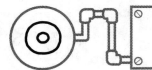 
Art Connections

Ocean Animal Creation

Look at the ocean animals Fuzzball and Motley create at the end of the story. Your students can create their own ocean fish using household items that they bring from home.

Materials:

- plastic bottle or jar, washed and dried, for each student
- paint (acrylic is recommended for painting plastic, though it stains)
- paint brushes and water
- buttons or "wiggly" eyes
- glue (a glue gun is recommended, for adult use only)
- 2 or 3 cone-shaped coffee filters per child or construction paper cut into fin and tail shapes

Teacher Preparation:

1. Assemble the materials.

Procedure:

1. Students paint their plastic jars.
2. Allow to dry.
3. While the jar is drying, students color the coffee filters with markers, then dip in water to diffuse the colors. Allow the filters to dry.
4. Glue or tape the filters onto the sides and back of the jar to resemble fins and a tail.
5. Glue on eyes.

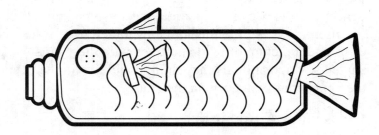

Music, Movement, Rhythm, and Rhyme

I Saw a Ship A-Sailing

I saw a ship a-sailing.
A-sailing on the sea,
And oh but it was laden
With pretty things for me.
There were comfits in the cabin,
And apples in the hold;
The sails were made of silk,
And the masts were all of gold.

The four-and-twenty sailors,
That stood between the decks,
Were four-and-twenty white mice
With jewels around their necks.
The captain was a duck
With a packet on his back,
And the ship began to move
The captain said, "Quack, Quack!"

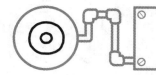 

Octopi in the Ocean

Music, Movement, Rhythm, and Rhyme (CONT.)

School of Fish

Read *Swimmy* by Leo Lionni (Knopf, 1991). Discuss how the school of fish looked like one big fish, but was actually made up of many little fish. One school of fish is made up of many individual fish. Assemble the children into a "school of fish." Have the group move together as one unit, with each student taking turns "leading" the school.

Centers

Set up centers to encourage students to explore the theme further during a free choice period, or assign small groups to parent-guided centers while you work with other students.

Science Center

Skills: observations, sensory exploration

At the Beach

Create a beach center with sand, shells, water, rocks, and other objects from the beach. Have students explore the texture of the sand, make prints with shells and rocks, and use the sand to trace letter shapes. Discuss what the sand and water feels like.

Snacks

Be sure to check with students' parents about allergies before serving any food.

Ocean Gelatin

Create an ocean gelatin mold using blue gelatin, with pieces of fruit as the ocean animals.

Ingredients:
- packaged boxes of blue gelatin
- pieces of fruit

Directions:
1. Mix the gelatin as directed on the package.
2. Add fruit.
3. Allow to set.

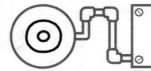

Octopi in the Ocean

Ocean Fish Cards

Directions: Use these cards with the Phonemic Awareness activity, "Fishing for **O**" on page 182. Copy and cut out the cards. Write **o** words on the cards. Have students fish for the **o** cards.

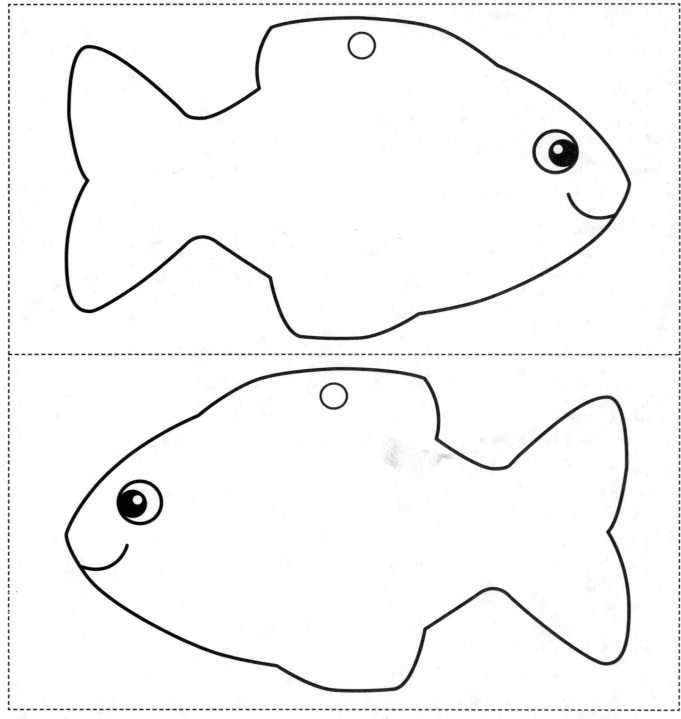

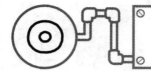

Octopi in the Ocean

The Eight-Armed Octopus

Directions: Use with page 184.

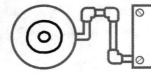

The Eight-Armed Octopus (CONT.)

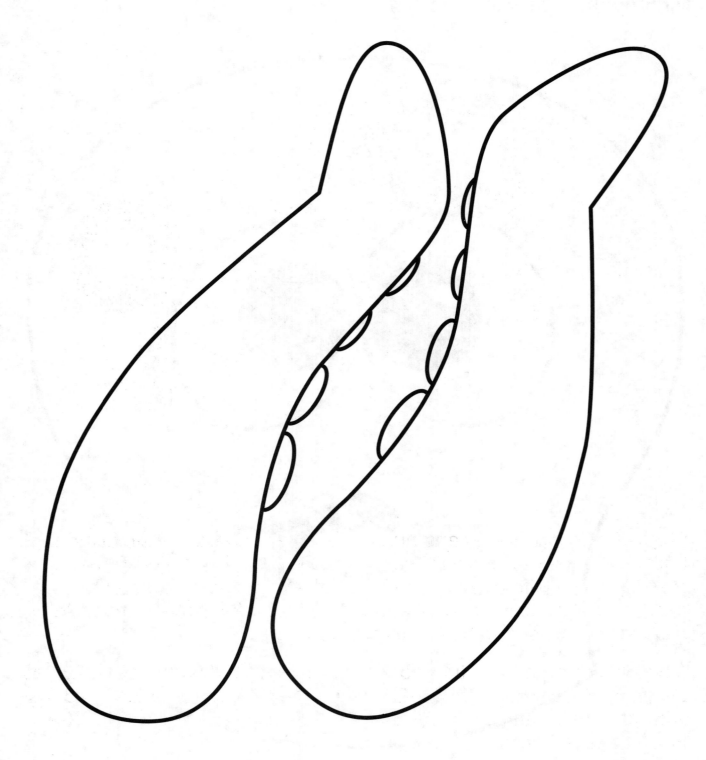

Unit Overview

Study **P** with pig stories and nursery rhymes. Share classic tales and traditional rhymes such as "The Three Little Pigs" and "To Market, To Market," along with modern retellings of the classics. Make piggy banks and introduce concepts about money; retell stories and build sequencing skills, and learn more about pigs.

Use this unit as a transition from an extended study of nursery rhymes and folklore ("K—Kings," "Q—Queens," "N—Nursery Rhymes," and "J—Jack and the Beanstalk") and then onto a farm unit ("F—Farm," "X—Fox, and "D—Dog).

Pigs

Language Arts Connections

Core Book

Scieszka, Jon. *The True Story of the Three Little Pigs.* Puffin Books, 1989.

The wolf corrects some misunderstandings in this hilarious version of "The Three Little Pigs." From his perspective, he's the victim, and those pigs, well, what would you do if you were presented with a free lunch? Walk away?

Read-Aloud Activities

Before Reading

- Read the title and the author's and the illustrator's names, pointing to the words as you read them.
- Point out the illustrations on the front and back covers. Discuss the similarities to a newspaper layout, and ask students why they think the cover illustrations might look that that.
- Relate the theme or story to students' previous knowledge by prompting them to retell the original tale.
- Ask for predictions about how the story in the book may differ from the traditional version.

During Reading

- As you read, make sure that students see the funny illustrations.
- Pause occasionally, to create suspense, or to ask for predictions.

After Reading

- Ask students what they think of this version of the story as compared to the original version.
- Have two adults act out the wolf telling his story to a judge who will decide whether the wolf was telling the truth. The students can be the jury and vote on the wolf's guilt or innocence.

Additional Books

Stock your class library with books about pigs. Students will enjoy looking at the illustrations and "reading" them to each other. When you read a story to your class, record yourself on tape. Then put the tape and the book in a literacy center so that your students can listen to it time and time again.

Amoss, Berthe. *The Three Little Cajun Pigs.* MTC Press, 1999.

Falconer, Ian. *Olivia.* Atheneum, 2000.

Galdone, Paul. *The Three Little Pigs.* Clarion Books, 1998.

Gibbons, Gail. *Pigs.* Holiday House, 1998.

Lowell, Susan. *The Three Little Javelinas.* Rising Moon, 1992.

Numeroff, Laura Joffe. *If You Give a Pig a Pancake.* Scholastic, Inc., 1998.

Miranda, Anne. *To Market, To Market.* Harcourt, Inc., 1997.

Trivizas, Eugene. *The Three Little Wolves and the Big Bad Pig.* Aladdin Library, 1997.

Wiesner, David. *The Three Pigs.* Clarion, 2001.

Wood, Don and Audrey. *Piggies.* Voyager Books, 1995.

Pigs

Language Arts Connections (CONT.)

Letter-Sound Introduction

Say the word *pig* slowly and deliberately, emphasizing the sound /p/. Ask students what beginning sound they hear in *pig*. Ask students if they know what letter makes that beginning sound of /p/. Tell students that the letter **p** makes the sound /p/.

Phonemic Awareness

Skill: Phoneme counting and phoneme blending

Say the word *pig*. Ask students to say only the first sound: /p/. Ask students what letter makes the sound /p/. Write the letter p on the board. Tell students to listen carefully for the next sound in *pig*. Say /p/, then pause slightly, and say /ĭ/. Ask students what that second sound was. Ask students what letter says the sound /ĭ/. Tell them that **i** says the sound /ĭ/. Write the letter **i** on the board to the right of the letter **p**. Tell students to listen carefully for the last sound in *pig*. Say /p/ /ĭ/ /g/, emphasizing the /g/. Ask students what the last sound was, and identify **g** as the letter that says the sound /g/. Write the letter **g** to the right of the letter **i**. Tell students that these letters make the sounds /p/ /ĭ/ /g/. When these sounds are blended together, they say, *pig*. Ask students how many sounds are in the word *pig*. Point to the letters and say the sounds /p/ /ĭ/ /g/. Tell students that the word *pig* has three sounds in it.

Letter Formation

After reading *The True Story of the Three Little Pigs* and introducing the letter-sound association, reinforce the association between the letter's formations and its sound by drawing the **P** and **p** into the shape of a pig's ears. Discuss that lower and upper case **P** look almost alike, but that the lower case **p** drops below the guide line on writing paper.

These activities will help to reinforce letter formation for students of all learning styles.

- Draw **P** onto 2 feet lengths pieces of butcher paper. Provide magazines that students can cut up. Students find pictures of objects that begin with the same letter sound, and glue them onto the letter **P**.

- Provide play dough for students to form the letter **P**.

- Cue auditory learners by verbally walking them through the letter formation. For example, say, "**P** . . . **p** . . . **p** . . . How do we form **p**? One line down, back to the top, curve around, then stop."

- Provide a variety of different shapes such as lines, circles, ovals, rectangles, and squares. Which shapes can be used to form the letters?

Language Arts Connections (CONT.)

"The Three Little Pigs" Story Set

Have students use scenes from "The Three Little Pigs" to retell the story, or to make up their own versions. Use this activity at a literacy center with small groups.

Skills: story retelling, sequencing

Materials:

- "The Three Little Pigs" Characters (pages 198–200)
- laminate machine access or clear contact paper
- Velcro tabs

Teacher Preparation:

1. Make a copy of the "Three Little Pigs" character set.
2. Color, cut and laminate or cover with clear contact paper.
3. Affix a Velcro tab to the back of each figure. The Velcro will hold the figures onto a flannel board.

Procedure:

1. Tell or read at least one of the traditional versions of "Three Little Pigs" such as *The Three Little Pigs* by Paul Galdone (Clarion Books, 1998).
2. Have the student, in pairs or in groups, retell the story to each other using the story set.

Math Connections

The Pigs' Money

The three little pigs will need money if they are going to buy some land and build their homes. Introduce money identification and put the piggy bank (page 195) to good use.

Skills: money identification, counting

Materials:

- plastic pennies, nickels, dimes, etc. (available at teacher supply stores)
- optional: Piggy Bank activity (page 199)

Procedure:

1. Tell the students that the pigs will need to know some things about money if they are going to buy land and construction supplies.
2. Distribute plastic money. Identify pennies, nickels, dimes, etc.
3. Make up story problems involving the money. For example, "The first little pig has found land that will cost a quarter. Which of the coins will he need?"
4. Have students role play pigs and merchants. For example, one pig could say, "I need to buy some sticks. How much will that be?" The stick sales person replies, "Two dimes."
5. Continue with creative play involving the fake money.

Extensions:

Discuss money values. For example, show that one nickel equals five pennies, or that a dime is worth two nickels or ten pennies.

                                                 ©Teacher Created Materials, Inc.

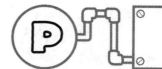 

Pigs

Science Connections

A Pig's Life

Discover whether pigs deserve the reputation of being smelly and dirty. Learn about pigs by consulting reliable pig resources such as a pig farmer, a veterinarian, or non-fiction books about pigs. If possible, take your class on a field trip to a farm. Read books about pigs, such as *Pigs* by Gail Gibbons (Holiday House, 1998).

Social Studies Connections

The Three Little Javelinas

The tale of the three little pigs has been told from the perspective of different cultures. Read other versions of the three little pigs, and discuss how the tale varies to reflect cultural differences. *The Three Little Javelinas* by Susan Lowell (Rising Moon, 1992) takes place in the Mexican desert. *The Three Little Cajun Pigs* by Berthe Amoss (MTC Press, 1999) is a Cajun version with a crocodile playing the villain's part.

Art Connections

Piggy Bank

Make piggy banks and begin to reinforce concepts about money.

Materials:

- clear plastic jar with lid. (Use jars for which the body of the jar is wider than its opening. The opening must be wider than a quarter.)
- pink construction paper
- chenille stems (one per student)
- wiggly eyes (two per student)
- toilet paper or paper towel rolls (1-2 per student)
- pink paint
- glue gun
- scissors

Teacher Preparation:

1. Arrange for at least one additional adult to assist with using the glue. Children should not be allowed to touch the glue gun.
2. Cut the paper towel or toilet paper rolls into 2" pieces. Every piggy bank will need four pieces as legs.

 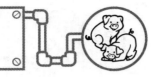

Art Connections (*CONT.*)

Procedure:

1. Have students paint the jars and toilet paper roll pieces with pink paint and allow to dry. Note: be sure that the lid is not sealed closed with paint.

2. Have students cut two ears from pink construction paper.

3. Once the jar "bodies" and paper roll "legs" are dry, have an adult assist the students with gluing the materials on to the jar, including:

   a. the pink construction paper ears

   b. the chenille stem tail (curled)

   c. the wiggly eyes

   d. the pink paper roll legs

4. Once dry, the piggy banks can be put to use. Take the lid off to put money in the pig's "mouth."

Music, Movement, Rhythm, and Rhyme

To Market, To Market

Read *To Market, To Market* by Anne Miranda, (Harcourt, Inc. 1997). This version of the traditional nursery rhyme will have your students laughing, pointing and enjoying the hilarious illustrations.

Dickery, Dickery, Dare

Dickery, dickery, Dare,

The pig flew up in the air;

The man in brown soon brought him down,

Dickery, dickery, Dare.

Higglety Pigglety Pop!

Higglety pigglety pop!

The dog has eaten the mop.

The pig's in a hurry,

The cat's in a flurry,

Higglety pigglety pop!

Modify the traditional nursery rhyme and finger play, "This Little Piggy," for an outside activity. Have students sit in a circle. Walk along behind them, tapping their heads or shoulders, saying one verse of the poem per child. On the last verse, the child jumps up, shouts, "Wee, wee, wee!" and runs around the yard to a pre-designated "home." That little pig gets to do the rhyme and the tapping the next time.

This Little Piggy

This little piggy went to market.

This little piggy stayed home.

This little piggy had roast beef.

This little piggy had none.

This little piggy said, "wee-wee-wee" all the way home.

Pigs

Centers

Set up centers to encourage students to explore the theme further during a free choice period, or assign small groups to parent-guided centers while you work with other students.

Shapes Center

Skills: identification and use of shapes

Stick Houses

Your students can help the three pigs build their houses. Draw a simple picture of a house. Set out craft sticks. Ask students to predict how many sticks it will take to build the house of sticks. Students glue sticks onto the house.

Imaginative Play Center

Skills: creative play, story retelling

"The Three Little Pigs"

Set out pig and wolf masks in the Imaginative Play Center. Students will enjoy using costumes in dress-up, imaginative play, and retelling "The Three Little Pigs."

Snacks

Be sure to check with parents about allergies before serving students any food.

Pigs in a Blanket

"Pigs in a Blanket" can be a quick snack or an entire meal, depending whether you use Vienna sausages or hot dogs. The recipe below will yield approximately eight servings. This is an easy recipe for children to assist with—they can roll the hot dogs or sausages in the rolls themselves, but an adult will be needed to slice the meat.

Ingredients:

- hot dogs or Vienna sausages
- package of crescent roll dough
- slices of cheese

Directions:

1. Pre-heat the oven to 375 degrees.
2. Slice the hot dog vertically; be careful not to slice it all the way through.
3. Put a slice of cheese into the slit of the hot dog.
4. Separate the crescent roll dough.
5. Put the hot dog on a piece of the dough and roll it up.
6. Put it on a cookie sheet and bake in the oven for 12-15 minutes or until the dough is golden brown.
7. Allow to cool, then serve.

 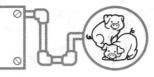
The Three Little Pigs Characters

Directions: Copy, color, cut and laminate these characters from the story. Attach a Velcro square to the back of each, and use with a flannel board to retell the story of "The Three Little Pigs."

The Three Little Pigs Characters (CONT.)

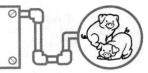

Pigs

The Three Little Pigs Characters *(CONT.)*

©Teacher Created Materials, Inc.

Overview

Continue the study of /k/ sounds with "Q—Queens." Either study
"K—Kings" and "Q Queens" at the same time, or introduce /k/ with
"K—Kings" and follow-up with an introduction to /kw/ with "Q—Queens."
Extend into a longer unit study of folklore with "N—Nursery Rhymes,"
"J—Jack in the Beanstalk," and "P—Pigs."

Queens

Language Arts Connections

Core Book

Steptoe, John. *Mufaro's Beautiful Daughters*. Lothrup, Lee & Shepard Books, 1987.

Set in southern Africa, this beautifully illustrated book tells the story of a king who invites the most beautiful daughters in the land to appear so that he can select a queen. Mufaro's daughter Manyara sneaks off to see the king first, but fortunately Nyasha's kindness and generosity make up for Manyara's jealous and selfish actions.

Read-Aloud Activities

Note: You may wish to show the illustrations and paraphrase the text for young children as this book is suitable for the average 8-year-old listener/reader.

Prior to Reading

- Read the title and the author's name, pointing to the words as you read.
- Point out the illustrations on the front and back covers.
- Tell students that this story is similar to the story of "Cinderella."
- Tell students that *Mufaro's Beautiful Daughters* takes place in southern Africa a long time ago. Show students southern Africa on a globe or a map.

During Reading

- As you read, make sure that each student can see the illustrations. Point out particularly beautiful scenes, such as the details of the city walls.
- Be expressive. Adopt voices for different characters.

After Reading

- Ask students how this story is like "Cinderella" and how it is different.

Additional Books

Stock your class library with books about queens and Cinderella tales. Students will enjoy looking at the illustrations and "reading" them to each other. When you read a story to your class, record yourself on tape. Then put the tape and the book in a literacy center so that your students can listen to it time and time again.

De Paola, Tomie. *Adelita: A Mexican Cinderella Story*. G.P. Putnam's Sons, 2002.

Craft, K.Y. *Cinderella*. Seastar Publishing Co., 2000.

Daly, Jude. *Fair, Brown and Trembling: An Irish Cinderella Story*. Ferrar Strauss & Giroux, 2000.

Gay, Marie-Louis. *Stella, Queen of the Snow*. Groundwood Books, 2000.

Gibbons, Gail. *The Honey Makers*. Harpercollins, 2000.

Lewis, J. Patrick. *Isabella Abnormella and the Very, Very Finicky Queen of Trouble*. Dorling Kindersley Publishing, Inc., 2000.

Jaffe, Nina. *The Way Meat Loves Salt: A Cinderella Tale from the Jewish Tradition*. Henry Holt and Company, 1998.

O'Neill, Alexis. *The Recess Queen*. Scholastic, 2002.

Queens

Language Arts Connections (CONT.)

Letter-Sound Introduction

Say the word *queen* slowly and deliberately, emphasizing the sound */kw/*. Ask students what beginning sound they hear in *queen*. Tell students that the letter **q** makes the sound */kw/*. It is almost always followed by the letter **u** so that it sounds similar to */k/*, but is blended with */w/*.

Phonemic Awareness

Skill: phoneme blending

Make one copy for each student of the "Q Cards" on page 208. Instruct students to cut the pictures into cards. Have them spread the square "Q Cards" on the table in front of them.

Say that you are thinking of one of the words on the cards, and that you will say it, but it will not sound quite right. When they have figured out which word you are saying, they are to hold the cards up over their heads to face you.

Say, "*Qu – een*," segmenting the */kw/* from the rest of the word. Students hold up the picture of the queen. Follow with the remaining words: *quack, quilt, quiet, quick, quarter, question,* and *quail*.

Letter Formation

After reading *Mufaro's Beautiful Daughters* and introducing the letter-sound association, reinforce the association between the letter's formations and its sound by drawing the **Q** and **q** into the shape of a queen.

These activities will help to reinforce letter formation for students of all learning styles.

- Guide students in warming up their fingers, hands, and arms by "air writing" the circles, the primary shape of **Q** and **q**.
- Provide a variety of different shapes: lines, circles, ovals, rectangles, and squares. Which shapes can be used to form the letters **Q** and **q** ?
- Use stencils to trace the letter shapes **O, Q, p** and **q** onto sandpaper. Students close their eyes and try to identify the letter shapes by feel.

Comparing "Cinderella" Tales

Introduce the concept of story elements by comparing the traditional "Cinderella" tale with *Mufaro's Beautiful Daughters*.

Skills: identifying story elements, summarizing important details

Materials:

- butcher paper
- markers
- traditional Cinderella tale
- a copy of *Mufaro's Beautiful Daughters*

Queens

Language Arts Connections (CONT.)

Teacher Preparation:

1. Familiarize yourself with the traditional "Cinderella" tale to retell orally, or locate a book to read about Cinderella. *Cinderella* by K.Y Craft. (Seastar Publishing Co., 2000) is a beautifully illustrated version.

2. Prepare a chart on butcher paper to record story elements.

   a. Include story elements terms that are appropriate for the students. Include "Characters" or "Who"; "Setting" or "Where"; "Problem;" "Important Events" or "Things that Happen;" and "Solution" or "The End".

   b. Include the names of the versions. ("Cinderella" and *Mufaro's Beautiful Daughters*).

	Who	Where	Problem	Things that Happen	The End
Cinderella					
Mufaro's Beautiful Daughters					

   c. Optional: draw picture symbols next to the words.

Procedure:

1. Tell or read the traditional version of "Cinderella."

2. Ask students how the traditional version is the same and how it is different from *Mufaro's Beautiful Daughters*.

3. Tell students that every good story is about someone and something happening to that someone. The "someones" are called "characters." The "something" is things that happen in the story. Most stories have some sort of a problem that needs to be solved, and in the end, the problem is solved. All stories happen somewhere, and the "somewhere" is call the "setting."

4. Show students the chart and identify the story elements on the chart in context with the explanations just provided.

5. Tell students that they can use this chart to help keep track of the details. This way they can easily compare the stories.

6. Begin to fill in the chart by asking key questions. "Who are the characters in 'Cinderella?'" "Who are the characters in *Mufaro's Beautiful Daughters?*" Write students' answers or draw pictures in the appropriate squares on the chart.

Follow-up Activity:

Have the students act out the different versions of Cinderella tales.

Queens

Math Connections

The Shape Castle

Reinforce identification and use of shapes as students create "shape castles."

Skills: shape identification and use of shapes

Materials:

- various shapes (circles, triangles, rectangles, squares, hexagons, etc.) cut from paper or foam, or stencils of shapes for students to trace. Shape templates are on pages 80–82.
- paper or foam, if students will be tracing and cutting shapes
- construction paper
- glue
- felt
- flannel board

Teacher Preparation:

1. If the shapes need to be made, students can trace shapes onto construction paper using stencils, and then cut. Otherwise, distribute shapes.
2. Cut flannel shapes to be used as samples on a felt board.

Procedure:

1. Direct students' attention to the flannel shapes, and ask what shapes they could use to create a shape castle.
2. Following the students' suggestions, create a shape castle with the flannel pieces on the felt board.
3. Tell students that they can each create their own shape castle, using the paper or foam shapes.
4. After students have created their shape castles, have students share and compare their castle creations. Discuss the many different styles of castles that were created using the same shapes.

Extensions:

Have students identify and write the names of the shapes they used. You may wish to provide a list showing each shape and its name for student reference.

Science Connections

The Queen Bee

Learn about the fascinating life of bees, from the worker bee to the queen. Consult books about bees to gain more information about the role of the queen bee and the work that bees do such as Gail Gibbons' *The Honey Makers* (Harpercollins, 2000). After this lesson, make honey-flavored treats (page 207) for a snack.

Social Studies Connections

Multicultural Cinderella Tales

Cinderella tales have been told and retold in many different cultures, and there are dozens of multicultural Cinderella tales available in picture book format. Read and discuss the differences in some of these versions.

Queens

Art Connections

"Queen or King for a Day" Cape

Select a day on which everyone can be a "Queen or King for a Day." Students will design, make, and decorate their own capes. If you are doing the "Q—Queen" unit at the same time as "K—Kings," then make the "King or Queen for a Day" crown (page 131) to wear with the cape.

Materials

- felt, sheets, or other large pieces of material that can serve as a cape
- "adornments," such as fake jewels, glitter, ribbons, etc.
- glue
- glue gun (for adult use only)
- scissors

Teacher Preparation:

Make the capes.

1. Cut a strip of material and glue it with a glue gun to the top (at the neck) to serve as a tie, or cut an opening for the head in the top of the cape.

Procedure:

1. Have the students glue "adornments" to their capes. Adult assistance may be required, particularly if glue guns are used.

Music, Movement, Rhythm, and Rhyme

Little Girl and Queen

Little girl, little girl,
Where have you been?
Gathering roses
To give to the Queen.
Little girl, little girl,
What gave she you?
She gave me a diamond as big as my shoe.

Pussy Cat, Pussy Cat

Pussy cat, pussy cat,
Where have you been?
I've been to London
To visit the queen.
Pussy cat, pussy cat,
What did you there?
I frightened a little mouse
Under her chair.

Music, Movement, Rhythm, and Rhyme (CONT.)

Follow the Queen

Play "Follow the Queen (or King)." Have students march in procession around the school or classroom as kings and queen wearing capes (page 206) and crowns (page 131) . One student leads the line as "queen" or "king" and the rest of the student imitate movements and actions.

Centers

Set up centers to encourage students to explore the theme further during a free choice period, or assign small groups to parent-guided centers while you work with other students.

Creative Play Center

Dress Up

Provide crowns, capes and other royal attire for the students to use in creative play. Students can retell traditional folk tales (such as "Cinderella" or "Sleeping Beauty") or make up their own stories.

Snacks

Be sure to check with parents about allergies before serving students any food.

Sweet as Honey

After discussing queen bees, make snacks using honey as a sweetener.

Honey Vanilla Yogurt

Ingredients:

- plain yogurt
- blueberries or sliced strawberries
- vanilla
- honey

Directions:

1. Mix the yogurt and the berries.
2. Add vanilla and honey to taste.

Honey Butter

Ingredients:

- freshly baked biscuits (mix and bake as a supervised center activity)
- butter
- honey

Directions:

1. Mix butter and honey until smooth and creamy.
2. Spread on warm biscuits.

Q Cards

Use with Phonemic Awareness Mini-Lesson in this unit. Copy, cut and distribute "Q Cards" to students.

queen	quilt
quack	quiet
quick	quart
question	quail

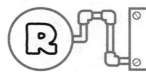 

Overview

It may be raining and pouring outside, but inside your classroom, there is a world of exploration waiting for your students' imaginations. Read the repetitive story of Ki-Pat who brings the rain to Kapiti plain. Explore science topics such as the water cycle and what plants need to grow. Conduct a symphony of rain music with your students.

This is a fitting theme to explore as the seasons change, either as a follow-up to the "L—Leaves" unit in the fall, or as an introduction to spring. Continue to explore weather with "H—Hats."

Rain

Language Arts Connections

Core Book

Aardema, Verna. *Bringing the Rain to Kapiti Plain.* Penguin Putnam Books, 1981.

This cumulative book tells the story of Ki-pat who helped end the drought in Africa by shooting his arrow into a cloud. The illustrations show African wildlife as well as Ki-pat's domesticated cattle herd. The story is based on a Nandi (from Kenya, Africa) folktale.

Read-Aloud Activities

Prior to Reading

- Read the title *Bringing the Rain to Kapiti Plain*, pointing to the words as you read.
- Read the author's name, Verna Aardema, and the illustrator's name, Beatriz Vidal. If you have read aloud other books by Verna Aardema, such as *Why Mosquitoes Buzz in People's Ears* (Scholastic, Inc.,1975), recall some story details.
- Point out the illustrations on the front cover.
- Ask students where they think the story might take place based on the title and illustrations.
- Show students where Africa is on a globe or world map.

During Reading

- The story is a cumulative tale, and uses repetitive text. Invite students to participate in reading with you by saying the verses that are used over and over.
- Point to the illustrations and words as your read. Name the African animals that are pictured in the illustrations.

After Reading

- Ask if the way that this story was told (cumulative, repetitive text) reminds them of any other stories they have heard.

Additional Books

Stock your class library with books about rain. Students will enjoy looking at the illustrations and "reading" them to each other. When you read a story to your class, record yourself on tape. Then put the tape and the book in a literacy center so that your students can listen to it time and time again.

Archambault, John and Martin, Bill Jr. *Listen to the Rain.* Henry Holt and Company, 1988.

Barrett, Judi. *Cloudy with a Chance of Meatballs.* Atheneum Books for Children, 1978.

Base, Graeme. *The Water Hole.* Harry Abrams, Inc., 2001.

McKinney, Barbara Show. *A Drop Around the World.* Dawn Publishers, 1998.

Schaefer, Lola. *This is the Rain.* Greenwillow, 2001.

Shannon, David. *The Rain Came Down.* The Blue Sky Press, 2000.

Spier, Peter. *Peter Spier's Rain.* Delacorte Press, 1982.

Stojic, Manya. *Rain.* Crown Publishers. 2000.

Rain

Language Arts Connections (CONT.)

Letter-Sound Introduction

Emphasize the /r/ sound as you say *rain*. Tell students that the letter **r** says the sound /r/. Brainstorm other words that begin with /r/.

Phonemic Awareness

Skill: sequence of sounds—identifying where /r/ is heard in a word (beginning, middle, or ending).

The Word Train—Choo! Choo! Where /R/ You?

The word train is seeking /r/ words. Help load /r/ words onto the correct train car according to where the /r/ sound is heard.

Make one copy of Word Train Picture Cards (pages 218–220) for each small group of students. Cut out picture cards and shuffle well. Put the picture cards in a bag or face down on the table.

Cut out the three train pictures and glue (one each) onto three brown paper bags. The train engine bag holds the beginning /r/ words; the train car bag will hold the middle /r/ word; and the train caboose bag will hold the ending /r/ words. Put the three bags in that order on a surface so that the students can see them.

Each student pulls out one picture card and determines the /r/ word that goes with it. Depending on where the /r/ sound is heard (beginning, middle, or end) the student drops the card into the appropriate train bag.

Letter Formation

After reading *Bringing the Rain to Kapiti Plain* and introducing the letter-sound association, write the letters **R** and **r** so that all the students can see them. Reinforce the association between the letter's formation and its sound by drawing the **R** and **r** to a rain scene.

These activities will help to reinforce letter formation for students of all learning styles.

- Provide a variety of different shapes: lines, circles, ovals, rectangles, and squares. Which shapes can be used to form the letters **R** and **r**?

- The letters **R** and **r** are made up of curves and lines. Look for curves and lines in the classroom.

- Carve the shapes **R** and **r** into a piece of flattened clay, and then allow the clay to dry until hard. With eyes closed, trace over the letters with fingers.

- Trace the letters **R** and **r** onto red paper. Have students cut out the **R** shapes.

- Provide trays of uncooked rice to practice forming the letters **R** and **r**.

Language Arts Connections (*CONT.*)

Rainy Day Fun

Everyone has their favorite rainy day activities, whether it's sipping hot apple cider with Mom and Dad, playing games with a sibling or a friend, or stomping in puddles. Now is the time for your students to share a favorite rainy day activity.

Skills: writing, oral language

Materials:

- Rain Drop Story Template (page 217)
- writing paper
- pencils
- optional: a recording of rain sounds

Teacher Preparation:

1. Make one copy for each student of the Rain Drop Story Template.
2. As a suggestion, set up this activity as a center so that you can work with very small groups. Arrange for a parent volunteer or aide to assist with the rest of the class.

Procedure:

1. Play the recording of rain sounds.
2. Tell the students that hearing those sounds reminds you of what you like to do when it is raining. Verbally share your favorite activity with students. If you have any photos of you doing your favorite activity, show them to the students.
3. Tell students that you know that they all have wonderful stories to share as well and that today everyone will have a chance to do that.
4. Explain that each student will tell you about his or her activity, and that you will write it down on the rain drop story sheet. Then each student can make a picture to go with his or her story.
5. Take dictation from individual students. Note: Some students may not need to use the story template. Allow those students to dictate their individual stories.
6. For the students who will use the template, start off with the phrase, "When it's raining outside, I like to…" Fill in the blank with the student's words.
7. After working with each student, give the paper back to him or her to illustrate.
8. Glue the stories onto large rain drops.

Follow-up:

To exhibit the students' work, create a large bulletin board display.

1. Draw or cut out large clouds. Use the rain drop stories as rain drops.
2. Draw or cut out a picture of a child walking with an umbrella.
3. Write or cut out the phrase, "Rainy Day Fun."

Rain

Math Connections

Comparing Plant Sizes

As told in the story *Bringing the Rain to Kapiti Plain* by Verna Aardema, plants need water to grow. Also, some plants grow bigger than others. Compare the measurements of different plants.

Skills: counting, measuring, comparing plant sizes

Materials:
- five different plants (potted house plants, seedlings, garden plants)
- rulers and measuring tapes
- index cards or post-its notes
- marker

Teacher Preparation:
1. Assemble materials.

Procedure:
1. Remind your students about the story, *Bringing the Rain to Kapiti Plain.* Ask your students why Ki-Pat wanted the rain to come.
2. Discuss that plants need rain to grow, and that without the rain in Africa, the plants were dying. The animals and people needed those plants to eat. Point out that some plants live indoors, and since they don't get rain, you must give them water from the sink to help them grow. Some plants grow bigger than others.
3. Show the class the plants that you have selected for the lesson. Ask them which one is the biggest plant. Respond, "Yes, that does look like the biggest plant. I wonder how big it is? Why don't we measure it to find out."
4. Measure the plant, and talk about how you are reading the measurement. For example, "This plant comes up to this point on the ruler. Let's count how many inches high that is: 1, 2, 3, 4, 5, 6—this plant measures 6 inches."
5. Write the number of inches on the index card or sticky note. Place the card in front of the plant. Note: Unless children understand the concept of measuring in feet as well, use only inches as your unit of measure.
6. Measure the remaining plants, and write the heights on the cards. Place the cards in front of the plants.
8. Ask your students to compare the results of the measurements and order the plants by height. For example, "Which plant was the biggest? That's right, this one was 18 inches tall. All the other plants were shorter than 18 inches. Which was the next biggest?"

Follow-up:
1. Measure the plants again in a couple of weeks, and see if any have grown.
2. Measure the students, and compare heights.

Rain

Science Connections

Weather

Check the weather daily with your students, and track the changing seasons. If it is raining, place a bucket to gather falling rain. Measure the amount of water that fell into your bucket that day.

What Do Plants Need?

Besides water, plants need soil and sun. Experiment with the growing plants in different conditions. What happens if we don't water one plant? What happens if one plant doesn't get sun? What happens if we take one plant out of the soil?

The Water Cycle

Where does rain come from? Boil a pot of water on a burner. Show the students the steam as the water evaporates. Then put a lid on the pot of boiling water. What happened to the steam? Take the lid off, and show the condensed water that has gathered on the inside. Shake the lid, and show students how it looks like rain.

Explain that the pot is like our planet Earth. The water in the pot is like the water in our oceans, lakes and rivers. The burner is like the sun. When the sun heats up the water, the water evaporates, or turns into steam. Then it comes down to Earth again in the form of rain. Note: Please use caution in this science exploration to prevent injuries to children or yourself. Instruct the children to stand back and watch with their eyes only.

A great resource for teaching children about the water cycle is *This Is the Rain* by Lola Schaefer (see "Additional Books" page 210.) The simple text and vivid illustrations provide a clear explanation of where rain comes from.

The author of *A Drop of Rain around the World*, Barbara Shaw McKinney (Dawn Publishers, 1998), has also authored *A Teacher's Guide to A Drop of Rain Around the World* (Dawn Publishing, 1998).

Social Studies Connections

Living Without Water

In *Bringing the Rain to Kapiti Plain*, Ki-Pat manages to pierce a rain cloud, bringing the rain to his herds on the plains of Kenya, Africa. Many people and animals around the world live with little water. After reading the core book, show the students where the story took place on a map or a globe. Then read *The Water Hole* by Graeme Base (Harry Abrams, Inc., 2001), and locate where in the world the animals depicted in the story are from.

Rain

Art Connections

Rain Drop Painting

Use colored water and straws to make raindrop paintings.

Materials:

- tempera paint (red, blue, yellow)
- water in several small containers
- straws
- heavy art paper
- crayons

Teacher Preparation:

1. Make water paint by squirting paint into each container (approximately one to two teaspoons of paint per cup of water).

Procedure:

1. Show students how to use their straws to hold water by putting one end of the straw in the colored water, placing a finger over the exposed end, and picking up the straw. The water will be trapped.
2. Students then drop the colored water over the art paper. They will need to experiment with how much water to drop—too much will result in a very wet sheet of paper.
3. Encourage them to experiment with mixing colors by dropping different colors of water in the same places.

Alternative:

1. Have the students use crayons to draw a picture.
2. Then have them drop watered paint onto the picture with staws. The paint will look like raindrops.

Music, Movement, Rhythm, and Rhyme

Rain, Rain, Go Away

Rain, rain, go away
Come again some other day!

It's Raining, It's Pouring

It's raining, it's pouring,
The old man is snoring,
He bumped his head
When he went to bed,
And he couldn't get up
In the morning!

Rainy Day Walk

After the rain has fallen, take students for a walk. Smell the fresh air, and hunt for rain drops on leaves. Make sure students are appropriately attired with rain boots and jackets.

Music, Movement, Rhythm, and Rhyme *(CONT.)*

A Symphony of Rain

Divide the class into four groups. Assign each group the following actions.

- Rub hands together
- Pat thighs, one at a time
- Drum fingers on table
- Clap hands (just 2–3 students)

Tell your students that a rainstorm is coming in a few moments. If they listen carefully, they will be able to hear music of the rain.

1. Say, "I think it's starting." Rub your hands together, gently at first, then picking up speed. Invite the hand rubbing group to join in. Tell them to keep going.
2. Say, "I'm beginning to hear rain drops." Drum you fingers lightly on the table, increasing the intensity gradually. Invite the finger drummers to join in. Tell them to keep going.
3. Say, "It's starting to rain harder." Pat your thighs, gently at first, then harder and faster. Invite the thigh patters to join in. Tell them to keep going.
4. Say, "It's raining hard now. I hear thunder. Clap your hands together. Invite the clappers to make thunder.
5. Then say, "I think the storm is ending. The thunder is getting softer." Tell your clappers to soften and then stop their clapping.
6. Say, "The rain is slowing down." Tell your thigh patters to soften and then stop their patting.
7. Say, "The rain is stopping." Tell your finger drummers to slow and then stop their drumming.
8. Say, "It's almost over now." Tell your hand rubbers to slow and stop their rubbing.
9. Say, "The storm has passed. Now we can breathe the fresh air." Have your students stand and stretch and breathe in deeply.

Centers

Sensory Center

Skills: sensory awareness

Set up a water play station in which students can experiment with the properties of water. Provide pouring and measuring tools, paint brushes, and water toys.

Snacks

Be sure to check with parents about allergies before serving students any food.

Potluck Snack Day

Cloudy with a Chance of Meatballs by Judi Barrett (Atheneum Books for Children, 1978) tells the tall tale of the land of Chewandswallow, where food falls from the sky! Read this book to your class, and then plan a potluck in which students bring their favorite foods.

Rain

Rain Drop Story Template

When it rains, I like to _____

_____

by _____

Rain

Word Train Picture Cards

Directions: Use with the Phonemic Awareness activity on page 211.

rain

rice

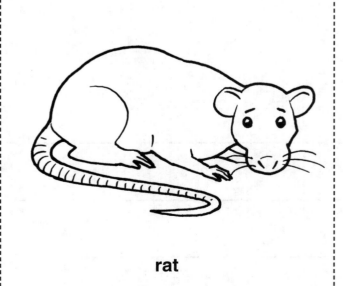

rat

rabbit

Word Train Picture Cards *(CONT.)*

Directions: Directions: Use with the Phonemic Awareness activity on page 211.

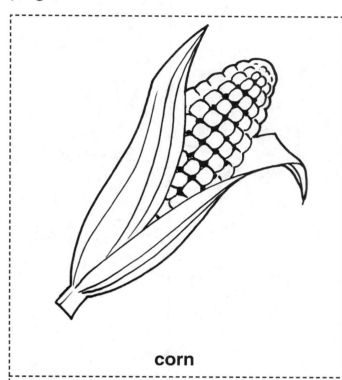

corn

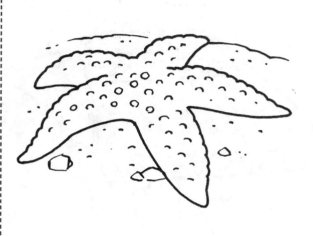

starfish

farm

giraffe

Word Train Picture Cards *(CONT.)*

Directions: Use with the Phonemic Awareness activity on page 211.

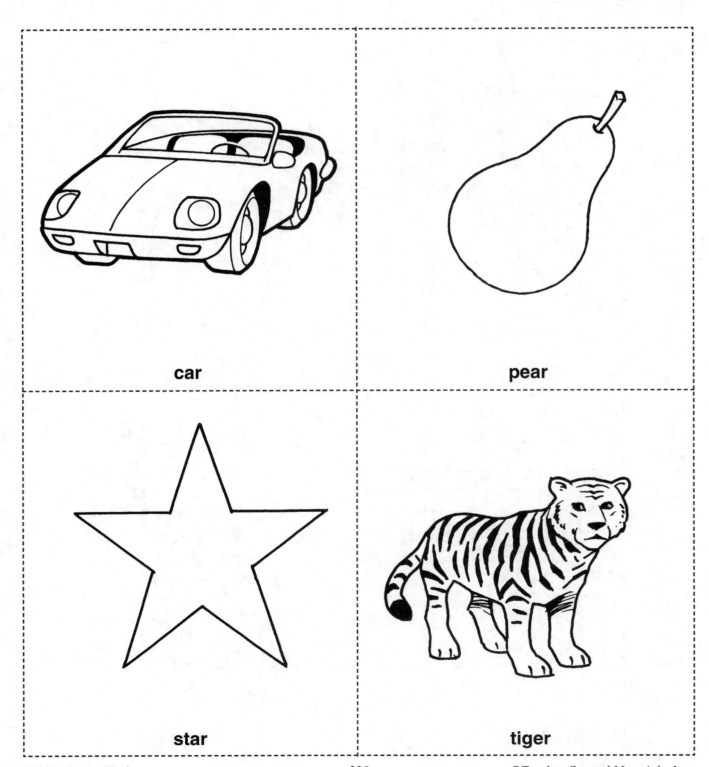

car

pear

star

tiger

Rain

Word Train Paper Bag Pictures

Directions: Copy and paste each illustration on a small brown paper bag. Place the paper bags next to each other with the train engine first, the train car in the middle, and the train caboose at the end. Use with the Phonemic Awareness activity on page 211.

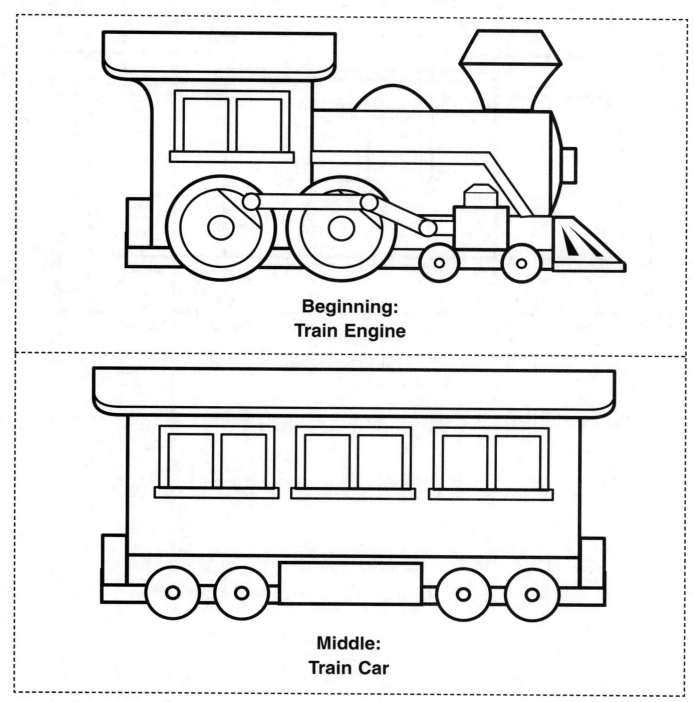

Beginning:
Train Engine

Middle:
Train Car

Rain

Word Train Paper Bag Pictures (*CONT.*)

Directions: See page 221. Use with the Phonemic Awareness activity on page 211.

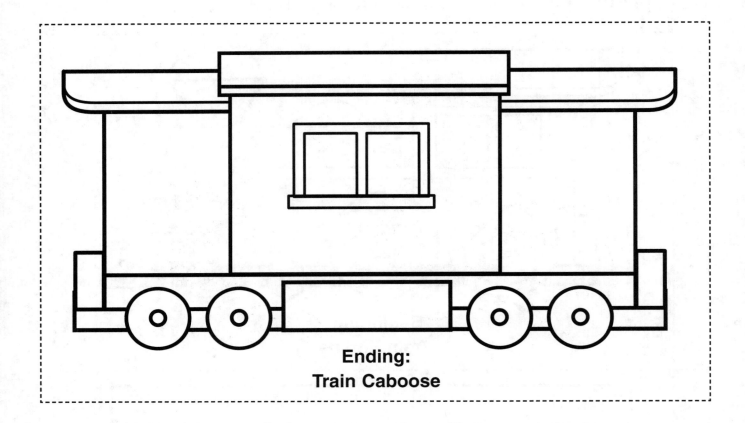

Ending:
Train Caboose

Overview

Explore /s/ with a study of snakes and salamanders. Begin by reading *The Salamander Room* by Anne Mazer (Alfred Knopf, 1991), and design habitat rooms suitable for wildlife. Make, measure, and decorate spiral snakes in an integrated math and art activity, and reinforce phonemic awareness skills with songs and rhymes about snakes and salamanders. Include this unit in an extended study of "Creatures, Creepers, and Crawlers" by teaching it between "T—Trees" and "M—Mouse."

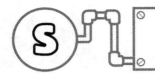 

Salamanders and Snakes

Language Arts Connections

Core Book

Mazer, Anne. *The Salamander Room.* Alfred Knopf, 1991.

When Brian finds a salamander in the woods, he decides to take it home. In response to his mother's questions regarding the salamander's comfort, Brian begins to imagine how he could bring the creature's comforts into his room. In a short time, Brian's bedroom is transformed into a forest habitat suitable for a salamander, and all its friends.

Read-Aloud Activities

Prior to Reading

- Introduce the book with a question or a statement such as, "Have you ever imagined what it might be like to bring an animal home? This is the story about a boy who really wants to keep a salamander he has found, and then he begins to think about everything that the salamander will need to be happy and healthy."
- Ask the students if they know what a salamander is. Describe it as a type of animal that looks like a lizard, but lives in the woods or the water, like a frog. Show the picture of the salamander on the front cover.

During Reading

- While reading, allow plenty of time for the students to look at the rich illustrations. Talk about how Brian's room is looking more and more like a forest.
- Provide opportunities for students to make predictions. Ask questions, between pages, such as, "What else do you think the salamander will need?"

After Reading

- Ask the students whether they think Brian decided to keep the salamander after all.
- Ask the students to imagine that they could bring home an animal. Have them draw pictures of what their rooms might look like after they turned them into suitable habitats for the animals. After the read-aloud session, extend this activity by having the students write a story about their pictures.

Additional Books

Stock your class library with books about snakes and salamanders. Students will enjoy looking at the illustrations and "reading" them to each other. When you read a story to your class, record yourself on tape. Then put the tape and the book in a literacy center so that your students can listen to it time and time again.

Arnosky, Jim. *Rattlesnake Dance.* G.P. Putnam's Sons, 2000.

Baker, Keith. *Hide and Snake.* Harcourt, 1991.

Banks, Kate. *The Bird, the Monkey and the Snake in the Jungle.* Frances Foster Books, 1999.

Buckley, Richard. *The Greedy Python.* Simon and Schuster, 1993.

Burns, Diane. *Snakes, Salamanders, and Lizards.* NorthWord Press, 1998.

Davis, Katie. *Who Hops?* Harcourt Brace, 1998.

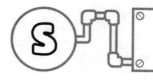 

Salamanders and Snakes

Language Arts Connections (CONT.)

Additional Books (CONT.)

Davol, Marguerite. *How Snake Got His Hiss: An Original Tale.* Orchard Books, 1996.

Gray, Libba Moore. *Small Green Snake.* Orchard Books, 1994.

Himmelman, John. *A Salamander's Life.* Children's Press, 1998.

Kudrna, Imbior. *To Bathe a Boa.* Scott Foresman, 1988.

Ling, Mary. *The Snake Book.* DK Publishing, 1997.

Nygaard, Elizabeth. *Snake Alley Band.* Doubleday, 1998.

Noble, Trinka Hakes. *The Day Jimmy's Boa Ate the Wash.* Penguin, 1980.

Olaleye, Issac. *Lake of the Big Snake.* Boyds Mills Press, 1998.

Pratt-Serafina, Kristin Joy. *Salamander Rain: A Lake and Pond Journal.* Dawn Publications, 2001.

Silverstein, Shel. *Where the Sidewalk Ends.* Harper and Row, 1974.

Letter-Sound Introduction

What is first sound of the words *salamander* and *snake*? A snake says, "Sssss," just like the beginning letter of the word *snake*. That letter is **s**. The letter **s** makes the sound /*s*/. Encourage students to practice saying the sound /*s*/ whenever they see or write the letter **s**.

Phonemic Awareness

Skill: identifying beginning /*s*/ words

Sally Snake

Sally Snake slithers through the grass seeking **s** words. Draw a large picture of Sally Snake (in an **S** shape) slithering through the grass. Help Sally find her words by having the students seek **s** words around the classroom. Write the words on squares of paper, (or have the students write the words on paper squares) and tape them to the picture, surrounding Sally.

Letter Formation

Show the cover of *The Salamander Room* by Anne Mazer to the students. Point out the S-shape of the salamander. Reinforce the association between the shape of the letter **S** and a snake by drawing it into the shape of a snake and a salamander.

These activities will help to reinforce letter formation for students of all learning styles.

- Have students make **S** shapes in sand while they say, "Sssss."
- Use stencils to trace **S** shapes onto sandpaper. Have the students close their eyes as they feel the letter shapes.
- Provide silky, soft, or smooth pieces of materials that the students can use to form **S** shapes.

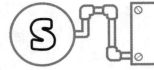

Language Arts Connections (*CONT.*)

My Animal Room

Have students imagine that they could bring an animal home. What would they need to do to help the animal be happy and healthy? This activity may need to be extended over a couple of days: one to brainstorm ideas, and one to draw the pictures.

Skills: creative writing, illustrating ideas

Materials:

- art paper
- crayons and markers

Procedure:

1. After reading *The Salamander Room*, discuss how Brian imagined that his room would change as he tried to make his salamander feel comfortable.

2. Ask the students to imagine what they would need to do to their rooms to make an animal feel safe, happy, and healthy.

3. Provide prompts to initiate brainstorming, such as:

   a. "What kinds of animal would you bring home?"

   b. "Where does that animal normally live?"

   c. "Where does the animal sleep?"

   d. "What does it eat?"

   e. "What does it need to keep it happy?"

4. Have the students draw pictures of their "Animal Rooms," including a picture of the animal.

5. As the students are drawing, write their dictated descriptions of the rooms and the changes they are imagining.

6. Allow students to share their "Animal Rooms" with each other.

7. At some point, emphasize the importance of keeping animals safe, happy and healthy by letting them live in their own natural habitats.

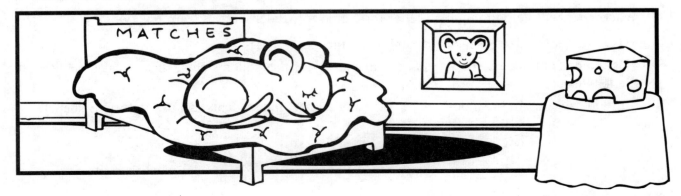

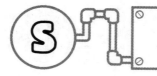 
Math Connections

Snakes are Sooo Long!

In this activity, students cut spiral paper "snakes" and then compare the lengths and widths. Extend this lesson into an art activity (page 228) and decorate the snakes with geometric shape patterns.

Skills: comparing lengths and widths, fine motor skills

Materials:

- butcher paper or large square of paper
- scissors

Teacher Preparation:

1. Cut the paper into large circular shapes, minimum of one per student.
2. Optional: Draw large spirals on the circle-shaped paper for the students to cut.

Procedure:

1. Demonstrate how to cut a spiral, beginning at the outer edge of a circle and spiraling inward.
2. Have students cut their circles into spirals, either on their own or along pre-drawn lines.
3. Once cut, have students extend the spirals to look like snakes.
4. Compare the lengths and widths of the different "snakes," using terms such as "wider than," "shorter than," "thinner than," and "longer than."

Extension:

Measure the snakes' lengths and widths with tape measurers, and compare the numbers.

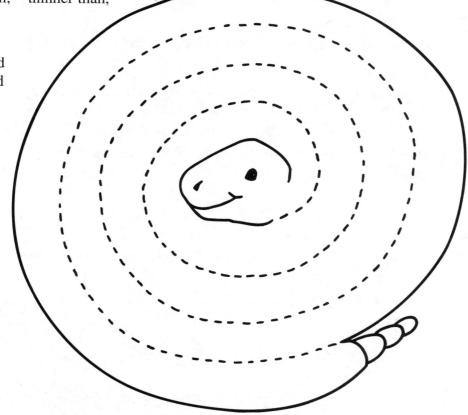

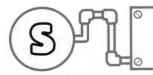

Salamanders and Snakes

Science and Social Studies Connections

Snake or Salamander Habitat

Set up a habitat for a snake or a salamander in the classroom. Refer to books about snakes and salamanders to determine what types of habitats they need. Ask a local pet store or veterinarian to recommend which animal would be most suitable for a classroom environment.

After learning about the characteristics of snakes or salamander habitats, look at maps to determine where snakes and salamanders might live.

Art Connections

Snake Skin Patterns

Decorate the spiral snakes from the Math Connections Activity on page 225 with geometric shapes and patterns.

Materials:

- geometric shapes (pages 80–82)
- scissors
- spiral snakes (from the Math Connections activity "Snakes Are Sooo Long!" on page 227)
- glue sticks

Teacher Preparation:

1. Copy the geometric shapes onto several different colors of paper.

Procedure:

1. Look at books that have pictures of snakes, such as *The Snake Book* by Mary Ling (DK Publishing, 1997). Discuss the different colors and patterns of snakes' skin.
2. Have the students identify and then cut out the shapes.
3. Have the students use the shapes to create patterns to decorate their snakes, and then glue the pattern shapes onto the snakes.

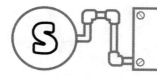

Salamanders and Snakes

Music, Movement, Rhythm and Rhyme

Snake and Salamander Songs

Bring Shel Silverstein's music and poetry into the classroom with his book Where the Sidewalk Ends (Harper and Row, 1974). Read and recite his poem, "Boa Constrictor." Peter, Paul and Mary sing "Boa Constrictor" on their album *Peter, Paul and Mommy* (Warner Brothers Records, Inc, 1969). For a salamander song, try the title song of Peter Himmel's album, *My Best Friend is a Salamander* (Baby Boom Music, 1997).

I'm a Snake!

By Barbara Knarr Ramming

I'm a snake!

Long and thin.

I have no legs.

I have no fins.

I'm a snake!

Just watch me wiggle.

And when I wiggle,

I make you giggle.

I'm a snake!

Just watch me slide.

Across the ground,

I gently glide.

I'm a snake!

From an egg I hatch,

With brothers and sisters

From the same egg batch.

I'm a snake!

I'm awake at night,

I sleep all day,

When the sun is bright.

Slithering Snakes and Salamanders

Have your students move like "Snakes and salamanders slithering silently in the grass." Emphasize that this is a "silent" (no voices) activity, and put some soft music on to help set the mood. As an alternative outside activity, have the students hop, "fly," slither, crawl, creep and run like animals. Read *Who Hops?* by Katie Davis (Harcourt Brace, 1998) to introduce this activity.

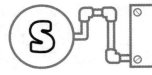 **Salamanders and Snakes**

Centers

Set up centers to encourage students to explore the theme further during a free choice period, or assign small groups to parent-guided centers while you work with other students.

Math Center

Skills: creating patterns, cooperative learning, fine motor skills

The Chain Snake

Provide multiple colors of construction paper cut into 6" x 2" strips and glue sticks. Have students make a chain snake by gluing the two ends of a construction paper strips together so it forms a circle, then looping the next strip though the circle and gluing the second strips ends together. The students continue adding onto the chain to increase the length of the "snake." When complete, they can glue on a snake head (an oval cut out of paper), and add eyes and tongue. Students can work cooperatively to make a very long snake, or work individually and create a pattern with the colors of strips they choose.

Snacks

Be sure to check with parents about allergies before serving students any food.

Breadstick Snakes

Bake delicious cheese breadsticks in the shape of slithering snakes!

Ingredients:

- strips of bread dough (such as Pillsbury Breadsticks™)
- finely shredded cheese
- raisins

Directions:

1. Have students twist their breadsticks into desired shapes. (This could be a great opportunity to have students practice forming **s** shapes.)
2. Add raisin "eyes."
3. Sprinkle with cheese.
4. Bake as directed.

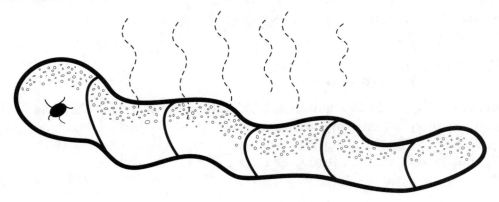

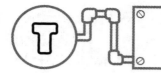 

Tree

Overview

Study trees as a focus for the letter **T**, and discover that trees are not only beautiful to look at, but also serve as homes to many creatures. Read *The Great Kapok Tree* by Lynne Cherry (Harcourt Brace Jovanovich, 1990), and discover how many animals depend on the kapok tree as a habitat. Build comprehension skills by reenacting the story in a class play; create rainforest collages in the Art Connections activity, and make a "Rhyming Tree."

Use this unit as part of an extended study of "Creatures, Creepers and Crawlers" with "S—Salamanders and Snakes," "M—Mouse," "I—Insects," "C—Caterpillars" and "B—Butterflies."

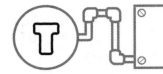 

Tree

Language Arts Connections

Core Book

Cherry, Lynne. *The Great Kapok Tree*. Harcourt Brace Jovanovich, 1990.

In the dense, green Amazon rain forest, a man strikes a great Kapok tree with his ax. When he tires, he lies at the foot of the tree and falls asleep. One by one, the forest creature emerge to whisper in his ear not to destroy their home and remind him of the importance of rain forest trees. When he awakens, he finds he must make a decision.

Read-Aloud Activities

Prior to Reading

- Introduce the book by reading the title and the author's name.
- Provide background information that the students will need for comprehension. For example, explain that a kapok tree is a great big tree that lives in a rain forest and is home to many animals. If necessary, describe a rainforest.
- Consider introducing other words that will be read in the story, such as "canopy" and "underbrush." The book's introduction explains many of these terms.

During Reading

- Use different voices when reading the words of the animals. For example, when reading the part of the boa constrictor, draw out the /s/ to "Ssss."
- As needed, define words that may be unfamiliar. Explain that *señor* is a Spanish word for *mister* or *man*.
- Allow ample time for students to look at the illustrations on each page.

After Reading

- Ask students which of the animals they recognized in the story.
- Discuss why the man decided to leave his ax and walk away from the tree.

Additional Books

Stock your class library with books about trees. Students will enjoy looking at the illustrations and "reading" them to each other. When you read a story to your class, record yourself on tape. Then put the tape and the book in a literacy center so that your students can listen to it time and time again.

Baker, Jeannie. *Where the Forest Meets the Sea*. William Morrow and Company, 1988.

Brenner, Barbara. *The Tremendous Tree Book*. Boyds Mills Press, Inc., 1979.

Carle, Eric. *Slowly, Slowly, Said the Sloth*. Philomel Books, 2002.

Christelow, Eileen. *Five Little Monkey Sitting in a Tree*. Clarion Books, 1991.

Ehlert, Lois. *Red Leaf, Yellow Leaf*. Harcourt Brace Jovanovich, Publishers, 1991.

George, Kristine O'Connell. *Old Elm Speaks: Tree Poems*. Houghton Mifflin, 1998.

George, Lindsay Barrent. *In the Woods: Who's Been Here?* Mulberry Books, 1998.

Gibbons, Gail. *The Seasons of Arnold's Apple Tree*. Harcourt Brace Jovanovich, 1984.

Gibbons, Gail. *Tell Me Tree: About Trees for Kids*. Little Brown and Company, 2002.

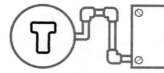 

Tree

Language Arts Connections (CONT.)

Additional Books (CONT.)

Hiscock, Bruce. *The Big Tree*. Boyds Mills Press, Inc., 1999.

Houghton, Eric. *The Crooked Apple Tree*. Barefoot Books, 1999.

Lionni, Leo. *The Alphabet Tree*. Knopf, 1990.

Manson, Christopher. *The Tree in the Wood: An Old Nursery Song*. North South Books, 1993.

Silverstein, Shel. *The Giving Tree*. Harper & Row, Publishers, 1964.

Udry, Janice May. *A Tree is Nice*. Harper Trophy, 1987.

Letter-Sound Introduction

What is first sound of the word *tree*? Say *tree* slowly and deliberately, emphasizing the /t/ sound, and segmenting it from /r/. Tell students that the letter **t** makes the sound /t/. Encourage students to practice saying the sound of the letter **t** whenever they see or write it so they can begin to learn the letter-sound association.

Phonemic Awareness

Skill: identifying similar word patterns

The Rhyming Tree

Make a large tree trunk and branches from brown paper and display it on a wall in the class room. Copy the leaves from the "C—Caterpillar" unit (page 38) onto green paper and cut out. Identify several groups of word families in which you want to focus. Write these on the branches of the tree. For example, on one branch, write *-at*; on another, write *-op*. Brainstorm words that belong in these word families with the students, and write the words on the leaves. Put the leaves on the appropriate branches. Encourage students to add leaves to branches as they think of new words.

Letter Formation

After reading *The Great Kapok Tree* and introducing the letter-sound association, write the letters **T** and **t** so that all the students can see them. Reinforce the association between the letter formations and its sound by drawing the **T** and **t** into shapes of trees.

These activities will help to reinforce letter formation for students of all learning styles.

- Make **T** and **t** shapes with wide tape. Have students trace the tape to make **t**.
- Have students use two, ten, twelve or twenty twigs to form the letters **T** and **t**.
- Put magnetic letters with similar shapes (**T, I, J, L, t, i, j, l**,) into a paper bag stapled shut or a closed box with a hole in its side. Students reach in and feel each letter. They say its name, its sound, and then pull it out of the box to check their answer.

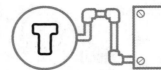 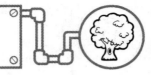

Tree

Language Arts Connections (CONT.)

The Great Kapok Tree Class Play

Reinforce comprehension by having students act out the story from the book. Adapt this activity according to student's abilities.

Skills: story retelling, comprehension

Materials:

- tree prop (such as a pole or a picture of a tree on a wall)
- a copy of *The Great Kapok Tree*
- optional: face paints
- optional: animal costumes

Teacher Preparation:

1. Determine how students will act out the story.
2. Determine how to assign parts.

Procedure:

1. Assign parts of the man and the animals to students.
2. Older students can discuss options for acting out the story. For example, they could rewrite the animals' words into lines to memorize. Or they could just say lines similar to what the animals said. Keep the lines as simple as possible.
3. Younger students can simply stand in front of the man, slowly shaking their heads and looking sad. The student who plays the man can act out that part without saying any lines, but may need guidance about how to act.
4. Use face paints to make children's faces look like animals, or make costumes, if desired.

Math Connections

A Tree Is a Habitat

After reading the story of the kapok tree, count the many animals that made their home in the tree. This activity is best done with very small groups, unless multiple copies of the book are available.

Skills: counting, bar graphing, comparing numbers

Materials:

- a copy of *The Great Kapok Tree*
- markers
- butcher paper

Teacher Preparation:

1. Review the book to identify the number of animals in each illustration.
2. Refer to the illustrations on the inside of the back and front covers. These identify the animals in the book.
3. Prepare the grid for the bar graph to be used. Across the bottom, write "Animal." On the left of the grid, write "Number." Make squares for up to fifteen animals.

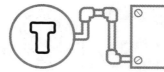 

Tree

Math Connections (CONT.)

Procedure:

1. On each page, have students count the number of animals that visit the man, beginning with the visits of the iguanas and the boa constrictors.
2. Write the name and have students fill squares of the number of animal observed in the illustrations. Optional: Next to each animal name, tape its picture.
3. Compare the results of the bar graph. Which types of animals made up the largest groups?

Science Connections

The Life of a Tree

Explore the life cycle of trees. Read books about trees such as *The Seasons of Arnold's Apple Tree* by Gail Gibbons (Harcourt Brace Jovanovich, 1984) or *Tell Me Tree: About Trees for Kids* by Gail Gibbons (Little Brown and Company, 2002). Encourage students to observe trees around them in the coming year. For example, have them adopt a tree near school or home and observe what happens to it throughout the year. Or plant a tree for Arbor Day. (Find out when Arbor Day will be celebrated in your states on the official Arbor Day *website, www.arborday.org*).

Social Studies Connections

The Great Kapok Tree has wonderful maps, located on the inside cover of the book, that display the locations of the world's rainforests. On a large map, locate the rain forest regions, and identify the closest rain forest.

Art Connections

Rainforest Collage

Create collages of the rain forest using pieces of tissue paper and pictures of animals.

Materials:

- assorted shades of green tissue paper, cut in squares and strips
- other colors of tissue paper for flowers and trees
- rubber cement or glue sticks
- pictures of animals from nature magazines

Teacher Preparation:

1. Assemble materials.

Procedure:

1. After reading the story, ask the students to recall some of the animals from the story.
2. Discuss how sometimes animals use to hide. Some animals blend in with the plants around them. This is called *camouflage*.
3. Have students glue overlapping green tissue paper to create images of trees and plants in the rainforest. They can use bright red, pink or orange tissue paper to create flowers.
4. Have them "hide" pictures of rain forest animals within the collage.

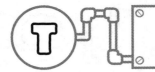

Tree

Music, Movement, Rhythm and Rhyme

The Green Grass Grows All Around (Traditional)

There was a tree (there was a tree)
All in the wood (all in the wood)
The prettiest tree (the prettiest tree)
That you ever did see (that you ever did see)
The tree in a hole and the hole in the ground
And the green grass grows all around,
  all around
The green grass grows all around

And on that tree (and on that tree)
There was a limb (there was a limb)
The prettiest limb (the prettiest limb)
That you ever did see (that you ever did see)
The limb on the tree, and the tree in a hole,
And the green grass grows all around,
  all around
The green grass grows all around.

And on that limb (and on that limb)
There was a branch (there was a branch)
The prettiest branch (the prettiest branch)
That you ever did see (that you ever did see)
The branch on the limb,
  and the limb on the tree,
And the tree in a hole,
And the green grass grows all around,
  all around
The green grass grows all around.

And on that branch (and on that branch)
There was a nest (there was a nest)
The prettiest nest (the prettiest nest)
That you ever did see (that you ever did see)
The nest on the branch, and the branch on the
  limb,
And the limb on the tree, and the tree in a hole,
And the green grass grows all around,
  all around
The green grass grows all around.

And in that nest (and in that nest)
There was an egg (there was an egg)
The prettiest egg (the prettiest egg)
That you ever did see (that you ever did see)
The egg in the nest,
  and the nest on the branch,
And the branch on the limb,
  and the limb on the tree,
And the tree in a hole,
And the green grass grows all around,
  all around
The green grass grows all around.

And in that egg (and in that egg)
There was a bird (there was a bird)
The prettiest bird (the prettiest bird)
That you ever did see (that you ever did see)
The bird in the egg, and the egg in the nest,
And the nest on the branch,
  and the branch on the limb,
And the limb on the tree, and the tree in a hole,
And the green grass grows all around,
  all around
The green grass grows all around.

And on that bird (and on that bird)
There was a wing (there was a wing)
The prettiest wing (the prettiest wing)
That you ever did see (that you ever did see)
The wing on the bird, and the bird in the egg,
And the egg in the nest,
  and the nest on the branch,
And the branch on the limb,
  and the limb on the tree,
And the tree in a hole,
And the green grass grows all around, all around
The green grass grows all around.

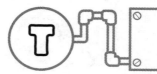 
Music, Movement, Rhythm and Rhyme (CONT.)

The Green Grass Grows All Around (CONT.)

And on that wing (and on that wing)

There was a feather (there was a feather)

The prettiest feather (the prettiest feather)

That you ever did see (that you ever did see)

The feather on the wing,
  and the wing on the bird,

And the bird in the egg, and the egg in the nest,

And the nest on the branch,
  and the branch on the limb,

And the limb on the tree, and the tree in a hole,

And the green grass grows all around,
  all around

The green grass grows all around.

And on that feather (and on that feather)

There was a bug (there was a bug)

The prettiest bug (the prettiest bug)

That you ever did see (that you ever did see)

The bug on the feather,
  and the feather on the wing,

And the wing on the bird,
  and the bird in the egg,

And the egg in the nest,
  and the nest on the branch,

And the branch on the limb,
  and the limb on the tree,

And the tree in a hole,

And the green grass grows all around,
  all around

The green grass grows all around.

And on that bug (and on that bug)

There was a germ (there was a germ)

The prettiest germ (the prettiest germ)

That you ever did see (that you ever did see)

The germ on the bug,
  and the bug on the feather,

And the feather on the wing,
  and the wing on the bird,

And the bird in the egg,
  and the egg in the nest,

And the nest on the branch,
  and the branch on the limb,

And the limb on the tree,
  and the tree in a hole,

And the green grass grows all around,
  all around

The green grass grows all around.

Yes, the green grass grows all around,
  all around

The green grass grows all around!

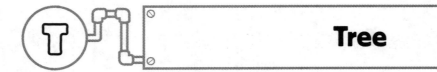 

Tree

Music, Movement, Rhythm, and Rhyme *(CONT.)*

Nature Walk

Take a nature walk, and observe the trees. Look at the animals that are living in and around the trees and discuss how the trees are habitats that provide the animals with the things they need to be happy and healthy. The book *In the Woods: Who's Been Here?* by Lindsay Barrent George (Mulberry Books, 1998) is an excellent resource for introducing nature walks.

Centers

Set up centers to encourage students to explore the theme further during a free choice period, or assign small groups to parent-guided centers while you work with other students.

Science and Math Center

Skills: sorting, habitat identification

Here is My Habitat

Make "habitats" by taping a picture of a habitat onto a tray or shallow box. Habitat pictures could include ocean, forest and desert. Provide pictures of various animals cut from nature magazines that live in these habitats. Students sort the animals into the appropriate habitat.

Snacks

Be sure to check with parents about allergies before serving students any food.

Tree Treats

Eat foods that come from trees and celebrate the wonderful treats that trees give us.

Ingredients:

- fruits: cherries, apples, oranges, lemons, grapefruits, pears, plums, apricots, bananas
- nuts: walnuts, almonds

Directions:

1. Prepare fruits by washing, peeling and slicing.
2. Shell nuts.
3. Make juices from fruits such as lemons, oranges and grapefruits. If an electric fruit juicer is available, make juices from all the fruits (except bananas).

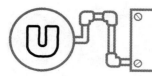 

Overview

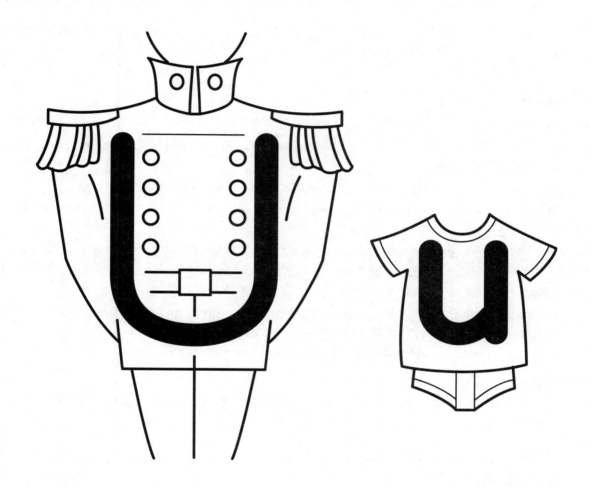

Focus on things that people wear, such as underwear and uniforms in this unit study for the letter **U**. Read *Jesse Bear, What Will You Wear?* by Nancy White Carlstrom (Macmillan Publishing Company, 1986). Reinforce sequencing skills in language arts and math, mix and match patterned and colored clothing, and have the students design their own "uniforms." Teach this unit after "H—Hats," then read "The Emperor's New Clothes," by Hans Christian Anderson, as a transition to "K—Kings."

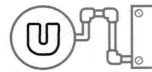 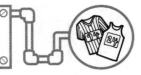

Underwear and Uniforms

Language Arts Connections

Core Book

Carlstrom, Nancy White. *Jesse Bear, What Will You Wear?* Macmillan Publishing Company, 1986.

The routine of Jesse Bear's day is brought to life with bright illustrations and clever descriptions of what he "wears." From ants in his pants to rice in his hair, Jesse Bear's "clothing" is described with rollicking rhythm and rhyme.

Read-Aloud Activities

Prior to Reading

- Discuss daily routines with students. What do they do first thing in the morning? Discuss getting dressed as one of the routines.
- Introduce the book by reading the title, the author's, and the illustrator's names.
- Tell students that in this story, Jesse Bear wears some things that may be different from regular clothes.
- Say that in this story, there are many rhyming words. When students hear a pair of rhyming words, they can demonstrate that they have identified them by putting their fingers on their noses.

During Reading

- Read in rhythm with the text. Tap your foot, or use some other means to "track" the rhythm. Discuss the rhythm of the text with the students.
- In some places, pause to allow students to fill in the rhyming words.

After Reading

- Ask the students to recall some of the things that Jesse Bear wore throughout his day.
- Compare Jesse's day with the daily routines of the students.

Additional Books

Stock your class library with books about things that people wear. Students will enjoy looking at the illustrations and "reading" them to each other. When you read a story to your class, record yourself on tape. Then put the tape and the book in a literacy center so that your students can listen to it time and time again.

Barrett, Judi. *Animals Should Definitely Not Wear Clothing.* Atheneum, 1970.

Boynton, Sandra. *Blue Hat, Green Hat.* Little Simon, 1995.

Calmenson, Stephanie. *The Principal's New Clothes.* Scholastic, 1991.

Kuskin, Karen. *The Philharmonic Gets Dressed.* HarperTrophy, 1996.

London, Jonathan. *Froggy Gets Dressed.* Viking Children's Books, 1997.

Neitzel, Shirley. *The Dress I'll Wear to the Party.* Mulberry Books, 1995.

Neitzel, Shirley. *The Jacket I Wear in the Snow.* Greenwillow, 1998.

Stinson, Karen. *The Dressed Up Book.* Firefly Books, 1990.

Language Arts Connections (CONT.)

Letter-Sound Introduction

Say *uniform* slowly and deliberately, emphasizing the /ū/. Ask students to identify the beginning sound. Then say *understand*, and ask students to identify the beginning sound. Tell students that the same letter, **u**, makes both sounds, /ū/ and /ŭ/.

Phonemic Awareness

Skill: Identifying similar word patterns, substituting phonemes.

Have the students identifying rhyming words in *Jesse Bear, What Will You Wear?* Record the words on sheets of white paper: *red/head*; *pants/dance*; *rose/toes*; *sun/run*; *sand/hand*; *bear/wear/chair/there*; *peas/please*; *crunch/bunch*; *bite/white*; *hair/hair*; *shirt/dirt*; *pants/ants*; *float/boat*; *feet/seat*; *blue/peek-a-boo*; *you/too*; *eyes/skies*; *bed/head*. On another day, have individual, pairs, or small groups of students illustrate some of the word pairs. (Determine the word pairs that can be easily illustrated, such as a "red head.") For a third activity, circle the parts of the words that are the same. Have the students brainstorm other words that could be created by substituting different beginning letters. (*crunch, bunch, munch* and *lunch*, for example, plus nonsense words including *dunch, funch*, etc...)

Letter Formation

After reading *Jesse Bear, What Will You Wear?* and introducing the letter-sound association, reinforce the association between the formations of the letter **U** and **u** and its sounds by drawing the shape into a picture of clothing. For example, the **U** could be the shape of an undershirt.

These activities will help to reinforce letter formation for students of all learning styles.

- Have the students swing their fingers and arms down and up, forming **u** shapes. As they form **U**, have them say, "Down, up." (To reinforce the concept that the **U** is written left to right, have the students move their fingers and arms left to right, not right to left.

- Reinforce letter formation and build fine motor coordination. Provide play dough for the students to roll and shape into **U**.

- Make thick mud, and have the students make **U** mud letters. (Reinforce the letter/sound association by reminding students that /ŭ/ is the middle sound of mud.)

- Cue auditory learners with a rhythm and rhyme. "**U** slides down, then up. It's like a curved cup."

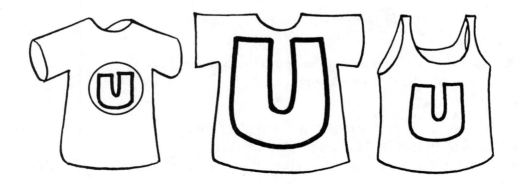

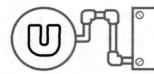 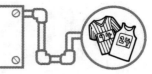

Language Arts Connections *(CONT.)*

My Getting Dressed Booklet

Practice sequencing skills by having the students sort "Getting Dressed" picture cards.

Skills: sequencing, identifying colors, reading, fine motor skills

Materials:
- "My Getting Dressed Booklet" (pages 246–247)
- crayons and markers
- scissors

Teacher Preparation:
1. Make a copy of the "Getting Dressed" booklet for each student.

Procedure:
1. Have students color and cut out the booklet pages.
2. Discuss the scenes illustrated on each page. Have the students discuss what the child is doing in each picture.
3. Read the words on each page. Have the students follow along, using their "pointer" fingers as they read the words.
4. Discuss the order of getting dressed.
5. Assist the students with assembling the pages in order. Then staple, with the booklet cover first.

Alternative:
1. Simplify this activity for younger students by cutting and assembling the booklets. Have them color the pages.

Math Connections

Mix and Match Outfits

Provide opportunities for creative play and at the same time reinforce concepts about matching, sorting and identifying patterns. Play mix and match with paper dolls and clothes

Skills: matching and sorting colors, identifying patterns

Materials:
- Boy and Girl Figures (page 249)
- clothing (page 248)
- optional: laminate paper or clear contact paper
- scissors
- colored paper (5–7 colors minimum)

Teacher Preparation:
1. Copy the boy and girl figures and clothes onto the colored paper.
2. Cut out and laminate the figures and clothing.

Procedure:
1. Have the students create outfits for the boy and girl figures by matching clothing colors. For example, blue hat, blue shirt, blue pants, blue shoes.
2. Once all the outfits have been sorted by color, begin creating mix and match outfits in patterns, such as blue hat, red shirt, blue pants, red shoes.

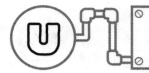 

Underwear and Uniforms

Science Connections

Where Do I Wear It?

Discuss where we wear certain pieces of clothing. Have the students dress the boy and girl figures (page 249) with clothing on page 248. A great book to introduce this activity is *Blue Hat, Green Hat* by Sandra Boynton (Little Simon, 1995). With very few words, the animal characters in this book wear clothing appropriately, with the exception of the one who does not.

Social Studies Connections

Uniformed Community Service Providers

Invite community service providers to speak to the students about their jobs—in uniform. Visit a fire station, and observe the firefighters in different types of clothing as they discuss fire safety. Invite a police officer to come to the classroom, in uniform, and discuss safety issues. Visit a veterinary clinic, and learn about veterinary medicine and animal care. Invite the local mail carrier to speak with the class about the postal service, and have the students write and post letters to home. Many of the parents of students in the classroom may wear uniforms at their jobs, as well. Invite parents to wear their uniforms to school and talk about their work.

Clothes of Other Cultures

People of other cultures do not dress in the same way. Share pictures of people wearing different types of clothing. Discuss how they are the same and different from the clothing worn by the students in your classroom. Reinforce the concept that underneath the clothing, everyone is basically the same: we all eat, drink, sleep, speak, etc., but there are differences in the way we look, where we live, the languages we speak, and the foods we eat.

Art Connections

Clothes Just For Me!

Trace the students' bodies on sheets of butcher paper, and then have them decorate their paper figures by drawing on clothing. This activity may take several days to complete.

Materials:

- butcher paper
- crayons, markers and paints
- construction paper
- pieces and scraps of material and ribbons
- yarn to use as hair (yellow, black, brown, red, etc.)
- large buttons or wiggly eyes
- glue
- scissors

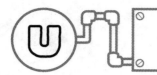 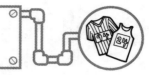

Art Connections (CONT.)

Clothes Just For Me! (CONT.)

Procedure:

1. Have students lie down on sheets of butcher paper. Outline the shapes of their bodies with marker.

2. Talk about what their bodies look like, and brainstorm things that are missing from their body pictures. Have students add eyes, hair, mouth, etc. by coloring them in with crayons and markers, or by gluing on button eyes, yarn hair, etc.

3. Discuss clothing that the students are wearing, or have them imagine clothing that they would like to wear. They can either draw the clothing on with crayons, markers, and paints, or glue on scraps of paper and material.

4. Allow to dry and then display.

Music, Movement, Rhythm, and Rhyme

What are you Wearing?

John's wearing a blue shirt, blue shirt, blue shirt.

John's wearing a blue shirt all day long!

(Substitute each student's name and something he or she is wearing.)

Put Your Finger on Your Shirt

Put your finger on your shirt, on your shirt.

Put your finger on your shirt, on your shirt.

Put your finger on your shirt, put your finger on your shirt,

Put your finger on your shirt, on your shirt.

(Repeat for socks, shoes, pants, etc.)

Getting Dressed Races

Have students race to put on as many articles of clothing as quickly as possible. Provide a large bag of clothing for each group of students. Have the groups work cooperatively to dress one person, or have everyone in the group dress as quickly as possible.

Centers

Set up centers to encourage students to explore the theme further during a free choice period, or assign small groups to parent-guided centers while you work with other students

Creative Play Center

Skills: creative play

Dress Up

Provide clothing and mirrors in a dress-up center. Have students use the clothing as costumes in creative play or when acting out stories, or to role play family routines and relationships.

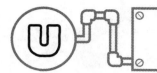 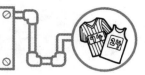
Snacks

Be sure to check with parents about allergies before serving students any food.

The Muffin Man

Students can wear the uniform of a baker. Make chef's hats and aprons, and then bake fresh blueberry muffins below, for snack time.

Materials:

- small white paper bags
- pieces of butcher paper
- string

Procedure:

1. Make the baker's hats by pulling the opening of the white paper bags over the students' heads and folding the edge up.
2. Make aprons out of squares of butcher paper. Tape string onto the paper in order to tie it around the students' waists.

Blueberry Muffin
Ingredients:

- 1 cup butter
- 1 cup brown sugar
- 4 eggs
- 2 cups milk
- 4 cups flour
- 1 teaspoon salt
- 2 ½ tablespoons baking powder
- 3 cups blueberries
- ½ cup of sugar
- oven
- two 12-muffin tins

Directions:

1. Mix together the butter and brown sugar.
2. Add the eggs and the milk.
3. Mix the dry ingredients (flour, salt, baking powder) in a big bowl.
4. Blend the wet and dry ingredients.
5. Mix the blueberries and the sugar in a bowl. Fold into the muffin batter.
6. Pour the batter into two 12-muffin tins (greased).
7. Bake at 400 degrees for 20 minutes or until golden brown.

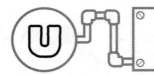 # Underwear and Uniforms

My Getting Dressed Booklet

Directions: Color and cut out the following sequencing cards. Put them into the correct order. Then assemble into a booklet.

I take my pajamas off. 	I put on my shoes. 
I put on my shirt and pants. 	I put on my jacket. 

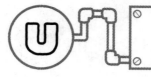

My Getting Dressed Booklet (CONT.)

I put on clean underwear.

I put on my socks.

Now I'm ready to play!

My Getting Dressed Book by

_____

I'm up and ready to start my day. After breakfast and washing, I'm ready to play! Before I do what I like best, I need to stop and go get dressed!

Underwear and Uniforms

Clothing

Directions: Copy onto several sheets of colored paper. Cut out and create outfits for the Boy and Girl Figures on page 249. Use with the Math Connections activity, "Mix and Match Outfits," on page 242.

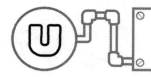 
Boy and Girl Figures

Directions: Make several copies. Cut out and use with the clothing sets on page 246. Use with the Math Connections activity, Mix and Match Outfits on page 242.

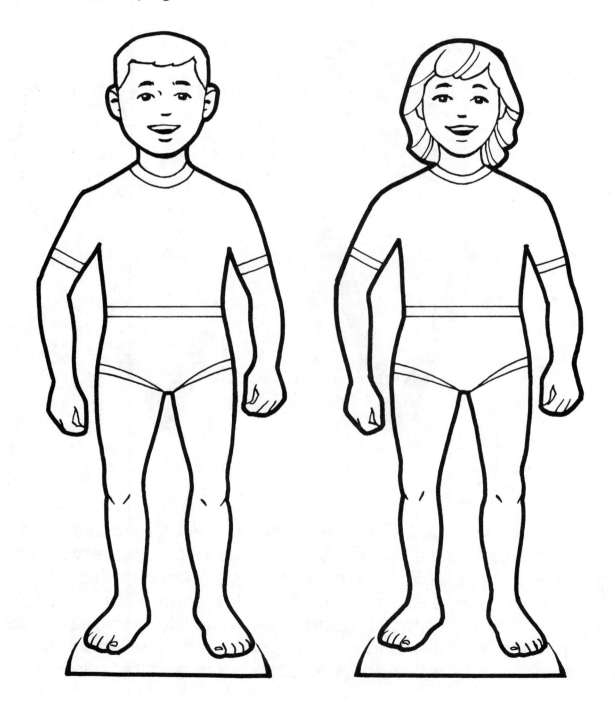

Vegetables

Unit Overview

While not many young children enjoy eating their vegetables, students will relish this unit focusing on vegetables, gardens and harvest time. Read *Growing Vegetable Soup* by Lois Ehlert (Harcourt, Inc., 1987), and learn how vegetables grow into food. Integrate other language arts and math skills while preparing to make delicious vegetable soup, counting seeds for math, and using vegetables as paint stamps in art. Use this unit as a follow-up to "A—Apples" and then transition to "L—Leaves."

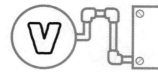 

Vegetables

Language Arts Connections

Core Book

Ehlert, Lois. *Growing Vegetable Soup*. Harcourt Inc., 1987.

Using simple text and bright illustrations, Lois Ehlert takes readers from the garden to the kitchen to grow vegetable soup. Vegetable seeds and seedlings are planted and watered, then cared for as they grow. When they are ready, the vegetables are picked for vegetable soup. A recipe for vegetable soup is included on the back cover.

Read-Aloud Activities

Prior to Reading

- Read the title, the author's, and the illustrator's names, pointing to the words as you read. Ask students to predict what they think the story might be about based on the title and cover illustrations.
- Ask students if any of them have a vegetable garden at home, and say that this story is about growing vegetables and making delicious soup.

During Reading

- As you read, make sure that each student can see the illustrations.
- Name the vegetables during reading.

After Reading

- Ask students what their favorite vegetables are, and eat vegetable snacks. Chart the result on a bar graph.

Additional Books

Stock your class library with books about vegetables. Students will enjoy looking at the illustrations and "reading" them to each other. When you read a story to your class, record yourself on tape. Then put the tape and the book in a literacy center so that your students can listen to it time and time again.

Carle, Eric. *The Tiny Seed*. Scholastic, Inc., 1987.

Ehlert, Lois. *Eating the Alphabet*. Harcourt Brace & Company, 1989.

Krauss, Ruth. *The Carrot Seed*. Harper Festival, 1993.

Martin, Bill Jr. and Sampson, Michael. *Rock it, Sock it, Number Line*. Henry Holt and Company, 2001.

Miranda, Anne. *To Market, To Market*. Harcourt, Inc., 1997.

Moore, Elaine. *Grandma's Garden*. Lothrup, Lee & Shepard Books, 1994.

Stewart, Sarah. *The Gardener*. Farrar, Straus & Giroux, 1997.

Wiesner, David. *June 29, 1999*. Clarion Books, 1992.

Letter-Sound Introduction

Say *vegetable* slowly and deliberately, emphasizing the /v/ sound. Tell students that the letter **v** says the sound /v/. /V/ is known as a "lip biter" letter because the top teeth gently bite the lower lip. Your students also should be able to feel their throat vibrate if they place their hand against their neck. It is a "motor on" or "noisy" sound, because the vocal cords vibrate when producing this sound. The formation of the lips and teeth are in the same position as the /f/ sound, except that /f/ is a "motor off" sound; the throat does not vibrate.

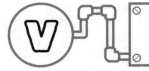

Vegetables

Language Arts Connections (CONT.)

Phonemic Awareness

Skill: syllable counting

One, Two, Three, Four!

Tell students to listen as you say *veg-e-ta-ble*. Speak slowly, pausing slightly between the syllables. Say it again, clapping with each beat. Ask how many beats they heard in the word "vegetable." They should have heard four. Tell students that all words have chunks of sounds that can be called "beats." Have the students cut out pictures of vegetables from magazines. (These can also be used in the center activity on page 255.) Once several vegetable pictures have been cut out, clap the beats as you say the name of each vegetable.

Letter Formation

After reading *Growing Vegetable Soup* and introducing the letter-sound association, reinforce the association between the letter's formation and its sound by drawing the **V** and **v** into the shape of vegetables, such as carrots in the ground.

These activities will help to reinforce letter formation for students of all learning styles.

- Guide students in warming up their fingers, hands, and arms by "air writing" **V** shapes.
- Encourage pairs of students to discover how to form a **V** shape using both sides of their bodies.
- Cue auditory learners with a verbal description: "The letter **V** is like a valley. Slide down the slope and climb up the other. That's how we make a **V**."
- Show students that their pointer and middle fingers spread apart form **V**.

How to Grow Vegetable Soup

Prepare students for making vegetable soup by recalling the sequence of events in the book *Growing Vegetable Soup*. This can be a center or whole group activity.

Skill: sequencing

Materials:
- How to Make Vegetable Soup (page 257)
- crayons or markers
- scissors
- construction paper
- glue sticks

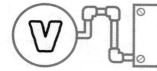
Language Arts Connections (CONT.)

How to Grow Vegetable Soup (CONT.)

Teacher Preparation:

1. Make one copy for each student of How to Make Vegetable Soup.

Procedure:

1. Instruct students to color and cut out each story square.
2. Tell students that they will be making their own vegetable soup, and that they will need to put the story squares in order so they know what to do.
3. Assist students as needed with sequencing the story squares.
4. Students glue squares onto construction paper in order.
5 Read the story sequence.

Follow-up Activity:

Prepare the vegetable soup recipe (page 256) with your class.

Math Connections

How Many Seeds?

Use the seeds from vegetables to introduce concepts of estimation, comparing numbers and counting numbers greater than twenty. This lesson could also serve as a science lesson.

Skills: estimating, counting, grouping by tens

Materials:

- assortment of vegetables with seeds (squash, peppers, cucumbers)
- shallow containers (such as paper plates) to hold seeds.

Teacher Preparation:

1. Cut the vegetables in halves or quarters so that the seeds are visible.
2. Optional: Remove seeds from some vegetables and allow to dry. Then bring dried seeds for students to handle along with sliced vegetables with seeds exposed.

Procedure:

1. Remind students about the seeds and seedlings that were planted in *Growing Vegetable Soup*. Explain that seedlings are small plants that started as seeds and are growing bigger.
2. Show the vegetables to students, and point out the seeds. Encourage students to explore the properties of the seeds.
3. Ask a variety of questions regarding the quantity of seeds and comparing the seeds. For example, do all vegetables have the same kinds of seeds?
5. For a comparing activity, suggest putting the seeds in groups of ten seeds each, and then seeing which vegetable has the most groups of seeds.
6. Review counting from 1 to 10, if appropriate, and then have students count out groups of ten seeds.
7. When all the seeds for the vegetables have been counted and grouped by tens, ask if now they know which vegetable has the most seeds.

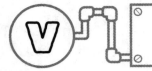

Vegetables

Science Connections

Vegetable or Herb Seedlings

Use the seeds from your math lesson to plant a vegetable or herb garden and watch it grow. You will need seeds, soil, water, and small pots. Most nurseries have small seedling starter kits that are fairly inexpensive. Plant the seeds. Provide sunshine and water, and watch them grow! Your students can chart and record the daily growth of their seedlings. When the seedlings are large enough, transfer them to pots or an outside garden. Don't forget to consider the best season for planting specific vegetables. For that reason, you may want to consider growing an inside herb garden.

As an introduction to this lesson, read *The Carrot Seed* by Ruth Krauss (Harper Festival, 1993), a classic story about a little boy who plants a carrot seed, and then patiently waits for his seed to grow.

Social Studies Connections

From the Farm to Your Table

Explore the question: How does food get from the farmer's field, onto the grocer's shelves, and end up on the dinner table? Try to arrange for a field trip to a farmer's market, or invite a farmer to come into your classroom as a guest speaker. You could also arrange for a visit to the produce section of a nearby grocery store.

Barring that, collect pictures of vegetables on farms and in stores. Create a chart illustrating how fruits and vegetables go from the farm to the store. For example, display pictures of the farm in one section with fruits and vegetables on plants and in the ground. Then draw a road with a picture of a truck, loaded with produce, headed to a picture of a store.

Art Connections

Vegetable Painting

Materials

- finger paints or tempera paints, assorted colors
- firm vegetables (potatoes, carrots, onions, firm squash, peppers, celery tops, lettuce leaves, corn on the cob)
- art paper
- soap, water, and towels for clean-up

Teacher Preparation:

1. Slice the firm vegetables into various shapes.
2. Set out vegetables, paints and paper at each station

Procedure:

1. Divide class into small groups.
2. Have students dip the vegetables into the paint and use as a stamp and brushes on the art paper.
3. Students can either experiment with the different shapes that can be made, or stamp a picture, such as a garden.
4. Allow to dry.

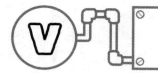 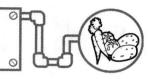

Vegetables

Music, Movement, Rhythm, and Rhyme

Old McDonald Had a Garden

Old McDonald had a garden, E-I-E-I-O,
And in this garden he had some carrots, E-I-E-I-O,
With a crunch, crunch here, and a crunch, crunch, there,
Here a crunch, there a crunch, every where a crunch, crunch,
Old McDonald had a garden, E-I-E-I-O.
Old McDonald had a garden, E-I-E-I-O,

And in this garden he had some tomatoes, E-I-E-I-O,
With a munch munch here, and a munch munch there,
Here a munch, there a munch, every where a munch, munch,
Old McDonald had a garden, E-I-E-I-O.
Old McDonald had a garden, E-I-E-I-O,
And in this garden he had some lettuce, E-I-E-I-O,
With a nibble, nibble here, and a nibble, nibble there,
Here a nibble, there a nibble, every where a nibble, nibble,
Old McDonald had a garden, E-I-E-I-O.

Old McDonald had a garden, E-I-E-I-O,
And in this garden he had some squash, E-I-E-I-O,
With a chomp, chomp here, and a chomp, chomp there,
Here a chomp, there a chomp, every where a chomp, chomp,
Old McDonald had a garden, E-I-E-I-O.

Take your students on a field trip where they can see vegetables growing and/or being harvested. Try to go to a working farm, a farmers' market, or a pumpkin patch.

During the field trip, have students sample the different types of vegetables they see. Take a class vote on the favorite vegetable tasted that day. (Note: Be sure to check with parents ahead of time about food allergies.)

Centers

Set up centers to encourage students to explore the theme further during a free choice period, or assign small groups to parent-guided centers while you work with other students.

Math Center

Skills: sorting

Fruits or Vegetables?

Have students cut pictures of fruits and vegetables out of magazines. Set out two containers (such as strawberry baskets) to be used as "baskets." Tape a picture of a vegetable on the outside of one container, and a fruit on the outside of the other. Students sort pictures according to whether they are fruits or vegetables.

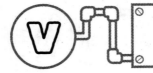

Snacks

Be sure to check with parents about allergies before serving any food.

Vegetable Soup

Make vegetable soup after the "How to Make Vegetable Soup" activity on page 252. Serve on a cool day with a roll for a warm and delicious meal. Follow the recipe provided below, or use the recipe provided in *Growing Vegetable Soup*. Have students assist with preparing the vegetables, although have an adult do the cutting! Don't miss out on the opportunity to integrate math skills as students measure the ingredients! This recipe yields 16 small servings.

Ingredients:

- 3 large carrots, scrubbed and sliced
- approximately 12 green beans, sliced in halves or thirds, with ends cut off
- 1 stalk celery, sliced
- 1 large onion, diced
- 2 medium potatoes (skin optional), cubed
- 1 14 oz can diced tomatoes
- 1 medium zucchini, sliced
- 1 small can or ¾ cup peas
- 1 small can or ¾ cup corn
- 2 16 oz cans vegetable or beef broth
- 6 cups water
- optional: spices such as salt, pepper, parsley, thyme, oregano

Directions:

1. Bring water to a boil in a large pot.
2. Add broth. Bring liquid to boil. Do not cover pot.
3. Add carrots, beans, celery, onion, potatoes, and tomatoes to boiling liquid.
4. Reduce heat to medium and simmer for ten to fifteen minutes.
5. Add zucchini, peas, and corn.
6. Taste and season, if needed.
7. Continue to simmer, uncovered, until vegetables are tender (without being mushy).
8. Allow to cool slightly, and then serve.

Vegetables

How to Make Vegetable Soup

Directions: Cut and color. Put into the correct order.

Wash and cut the vegetables

Cook the soup.

Eat the soup. Yummy!

Put the vegetables in the pot.

Whales in the Waves

Overview

Study the letter **W** with a whale unit. Read fiction and non-fiction books about whales, compare the measurements of whales and other large objects, and make a whale out of a paper bag. Use map reading skills to follow the migration of whales along from cold and warm ocean regions. Include this study in an ocean unit with "O—Ocean."

Whales in the Waves

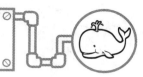

Language Arts Connections

Core Book

Sheldon, Dyan. *The Whale's Song*. Dial Books for Young Readers, 1991.

In this sweet story, Lilly is enthralled by her grandmother's memories of whales. Her grandmother recalls waiting by the sea, hoping for a glimpse of the wondrous sea creatures. She tells Lilly that if you bring the whales a special gift, they will come to you with a song. Determined to hear the whales' song, Lilly presents her own gift to the ocean, and patiently waits. She is finally rewarded with the whale's song.

Read-Aloud Activities

Prior to Reading

- Read the title, the author's and illustrator's names. Show the students the front cover illustration, and ask the students what they think the book might be about.
- Ask the students if they have ever hoped for something that they really, really wanted. Tell them that this is the story of a little girl, named Lilly, who really, really wanted to hear the whale's song.
- Ask students if they have any idea of what the whale's song is.

During Reading

- Talk about how the illustrations almost look like photographs.
- Vary the tone of your voice for the different characters. For example, when reading great-uncle Frederick' words, use a very grumpy tone.
- Ask students why they think Frederick uses such grumpy words.

After Reading

- Ask students if their grandparents tell them childhood stories.
- Ask students what they think a "whale's song" sounds like. If available, play a tape of whale vocalizations. (See "Science Connections" on page 261 for a recommendation of a whale tape).

Additional Books

Stock your class library with books about whales. Students will enjoy looking at the illustrations and "reading" them to each other. When you read a story to your class, record yourself on tape. Then put the tape and the book in a literacy center so that your students can listen to it time and time again.

Davis, Maggie Steincrohn. *A Garden of Whales*. Firefly Books, 1993.
Gibbons, Gail. *Whales*. Holiday House, 1991.
Himmelman, John. *Pipaluk and the Whales*. National Geographic, 2002.
London, Jonathan. *Baby Whale's Journey*. Chronicle Books, 1999.
Pallotta, Jerry. *Dory Story*. Charlesbridge Publishing, 2000.
Pfister, Marcus. *Rainbow Fish and the Big Blue Whale*. NorthSouth Books, 1998.
Raffi. *Baby Beluga*. Crown Publishers, 1997.
Schuch, Steve. *A Symphony of Whales*. Harcourt, 1999.
Steig, William. *Amos and Boris*. Ferrar, Strauss and Giroux, 1971.
Wolpert, Tom. *Whales for Kids*. NorthWord Press, 1991.

Whales in the Waves

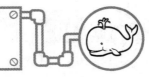

Language Arts Connections (CONT.)

Letter-Sound Introduction

What is first sound of the words *whales* and *waves*? Tell the students that the letter **w** makes the sound /w/. Have them hold their hand in front of their mouths as they say /w/ and feel the "wind" on their hands.

Phonemic Awareness

Skill: identifying beginning /w/ words

Where, Oh Where is /W/?

Provide the students with squares of paper, pencils and crayons. Have them think of things that begin with /w/. Have them write the words (using their developing writing skills) or draw pictures to represent the words on the paper squares. Have each student "read" their word/picture card(s) and put them in a box decorated as a whale.

Letter Formation

After reading *The Whale's Song* and introducing the letter-sound association, reinforce the association between the letter formation and its sound by drawing the **W** and **w** into a picture of a whale swimming in the waves.

These activities will help to reinforce letter formation for students of all learning styles.

- Provide water paints for the students to paint **W** and **w** shapes.
- In warm weather, give each student a large house paintbrush and a container of water. Have the students "paint" **W** and **w** on the sidewalks with water.
- Use corrugated bulletin board edging to form **W** and **w**. Have the students run their fingers over the "wavy" textured shapes.
- Guide students in "air writing" a **W**, saying, "Down, up, down, up."

A Whale of a Tale

Practice oral language skills, and discuss the difference between truth and fantasy by telling outlandish stories.

Skills: identifying real versus imaginary stories, oral language

Materials:
- paper
- pencils
- crayons/markers

Procedure:

1. Introduce the activity by telling a crazy, outlandish story. Afterwards, ask the students if they think this story really happened.
2. Discuss the terms *real* and *imaginary* (or truth and fiction, real and pretend or make believe, etc.),
3. Prompt an oral storytelling activity by having the students tell their own "imaginary" and "real" stories.
4. After a student tells a story, the rest of the class can try to determine whether the story is real or imaginary.

Whales in the Waves

Language Arts Connections (CONT.)

A Whale of a Tale (CONT.)

Alternative:

1. Provide prompts, such as, "Tell me a story that involves a whale and a space ship."

Follow-up Activity:

1. Record the students' stories, and display them on a bulletin board titled, "A Whale of a Tale."

2. Discuss that the term "A Whale of a Tale" means a story that is totally outrageous and beyond belief.

Math Connections

As Big as a Whale

With a long measuring tape, measure out the length of a whale. The blue whale is over 100' long. How big is that compared to a football field, a house, or a car?

Skills: measurements, comparing lengths

Materials:

- 100' measuring tape
- large open space in which a very long measuring tape can be used (minimum 100 feet)

Procedure:

1. Tell the students that the largest type of whale is the blue whale. It is the largest animal on earth, up to 100' long.

2. Ask the students to estimate how long 100' is. Ask questions, such as, "Is the blue whale larger or smaller than a car? What about a house?

3. Measure 100' with the measuring tape. Have half of the students stand at either end of the whale measurement.

4. Compare the length of the whale to other large objects, such houses.

Extension:

1. Compare the measurements of the blue whale to other whales or other ocean animals.

Science Connections

Whale Talk

Whales use extraordinary sounds to communicate with each other. "Whales of the World" is a tape of 11 songs about whales for kids, interspersed with recordings of actual whale songs and sounds. It is available from NorthSound, NorthWord Press, Inc. at (800) 336-6398.

Waves

Discover, on a very small scale, how the wind creates waves in the ocean. Experiment with waves by putting water in a shallow bowl. Have the students blow "wind" through a straw and watch the waves. Put plastic boats or sea creatures in the water, and discuss how the waves move the objects.

Whales in the Waves

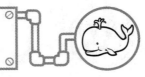

Social Studies Connections

Whale Migrations

Most whales migrate, or move from one area of the ocean to another, in warm and cold seasons. They travel to cold water for feeding, and to warm waters to breed and give birth. They breed and give birth in the warm waters along the southern coasts of Africa, Mexico, Central and South America and off the coasts of Australia and New Zealand. To feed, they travel to the cold regions, such as Antarctica or the Arctic. Discuss the cold and warm parts of the ocean, and locate these regions on a map.

Art Connections

Paper Bag Whale

Create a whale toy or puppet out of a brown paper bag. Have students use the paper bag whales in creative play.

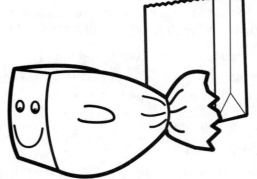

Materials

- paper bag
- newspaper or other stuffing
- tape or string
- marker
- blue or gray paint

Procedure:

1. Stuff the paper bag with the newspaper.
2. Tie the end closed, leaving the end flared out for the tale.
3. Paint the whales blue or gray.
4. Draw or paint a face on the whale and have fun!

Music, Movement, Rhythm, and Rhyme

If You Ever

If you ever, ever, ever, ever, ever,
If you ever, ever, ever meet a whale,
You must never, never, never, never, never,
You must never, never, never touch its tail.
For if you ever, ever, ever, ever, ever,
If you ever, ever, ever touch its tail,
You will never, never, never, never, never,
You will never, never, meet another whale.

Baby Beluga

Sing and listen to "Baby Beluga" by Raffi, available on *Baby Beluga* (Rounder, 1996). Raffi has written a book with the same words, *Baby Beluga* (Crown Publishers, 1997). Read the book and integrate the social studies discussion about cold regions. In the illustrations, a baby beluga is shown swimming in the Arctic.

 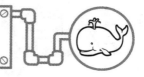

Whales in the Waves

Music, Movement, Rhythm, and Rhyme (CONT.)

Whales in the Waves

Have the students pretend to be sea creatures: whales swimming in the waves, fish floating silently under the surface, and octopi with eight arms swirling through the water. Come up with creative ways to imitate ocean animals: wiggle across the floor, jump (as though jumping in the waves) as high as possible, and wave arms like fins. Have four students stand together with the back touching and arms waving like an octopus. Can they manage to walk together?

Centers

Set up centers to encourage students to explore the theme further during a free choice period, or assign small groups to parent-guided centers while you work with other students.

Math Center

Skills: estimating, counting, comparing numbers

How Many?

Put fish-shaped crackers or gummy fish (perhaps something that resembles whales) in a jar or bowl. Have the students estimate how many they think are in the jar, and write that number down on a slip of paper. Have the students, with the assistance of the parent guide. Compare that number with the estimations.

Snacks

Be sure to check with parents about allergies before serving any food.

"Whale" Cracker in Soup

Add whale or fish shaped crackers to soup for a quick, delicious snack.

Ingredients and Materials:
- Fish- or whale-shaped crackers
- canned soup (tomato, chicken, etc.)
- water or milk for preparing the soup

Directions:
1. Prepare the soup as directed.
2. Add the crackers to the soup.

Fox

Overview

The sly fox has arrived, with plenty of tricks, including the tricky **x** sound. Study "F—Fox" following "P—Pigs" and "F—Farm" and continue with the Farm theme. Delight in the troubles of Hattie the Hen as she desperately tries to warn her barnyard companions about the fox emerging from the bushes in *Hattie and the Fox*, by Mem Fox. Learn about how and where foxes live in Science and Social Studies Connections, and complete your own version of a fox trickster tale for writing.

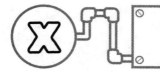 **Fox**

Language Arts Connections

Core Book

Fox, Mem. *Hattie and the Fox*. Simon and Schuster, 1986.

Hattie the hen sees a nose, two eyes, two ears, a body and then the whole fox emerging from the bushes. Despite her repeated warnings, none of the barnyard animals take her squawking seriously, until it's almost too late! This cumulative, suspense-filled book is a delight for young listeners.

Read-Aloud Activities

Prior to Reading

- Read the title, pointing at the words as you read. At the same time, open the book so that the front and back covers are visible to students. Ask students who they think Hattie is, based on the cover illustrations.
- Ask students to predict what they think the story might be about based on the title and cover illustrations.
- Read the author's, and the illustrator's names. Note the author's name is Mem Fox and the title of the story is *Hattie and the Fox*.

During Reading

- Be expressive. Use different voices for each barnyard animal.
- Point to your nose, eyes, and ears each time Hattie sees those fox parts emerging from the bushes. Encourage students to do the same.

After Reading

- Talk about how the story made you feel. For example, "Wow, I was so nervous when the other animals didn't take Hattie seriously! I wonder what they were thinking."
- Allow time for students to articulate responses and to discuss the story.
- Be open to students' needs to express themselves in different ways. Some students may want to draw a picture about the story, while others may want to talk about it. Still others may want to use music to describe their feelings.

Additional Books

Stock your class library with books about foxes. Students will enjoy looking at the illustrations and "reading" them to each other. When you read a story to your class, record yourself on tape. Then put the tape and the book in a literacy center so that your students can listen to it time and time again

Aylesworth, Jim. *The Tale of the Tricky Fox*. Scholastic Press, 2001.
Carle, Eric. *Hello, Red Fox*. Simon and Schuster Books for Young Readers, 1998.
Dr. Seuss. *Fox in Socks*. Random House, Inc., 1965.
Hogrogian, Nonny. *One Fine Day*. Macmillan Publishing Company, Inc., 1971.
Hutchins, Pat. *Rosie's Walk*. Simon and Schuster, 1968.
Laukel, Hans Gerold. *The Desert Fox Family Book*. North-South Books, 1996.
McBratney, Sam. *I'll Always Be Your Friend*. Harper Collins Publishers, 2001.
McKissack, Patricia C. *Flossie and the Fox*. Dial Books for Young Readers, 1986.

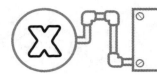

Fox

Language Arts Connections (CONT.)

Letter-Sound Introduction

What is ending sound of the word *fox*? Say fox slowly and deliberately, emphasizing the */ks/* sound. Tell students that the letter **x** makes the sound */ks/*. **X** and the */ks/* sound can be pretty tricky, just like the fox. Occasionally, **x** makes the */z/* sound, as in *xylophone*. Also, **x** is not the only letter that says */ks/*; the letters **cks** also say */ks/*.

Phonemic Awareness

Skill: manipulation of sounds: substituting beginning sounds in a word, identifying similar word patterns.

Make a copy of the "Fox Rhyming Words" (page 273). Cut out each card. Show students the "fox" card, and ask students what the picture shows. They respond, "fox." Model for the students how to write the word fox. For example, "Let's write *fox* on the board. Help me figure out the letters to write. What letters make those sounds? **F, o, x**—*fox*." Next, show the cards for fox and box. Ask, "How can I change the word from *fox* to *box*?" as you emphasize the beginning sounds. Continue to prompt students as needed. For example, ask, "What sounds are the same in the words *fox* and *box*?" as you emphasize the */o/* and */ks/* sounds. When students have told you to change the beginning letter, write the word box under the word "fox." Do the same for *ox*, but this time, omit a beginning letter. Ask, "What other words rhyme with *fox*?" If *blocks*, *socks* and *knocks*, are identified, acknowledge that these words do rhyme with *fox*. They each end in **-cks** which also makes the */ks/* sound.

Letter Formation

After reading *Hattie and the Fox* by Mem Fox, and after introducing the letter-sound association, reinforce the association between the letter formations and its sound by drawing the **x** into the illustration of a fox.

These activities will help to reinforce letter formation for students of all learning styles.

- Challenge students to find as many different things as possible in the classroom that could be used to form the letter **x**, for example, two crayons, two fingers, two craft sticks. Students can either collect objects in a bag, or draw pictures of them.

- Put plastic letter shapes into a paper bag stapled shut or a closed box with a hole in its side. Students put their hand in the hole and identify each letter that they feel. They check themselves by pulling the letter out of the box or bag.

- Draw a very large **x** on a several sheets of butcher paper that have been taped together. Have the entire class participate in painting the **x** with "extra bright colors" such as neon green, orange or yellow.

- At snack time, have the students make **x** shapes out of carrots, celery, and pretzel sticks. Stick the intersecting pieces together with peanut butter.

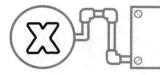

Fox

Language Arts Connections (CONT.)

The Tale of the Tricky Fox

The fox has a reputation for being a trickster. Many tales have been written about the clever fox. With this lesson, your class can write their own tricky fox tale. Your students supply names, places, actions, and describing words, and end up with their own version of a trickster tale.

Skills: vocabulary, comprehension, listening skills, grammar

Materials:

- The Tale of the Tricky Fox (page 274)
- pencil
- art paper
- crayons and markers

Teacher Preparation:

1. Make a copy of "The Tale of the Tricky Fox."
2. Review the tale so that you know what details will be repeated. For example, the Tricky Fox's name is repeated several times throughout the story.
3. Consider highlighting, circling, or identifying in some way the unique details that will be added. For example, since the Tricky Fox's name is not unique (it is repeated several times throughout the story), you will ask for it only one time, and then fill in that name throughout the rest of the story.

Procedure:

1. After reading *Hattie and the Fox*, discuss how the fox has a reputation for being a clever "trickster" who likes to play tricks.
2. Tell students that you are going to tell them a story, but many important parts are left out. They will help you to fill in these important parts.
3. Determine how you will handle student participation. There are 22 details needed, so consider having each student provide one detail.
5. Begin reading the story.
6. When you reach a blank space, identify which students will provide that detail. Then finish reading the entire sentence so that the students understand its meaning.
7. After all the blank spaces have been filled in, reread the story.

Follow-up Activity:

1. Make a class book of the story. Write the story on large pieces of art paper, with a few sentences on each page.
2. Have the class decide on a title for their story, and write the title on one piece of art paper for the book cover.
3. Divide the class into the same number of groups as the number of pages, with one additional group for the book cover.
4. Have the groups illustrate the pages of the books and the cover.
5. Assemble the book and add it to the class library.

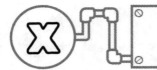

Fox

Math Connections

Measuring Foxes

The size of a fox varies, depending up on the type. Compare the measurements of the smallest fox (the fennec fox) to the largest (the red fox).

Skills: measuring and comparing numbers

Materials:

- measuring tape
- optional: butcher paper to draw the shape of a fox
- photographs of fennec and red foxes, from nature magazines, books or the Internet

Background Information:

The fennec fox is the smallest fox, about 14" to 17" (36–44 cm) long with an 8" (20 cm) tail. It weighs 2 to 3.5 pounds (1–1.5 kg). It lives in the sandy Sahara Desert in northern Africa. Fennecs have several characteristics that help them cope with desert heat. They have very large ears, which help them to radiate heat. They are primarily nocturnal, and rest during the heat of the day. Finally, they have fur on the pads of their feet so they can run across hot sand.

The red fox is the largest of the foxes. Its body measures 18" to 33" (45–90 cm), with the tail measuring 12" to 22" (30–55 cm), and it weighs 8 to 15 pounds. (3.5–7 kg). Red foxes live throughout the world in North America, Europe, and Asia. The red fox is actually reddish brown, and its long, bushy tail has a white tip.

Procedure:

1. Show photographs of fennec and red foxes, and discuss their physical characteristics.
2. Use a measuring tape to measure the sizes of the two types of foxes. Sketch the outlines of measurements on the butcher paper.
3. Discuss some of the characteristics, such as the fact that the tail is about one-third of the foxes' total length.
4. Compare the measurements of the foxes to objects in the room such as students, tables, and chairs.

Science and Social Studies Connections

A Fox's Life

Even though foxes have a reputation for being bold, cunning, and deceitful, in fact, they are shy and appear to be very intelligent. Study the fox to learn more about these interesting animals.

Compose a "KWL" chart with the questions, "What Do We Already **Know**?" "What Do We **Want** to Know?" and "What Did We **Learn**?" written in three large columns on a sheet of butcher paper. Have students brainstorm things that they already know about foxes and record these ideas in the appropriate column. Then have them brainstorm things that they would like to discover about foxes, and record these in the next column. Fill in the third column as your learn more about foxes.

Fox

Science and Social Studies Connections (CONT.)

A Fox's Life (CONT.)

Provide resources about foxes, such as *The Desert Fox Family Book*, by Hans Gerold Laukel (North-South Books, 1996). Assist students with researching the answers to their questions. Record these answers in the "What Did We Learn?" column.

Pull out a globe or map, and find the different homes of the fox in the world, in your state, or in your community. The fennec fox lives in the deserts of Northern Africa. Find pictures of the fennec fox in books (such as *The Desert Fox Family Book*) or on the internet. Identify the Northern African desert habitat on the globe or map.

Art Connections

Fox Masks

Promote creative play amongst your students as they create masks of the animals they are studying. The following fox mask is quick, easy and fun to make.

Materials:

- Fox Mask (page 273)
- heavy paper on which to copy the mask
- scissors
- glue or tape
- crayons or markers
- string or yarn
- single hole paper punch

Teacher Preparation:

1. Copy one Fox Mask for each student onto heavy paper.

Procedure:

1. Have each student color the fox mask with crayons or markers.
2. Have each student cut out the fox mask. Assist as needed.
3. Punch a hole on each side of the mask. Tie one piece of string onto each hole. Tie a second piece of string onto the other hole.
4. Place the mask on the student's face, and tie the string around his or her head.

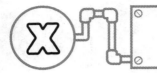 
Music, Movement, Rhythm, and Rhyme

A Hunting We Will Go

A hunting we will go, a hunting we will go,
Heigh ho, the derry-o, a hunting we will go,
A hunting we will go, a hunting we will go,
We'll catch a fox and put him in a box,
And then we'll let him go.

A hunting we will go, a hunting we will go,
Heigh ho, the derry-o, a hunting we will go,
A hunting we will go, a hunting we will go,
We'll catch a fish and put him on a dish,
And then we'll let him go.

A hunting we will go, a hunting we will go,
Heigh ho, the derry-o, a hunting we will go,
A hunting we will go, a hunting we will go,
We'll catch a bear and cut his hair,
And then we'll let him go.

A hunting we will go, a hunting we will go,
Heigh ho, the derry-o, a hunting we will go,
A hunting we will go, a hunting we will go,
We'll catch a pig and dance a little jig,
And then we'll let him go.

A hunting we will go, a hunting we will go,
Heigh ho, the derry-o, a hunting we will go,
A hunting we will go, a hunting we will go,
We'll catch a giraffe and make him laugh,
And then we'll let him go.

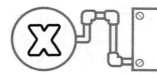 

Music, Movement, Rhythm, and Rhyme (CONT.)

Note: Refer to the Center Activity on page 272 prior to reading this poem to students.

Miss Fox's Box
by Barbara Ramming

The other day I saw a fox
And on her head she had a box
I wondered what she had inside
I walked up to her
And asked with pride,
"Miss Fox, up there, up on your head
I see a box and wonder, please,
What could you hold inside of it?
Is it something you might squeeze?"
"Why yes it is," said Miss Fox,
But you must guess what's in the box.
So I began to think and think.
I asked if it was something pink.
But she replied without a blink
"Inside the box there's nothing pink."
"I'll give you a hint
To help you along.
It's eatable and squeezable
And a little bit long,
It's white or it's brown,
And just like a ham,
It's oblong or round;
I like it with jam!
So I thought and I thought
Soon I knew what it was.
I invited Miss Fox
To breakfast because…
I had strawberry jam and butter, so much!
A toaster and plates, a knife and such.
The squeezable thing she had in a box
Was a fresh loaf of bread baked by Miss Fox.

Fox and Chickens

Play this version of tag by selecting one student to play the fox. The other students are chickens in the barnyard. Any chickens that the fox tags become foxes also. Continue playing until all chickens are foxes.

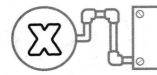

Fox

Centers

Set up centers to encourage students to explore the theme further during a free choice period, or assign small groups to parent-guided centers while you work with other students.

Critical Thinking Center

Skills: asking questions

Miss Fox's Box

Read Barbara Knarr Ramming's poem "Miss Fox's Box," excluding the last two verses. At the center, set out a box with a loaf of bread inside. Have the students try to guess what could be in the box. Encourage the students to ask questions to try to determine the contents of the box.

Snacks

Be sure to check with parents about allergies before serving students any food.

Fresh Bread and Strawberry Jam

After reading "Miss Fox's Box," bake a loaf of fresh honey whole wheat bread. Slice, toast and serve with butter and strawberry jam.

Ingredients:

- 1 package (.25 ounce) rapid rise yeast
- 1 teaspoon white sugar
- ½ cup warm water
- 1½ cups milk
- ¼ cup water
- ¼ cup melted butter
- ¼ cup honey

- 2 teaspoons salt
- 2 cups whole wheat flour
- 3 cups bread flour
- 2 tablespoons butter
- 2–3 bowls
- bread pans
- oven

Directions:

1. Dissolve the yeast and the sugar in ½ cup warm water.
2. In a separate bowl, combine the milk, ¼ cup water, ¼ cup melted butter, honey, salt, and wheat flour.
3. Mix in the yeast mixture. Let the mixture sit for 20 minutes.
4. Add white flour.
5. Mix until the dough forms a ball. Knead dough for an additional 10 minutes.
6. Coat the dough in butter, and put it in a bowl. Cover the bowl loosely with a towel. Let dough rise until almost doubled (35–45 minutes).
7. Punch down, and divide dough in half. Knead out the bubbles. Form into loaves, and place in buttered bread pans. Butter the tops of the dough, and cover loosely with towel. Let rise in a warm area until doubled (about 30 minutes).
8. Bake at 375 degrees for 25 to 35 minutes, or until tops are dark golden brown. Cool, and then slice.

 **Fox**

Fox Rhyming Words

Directions: Copy and cut out the cards. Use with the Phonemic Awareness activity on page 266.

fox

box

ox

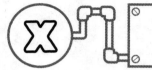 
The Tale of the Tricky Fox

Once upon a time, there was a clever young fox. His name was _____.
(Tricky Fox's name)

He had a _____ coat, a _____ tail, a _____
(describing word) (describing word) (describing word)

nose, and two _____ eyes. More than anything, he loved to play tricks.
(describing word)

Everyday, he managed to get into some sort of trouble with his tricks. Everyday, his mother would

say, "_____ , please try not to play any tricks today." And everyday,
(Tricky Fox's name)

_____ would try really, really hard to not any play tricks on
(Tricky Fox's name)

anyone! But he just couldn't help it! Playing tricks was so much fun! That is, it was fun until the

day that he tried playing a trick on the _____ .
(name of other animal)

It all started when _____ took _____ 's
(Tricky Fox's name) (name of other animal)

_____ . _____ looked everywhere for his/her _____ .
(thing) (name of other animal) (thing)

He/she soon figured out that _____ had taken it as one of his tricks.
(Tricky Fox's name)

_____ decided that enough was enough! He/She would play a trick on
(name of other animal)

_____ . Maybe then, _____ would stop playing tricks.
(Tricky Fox's name) (Tricky Fox's name)

_____ gathered everyone together. They had all had enough of _____
(name of other animal) (Tricky Fox's name)

tricks! Together, the animals came up with a plan.

That afternoon, _____ was walking along feeling pretty good about
(Tricky Fox's name)

the trick he had played on _____ , when suddenly, out of nowhere,
(name of other animal)

a _____ _____ _____ !
(describing word) (thing) (action word)

_____ _____ !
(Tricky Fox's name) (action word)

Suddenly all the animals came out of the _____ . They were all _____ ,
(place) (action)

and _____ realized that he had just been tricked! He looked around,
(Tricky Fox's name)

and said, "I guess it isn't so fun for the one who's being tricked. My trickster days are over!"

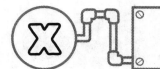

Fox

Fox Mask

Directions: Copy on heavy paper. Color and cut. Punch a hole, as indicated, in each side of the mask. Tie onto student's head with string.

 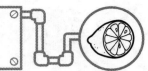
Unit Overview

The world is filled with bright, beautiful colors. Anytime of year is the perfect time to explore colors, and with *My Many Colored Days* by Dr. Seuss (Alfred A. Knopf, 1996), you can integrate discussions of feelings with color studies. In this unit, students write about feelings, experiment with blending colors, and use a chart to measure their favorite colors in math.

 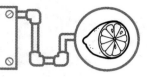

Yellow

Language Arts Connections

Core Book

Dr. Seuss. *My Many Colored Days*. Alfred A. Knopf, 1996.

Although Dr. Seuss wrote the manuscript for this book in 1973, it was not actually published until 1996. Dr. Seuss reportedly felt that it would take an extraordinary artist or artists to illustrate the text. Those artists, Steve Johnson and Lou Fancher, used striking colors and fairly abstract images to convey Dr. Seuss' message: that we all experience different moods and feelings from day to day.

Read-Aloud Activities

Prior to Reading

- Read the title, pointing to the words as you read.
- Read the author's, and the illustrators' names. Remind students of other Dr. Seuss books that they may have read.

During Reading

- As you read, make sure that each student can see the illustrations. Hold the book so that it is facing the students, and turn it slowly as you read.
- Be expressive. Your voice and facial expressions will draw students into the story.
- For example, during the happy parts, use a happy voice. During the more solemn parts, slow down and lower the pitch of your voice.

After Reading

- Allow time for students to articulate responses. Wait a few moments so they can think about what they would like to say.
- Respond to the story yourself. You might want to start by talking about how the book made you feel, or about what color you feel today.

Additional Books

Stock your class library with books about colors and feelings. Students will enjoy looking at the illustrations and "reading" them to each other. When you read a story to your class, record yourself on tape. Then put the tape and the book in a literacy center so that your students can listen to it time and time again.

Bang, Molly. *When Sophie Gets Angry—Really, Really Angry…* Scholastic, Inc., 1999.

Boynton, Sandra. *Blue Hat, Green Hat*. Little Simon, 1984.

Carle, Eric. *Hello, Red Fox*. Simon and Schuster Books for Young Readers, 1998.

Ehlert, Lois. *Color Zoo*. Harper Collins Publishers, 1989.

Joosse, Barbara. *I Love You the Purplest*. Chronicle Books, 1996.

Lionni, Leo. *Little Blue and Little Yellow*. Harper Collins Publishers, 1959.

Schwartz, Betty Ann. *What Makes a Rainbow?* Piggy Toes Press, 2000.

Walsh, Ellen Stoll. *Mouse Paint*. Harcourt Brace and Company, 1989.

 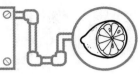

Yellow

Language Arts Connections (CONT.)

Letter-Sound Introduction

Say *yellow* slowly and deliberately, emphasizing the /y/ sound. Tell students that the letter **y** says the sound /y/. Tell students that **y** is one of those letters that says more than one sound; it also sometimes says the long /ē/ sound or the long /ī/ sound.

Phonemic Awareness

Skill: Syllable splitting

"Handling" Words

Say the word *yellow*. Say, "Let's break that word into chunks. *Yell–ow*. I hear two chunks. *Yell-ow*." As you say yellow the second time, spread your right hand open in front of you with *yell-* and your left hand open in front of you with *-ow*. Say, "What other color words have two chunks?" Go through the colors, trying to use the two hand motion with each. For example, say, "Blue—no, only one hand. How about purple? I used two hands." Since not many colors have two syllables, proceed to students names.

Letter Formation

After reading *My Many Colored Days* by Dr. Seuss, and after introducing the letter-sound association, reinforce the association between the letter's formation and its sound by drawing the **Y** and **y** into a scene with yellow colored objects. For example, the shapes **Y** and **y** could be parts of a sun's rays.

These activities will help to reinforce letter formation for students of all learning styles.

- Write **Y** onto a piece of paper. Students glue yellow yarn onto the lines of the **Y**.
- Assemble a variety of line-shaped objects (craft sticks, math rods, and strips of construction paper). Students can experiment with different sizes of lines to create **Y** and **y**.
- Put plastic letter shapes into a paper bag stapled shut or a closed box with a hole in its side. Students put their hand in the box and identify each letter that they feel. If they think they feel a **Y** or **y**, they pull the letter out of the box or bag.
- Draw **Y** onto pieces of butcher paper. Students paint in the letter **y** with yellow paint.
- Cue auditory learners with rhythm and rhyme when teaching about letter formations. For example, with lower case **y**, say, "Slide down, now stop. Back to the other side, on top. Slide down, don't stop! Pass the line. Now stop."

 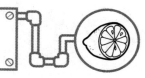

Language Arts Connections (*CONT.*)

Today I Feel . . . Class Book

The core book of this unit is a great tool to facilitate discussions about feelings. In this writing activity, your students can tell their own story about how they feel today. This activity is best done with very small groups of students at a writing center.

Skill: writing

Materials:

- a copy of *My Many Colored Days*
- "Today I Feel" (page 284)
- pencils
- writing paper
- construction paper (variety of colors)
- glue stick
- 3-hole punch and yarn, or staples and stapler

Teacher Preparation:

1. Make one copy for each student of the "Today I Feel."

Procedure:

1. After reading *My Many Colored Days*, have the students brainstorm how different colors make them feel.
2. Tell the class that each student will make one page of a class book. Each page will begin with the statement "Today I feel (choose color) because…" They will each choose a color to insert in the statement, and tell why they feel that way today. For example, "Today I feel blue because it's raining and I can't play outside."
3. Fill out each student's sheet as he or she dictates phrases.
  a. Optional: have students write in the color themselves. Provide a color chart with the spelling of each color.
  b. Some beginning writers may want to write out their own phrases, with assistance as needed, as a center activity.
4. After students have dictated their sentences, give them their pages to illustrate. The face has been started, and students can draw in the mouth according to the expressed emotion.
5. Have students glue their pages to sheets of construction paper that are the same color that they have written about.
6. Assemble the class book by stapling together or by using 3-hole punch and tying together with yarn.

Math Connections

"Our Favorite Colors" Bar Graph

Take a class poll of your students' favorite colors, and then chart the results to see what the most popular color is.

Skills: counting, bar graphing

Materials:

- one large piece of butcher paper
- squares of construction paper

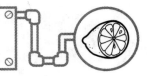
Math Connections (*CONT.*)

Teacher Preparation:

1. Cut squares of construction paper in blue, red, green, yellow, black and any other colors that your class chooses for "Our Favorite Colors" bar graph.

2. Draw a grid on the butcher paper. Write "Our Favorite Colors" across the top and "Colors" at the bottom. Write "Number of Students" next to the left column, and write numbers (1-10, for example) in each square of the left column. Glue or tape a square of each color in the squares in the bottom row.

Procedure:

1. Begin by telling your class that most people have a favorite color. Tell them that today, they will each have a chance to tell you what their favorite color is.

2. Show them the bar graph. Tell them that you this will help everyone to see what everyone's favorite colors are.

3. Have each student choose a color square, and write their name on it. Assist as needed.

4. Select one student to glue their color square into the bar graph in first position square of that color.

5. The next student chooses a color, and glues it on to the chart. If is the same color as the first students', they glue it into the second position square of that color.

6. Continue until all the students have glued their color square in place.

7. Summarize the results by counting the squares of each color.

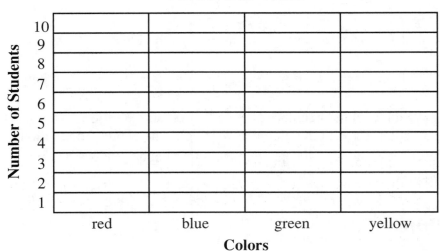

Science Connections

A Rainbow of Colors

In *What Makes a Rainbow* by Betty Ann Schwartz (Piggy Toes Press, 2000), a young rabbit tries to discover what makes a rainbow. He learns that the colors of the rainbow are made by rain drops and sun. Read the book on a sunny day, then make a rainbow outside using a sprinkler. You can also use a prism to reflect light and make rainbow patterns on the wall.

 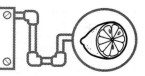

Yellow

Social Studies Connections

My Many Different Feelings

In *When Sophie Gets Angry—Really, Really Angry…* by Molly Bang (Scholastic, Inc., 1999), Sophie deals with her anger. The illustrations in the book, particularly the use of colors, convey Sophie's changing feelings. Read the story to your class and discuss ways to deal with feelings.

Art Connections

Handpainting

When students can blend colors themselves, they understand how to create new shades and colors. Have students use their own art medium—hand paints— and give "hands on" a whole new meaning! Two good books to introduce this concept are *Mouse Paint* by Ellen Stoll Walsh, and *Little Blue and Little Yellow* by Leo Lionni (both listed on page 277). This lesson is best done with small groups in centers.

Materials: (per groups of four students)

- ¾ cups cornstarch
- 3 cups cold water
- 3 cups boiling water
- food coloring
- liquid dish soap
- art paper
- art smocks
- a copy of *Mouse Paint* or *Little Blue and Little Yellow*

Teacher Preparation:

1. Mix cornstarch and cold water until smooth in a pan.
2. Add boiling water.
3. Stir constantly as you bring the mixture to a boil.
4. Remove from heat. Allow to cool thoroughly, stirring occasionally.
5. Mix in some liquid dish soap (to prevent any stains from setting).
6. Create a color chart that shows how to blend primary colors into other colors. For example, label Yellow (next to a yellow square) + Blue (next to a blue square) = Green (next to a green square). Other color combinations to include on your chart are: yellow + red = orange; red + blue = purple; purple + blue = indigo; blue + green = aqua.

Procedure:

1. Optional: *Read Mouse Pain*t and/or *Little Blue and Little Yellow*.
2. Distribute handpaint mixture to each group.
3. Have students add approximately six drops food coloring per cup of handpaint.
4. Students should mix the handpaint and food coloring well.
5. Students then paint using their entire hands.

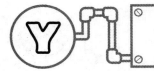 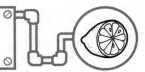

Yellow

Music, Movement, Rhythm, and Rhyme

Throughout this unit of study, recite nursery rhymes about colors.

Little Boy Blue

Little Boy Blue, come, blow your horn.

The sheep's in the meadow, the cow's in the corn.

Where's the little boy, who looks after the sheep?

He's under the haystack, fast asleep.

Roses Are Red

Roses are red,

Violets are blue,

Yellow is happy,

And so are you!

Chook, Chook

Chook, chook, chook, chook, chook,

Good morning, Mrs. Hen.

How many chickens have you got?

Madam, I've got ten.

Four of them are yellow,

And four of them are brown,

And two of them are speckled red,

The nicest in the town.

Little Green House

There was a little green house,

And in the little green house

There was a little brown house,

And in the little brown house

There was a little yellow house,

And in the little yellow house

There was a little white house,

And in the little white house

There was a little heart.

Color Hunt

Colors are everywhere in nature! Send students on a color hunt by assigning small groups one color for which they will hunt. When they find an object of that color, they draw a picture of it, and put it into a bag. Allow about twenty minutes for this activity, and then have students share their findings.

282

©Teacher Created Materials, Inc.

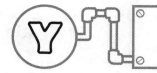 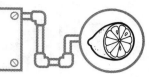

Yellow

Centers

Set up centers to encourage students to explore the theme further during a free choice period, or assign small groups to parent-guided centers while you work with other students.

Math Center

Skills: sorting, counting

Baskets of Colors

Assemble a variety of yellow, red, blue, green, purple, orange, brown, and black objects. Tape a square of each color onto a bag or basket. Students sort objects into the appropriate container, and then count them to see which container has the most objects.

Snacks

Be sure to check with parents about allergies before serving any food.

Color of the Day Snacks

Choose a different color to celebrate each day with snack. Students will enjoy predicting which color will be served today!

Yellow Day

- Yellow cheese, such as American or cheddar, sliced or diced and served with crackers.
- sliced bananas, Golden Delicious apples, and golden raisins
- pineapple rings, served with yogurt dip.

Red Day

- Red Delicious apples, sliced with skins on, and served with peanut butter
- tomatoes, sliced and served with bread. Make a tomato and cheese sandwich and pop it in the toaster oven until the cheese is melted.
- strawberries and watermelon, sliced and served chilled
- red bell pepper, seeded and sliced

Green Day

- celery sticks, served with cream cheese, peanut butter or cottage cheese
- avocado guacamole, mixed with fresh salsa, and served with corn chips
- fresh snap peas and green beans
- cucumber, sliced with the peel on, and served chilled

Orange Day

- carrots, sliced into circles or sticks, served with ranch dressing
- oranges slices and orange juice
- cantaloupe, sliced and served chilled

Blue Day

- blue gelatin, mixed as directed, with fruit chunks, and chilled until firm
- blueberries

 **Yellow**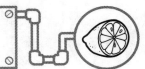

Today I Feel . . .

Directions: Add a mouth to show how you feel.

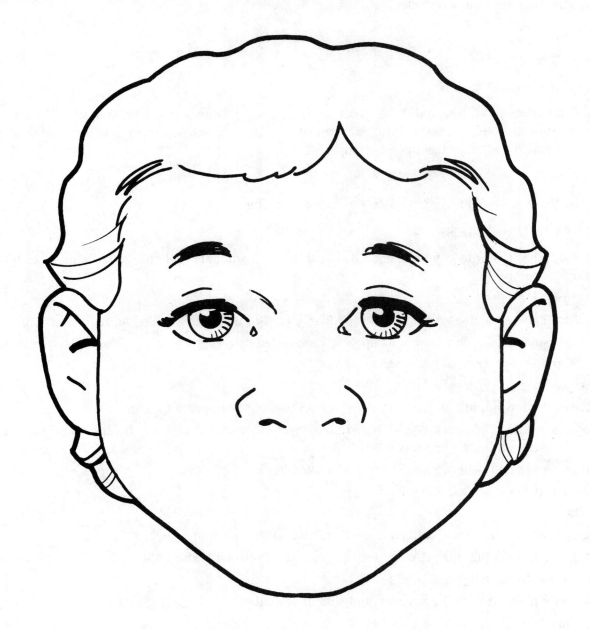

"Today I feel _____ because _____

_____ .

Zoo

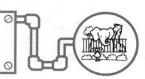

Overview

Explore zoos, and the animals that live in them, in this unit. Integrate language arts, math, science, and social studies. Begin by reading *If Anything Ever Happened at the Zoo* by Mary Jean Hendrick (Harcourt, Brace and Company, 1993). Make zoo animal alphabet and counting books, and celebrate the vivid artwork of Eric Carle.

Extend this unit with "G—Gorilla" and "E—Elephant."

Zoo

Language Arts Connections

Core Book

Hendrick, Mary Jean. *If Anything Ever Goes Wrong at the Zoo*. Harcourt, Brace and Company, 1993.

Every Saturday, Leslie and her mother visit the zoo. During her visits, Leslie tells the zookeepers that if anything should ever happen at the zoo, the animals can come over to her house to stay. Imagine her surprise, and her mother's, when one rainy night the zookeepers actually show up, with animals in tow!

Read-Aloud Activities

Prior to Reading

- Read the title, the author's, and the illustrator's names, pointing at the words as you read. Ask students to predict what the story might be about based on the title, *If Anything Ever Goes Wrong at the Zoo*.
- Ask students if any of them have ever visited a zoo, and take a few moments to discuss their experiences.

During Reading

- As you read, make sure that each student can see the illustrations.
- Discuss the descriptions that the zookeepers provide of what each type of animal needs, and compare those descriptions to the illustrations.
- When the animals begin to arrive at Leslie's house, allow time for the students to look at and respond to the illustrations.

After Reading

- Ask students how they think their parents (or caregivers) might respond if all those animals came to their homes.
- Ask students if they had to choose one of these animals to live at their home, which would it be, and why?

Additional Books

Stock your class library with books about zoos, and the animals that live in them. Students will enjoy looking at the illustrations and "reading" them to each other. When you read a story to your class, record yourself on tape. Then put the tape and the book in a literacy center so that your students can listen to it time and time again.

Alborough, Jez. *Hug*. Candlewick Press, 2000.

Base, Graeme. *Animalia*. Harry N. Abrams, Inc., 1986.

Campbell, Rod. *Dear Zoo*. Little Simon, 1986.

Carle, Eric. *Animals, Animals*. Philomel Books, 1989.

Carle, Eric. *From Head to Toe*. Harper Collins, 1999.

Carle, Eric. *Slowly, Slowly, Said the Sloth*. Philomel Books, 2002.

Carle, Eric. *The Art of Eric Carle*. Philomel Books, 1996.

Carle, Eric. *The Mixed Up Chameleon*. Harper Trophy, 1988.

Carle, Eric. *1, 2, 3 To the Zoo*. The Putnam & Grosset Group, 1968.

Ehlert Lois. *Color Zoo*. Harper Collins Publishers, 1997.

Hoban, Tana. *A Children's Zoo*. Greenwillow Books, 1985.

Knowles, Sheena. *Edward the Emu*. Harper Collins Publishers, 1988.

 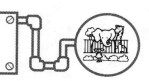

Zoo

Language Arts Connections (CONT.)

Additional Books (cont.)

Martin, Bill Jr. *Brown Bear, Brown Bear, What Do You See?* Henry Holt and Company, 1983.

Martin, Bill Jr. *Polar Bear, Polar Bear, What Do You Hear?* Henry Holt and Company, 1991.

Mazer, Anne. *The Salamander Room.* Alfred Knopf, 1991.

Morozumi, Atsuko. *My Friend Gorilla.* Farrar, Straus and Giroux, 1997.

Paxton , Tom. *Going to the Zoo.* William Morrow and Company, 1996.

Parr, Todd. *Zoo Do's and Don'ts.* Little, Brown and Company, 2000.

Polisar, Barry Louis. *Peculiar Zoo.* Rainbow Morning Music, 1993.

Rathman, Peggy. *Good Night, Gorilla.* G.P. Putnam's Sons, 1994.

Letter-Sound Introduction

What is first sound of the word *zoo*? Say *zoo* slowly and deliberately, emphasizing the /z/ sound. Tell students that the letter **Z** makes the sound /z/.

The sound /z/ is similar to the sound /s/, except that /z/ is a "noisy" sound. Have students say /s/, and tell them to think about the shapes of their mouths. Have them put their hands on their throats. What do they feel? (No vibration.) Then have them say /z/. Have them put their hands on their throats. This time what do they feel? A vibration. Sometimes, when **s** comes at the end of a word, it makes the /z/ sound.

Phonemic Awareness

Skill: Phoneme Blending

Which Animal?

Segment the names of zoo animals, and have your students put them back together again to practice blending phonemes. Say, "I'm thinking of an animal that lives in the zoo. The name of that animal is /z/ /e/ /b/ /r/ /a/. What is it?" (Zebra.) Continue segmenting words into phonemes with other zoo animal names. Then, reverse the process. Pick an animal, or have students pick and animal, and have students segment the blended word into phonemes.

Letter Formation

After reading *If Anything Ever Goes Wrong at the Zoo* and introducing the letter-sound association, reinforce the association between the letter formations and its sound by drawing **Z** into an illustration of a zoo.

These activities will help to reinforce letter formation for students of all learning styles.

- Provide three, four and seven craft sticks per student or group of students. What number of craft sticks best forms a **Z** and a **z**?

- Put magnetic letters with similar shapes (**M, N, V, W, Y, Z, m, n, h, u, v, w,**) into a paper bag stapled shut or a closed box with a hole in its side. Students reach in and feel each letter. They say its name, its sound, and then pull it out of the box or bag to check their answers.

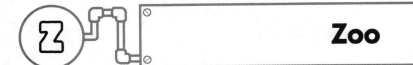
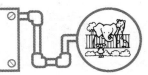
Language Arts Connections *(CONT.)*

Zoo Alphabet Book

Reinforce letter formation, letter/sound associations, and the alphabet by having the class create an alphabet zoo book. Have individuals, pairs, or small groups of students write and illustrate a letter (or two) of the alphabet with the name of an animal that begins with that letter. This activity may take two or three days to complete.

Skills: letter writing, letter identification

Materials:

- paper
- plastic magnetic letters
- crayons and markers
- wildlife or zoo magazines
- scissors
- glue

Teacher Preparation:

1. Determine how to divide the class and assign letters (that is, one or two letters per student, or several letters per small group).
2. Determine whether students will brainstorm animals to use in the book or you will predetermine the animals to be used. If you will make the choices, write the letter and the animal name for that letter on a single sheet of paper, for example, write **E** and *elephant* on the sheet.

Day One Procedure:

1. Read or display animal alphabet books, such as *Animalia* by Graeme Base (Abrams, Inc., 1986).
2. Introduce the activity by telling students that the class will be making its own animal alphabet book.
3. Have students brainstorm animals to use in the alphabet book, or select from the list on page 294. Write the final selection of animal names on sheets of paper and distribute to students.

Day Two Procedure:

1. Put the magnetic letters in a bag. Have each student or group of students pick one or two of the letters (depending upon the number you have determined each group will do).
2. Assist students with copying the letter and animal name onto the paper they will be making into the book page. To write the animal name, they can copy it from the sheet of animal names, or sound out the word.
3. Have students cut out pictures of the animals from magazines, and glue the pictures onto the paper. Remind them not to cover up the letter or animal name.
4. Make a cover for the alphabet book.
5. Allow pages to dry, and then assemble into a class book.

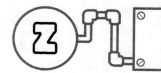 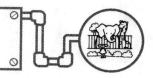

Zoo

Math Connections

Zoo Counting Book

In this math activity, students make their own animal counting books, using numbers one to five. Customize this lesson by selecting the types of mediums (stencils, stamps or stickers). This activity may take several days to complete.

Skills: number identification, number writing, number quantity

Materials:

- zoo animal stickers or zoo animal sponge stamps and paint, or zoo animal stencils, crayons and markers
- five blank sheets of paper, per student
- cover and first page of the Zoo Counting Book (pages 295–296)
- numbers one to five, written as numbers and as words (1, one) on pocket strips in a pocket chart or on the board.
- names of animals, with a picture of the animal next to it, written on pocket strips in a pocket chart or on the board.

Teacher Preparation:

1. Determine which materials to use for animal illustrations. If students will be using animal sponge stamps, make them by tracing animal shapes (from cookie cutters or stencils) onto thin sponges, then cut.

2. Compile book pages with the book cover on the top, the first page next, and the five blank pages. (Do not staple if paint will be used.)

3. Depending on the writing abilities of the students, or to save time, you may want to write the numbers and animal names on each page, or create "dot-to-dot" numbers and animal names for the students to trace. Copy these pages to assemble into booklets.

Day One/Two Procedure:

1. Read or display copies of animal counting books such as *1, 2, 3, to the Zoo* by Eric Carle (The Putnam & Grosset Group, 1968). Introduce the activity by telling students they will be making their own animal counting book.

2. Direct student attention to the written numbers and animal names. Discuss that if there is one animal, there is not an **s** at the end of the animal's name, but when there is more than one animal there is an **s**: two elephants, three monkeys, etc.

3. Distribute copies of numbers and animal names that have been made for students if they will be copying the numbers and words onto blank sheets of paper.

4. Distribute the book packets to students. Read the book cover and the first page with the students, having them use their "pointer fingers" to point at each word.

5. When finished reading, tell students that now they are going to make the rest of the book. Tell the students to look at the written number words and write the numbers on their book pages. They should write them the same way: with the number first, then the word. Assist them as needed.

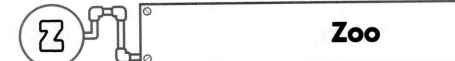 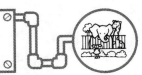

Math Connections (CONT.)

Zoo Counting Book (CONT.)

Day Two/Three Procedure:

1. When the numbers have been written, students can begin to illustrate their pages. Note: if the students will be using paint to illustrate their animals, they should write their names on the back of each number page prior to painting them. That way, the pages can be identified after drying.

2. After pages have been illustrated and are thoroughly dry, assist students with compiling pages in numerical order. Then staple each book.

Science Connections

Zoo Animal Research

Foster students' natural inquisitiveness by introducing them to the world of information and research. In this activity, students brainstorm questions about zoo animals and their natural habitats, and look for answers in books and on the Internet.

After reading *If Anything Ever Goes Wrong at the Zoo*, discuss what the zookeepers told Leslie about the needs of each type of animal. For example, the monkeys needed things to climb on. Talk about how all animals need special things in order to live. Some animals eat leaves from trees, and other animals need meat. Some like to live on wide, open plains, while others want a small, enclosed space. The places that animals live are called "habitats." Animals have everything they need to live in their habitat.

Have each student or the entire class select an animal to study. Before they begin looking for that information in books and on the Internet, they will need to think about what information they are looking for. To begin with, they need to think of questions that they want to have answered. Brainstorm questions, such as, what is the animal? Where does it like to live? What does it like to eat? What else does this animal need to have in order to live? Write these questions on a sheet of butcher paper or on the board, with some sort of pictorial symbol next to it so that beginning readers will be able to "read" the question.

Consult resources (books, nature magazines, and Websites) that will provide reliable information about the animals. Record the answers next to each research question.

Following are recommendations for Websites:

www.zoobooks.com: Zoobooks Magazine

www.seaworld.org: Sea World and Busch Gardens

www.lazoo.org: Los Angeles, California Zoo

www.oaklandzoo.org: Oakland, California Zoo

www.sandiegozoo.org: San Diego, California Zoo

www.phillyzoo.org: Philadelphia, Pennsylvania Zoo

www.natzoo.si.edu: Smithsonian National Zoo (Washington, D.C.)

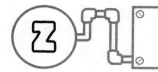
Zoo
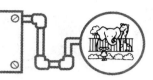

Social Studies Connections

Where in the World?

Animals' natural habitats are not zoos. Learn where some of the animals originated. Hang a large world map on the wall. Have students cut out pictures of animals from magazines, and glue or tape them on the part of the world they are from.

Africa—elephants, giraffes, zebras, monkeys
Arctic—polar bears
South America—monkeys
Asia—tigers, elephants
Antarctic—penguins
Australia—kangaroos, koalas

Art Connections

Eric Carle's Zoo

Author and illustrator Eric Carle is well known for his signature illustrations. Celebrate his work, and particularly his art, by transforming your classroom into an Eric Carle-like zoo.

Materials:

- butcher paper
- paint, assorted colors
- painting tools such as sponges, texturing tools, etc.

Teacher Preparation:

1. Determine which of the two methods (discussed below) will be used.
2. For more information on Eric Carle's art techniques, read *The Art of Eric Carle* (Philomel Books, 1996).

Procedure:

1. Share several of Eric Carle's books with students. Discuss the illustrations.
2. Talk about how Eric Carle makes his illustrations: First, he makes a pencil outline of an object on white paper. Then he tears colored paper into shapes that he will choose to fill in the object. The finished picture is a collage.
3. Tell students that they will be making illustrations like Eric Carle's.
4. Create animal illustration using either method described below.

Method One:

1. Group students, and give each group a large sheet of butcher paper, a single color of paint, and one type of painting tool.
2. Allow the sheets of painted butcher paper to dry thoroughly overnight.
3. Draw simple outlines of zoo animals on large sheets of butcher paper.
4. Have students cut out different shapes, using the large sheets of painted paper.
5. Students then glue these shapes onto the outlines.
6. Allow the collages to dry thoroughly and then cut out the outlines.

Art Connections (CONT.)

Eric Carle's Zoo (CONT.)
Method Two:

1. Draw the outlines of the animals on large sheets of white butcher paper.
2. Have students decorate these shapes using a variety of tools and colors. (See the first step of Method One.)
3. Allow to dry thoroughly and then cut out the animal shape.

Music, Movement, Rhythm, and Rhyme

Habitat (Have to Have a Habitat)
by Bill Oliver

Chorus

Habitat, habitat, have to have a habitat
Habitat, habitat, have to have a habitat
Habitat, habitat, have to have a habitat
You have to have a habitat to carry on!

The ocean is a habitat, a very special habitat
It's where the deepest water's at
It's where the biggest mammal's at
It's where out future food is at
It keeps the atmosphere intact
The ocean is a habitat we depend on! (*Chorus*)

The forest is a habitat, a very special habitat
It's where the tallest trees are at
It's where a bear can scratch her back
(*ch-ch-ch-ch-ch-ch-ch*)
It keeps the ground from rolling back
Renews the oxygen, in fact
The forest is a habitat we depend on! (*Chorus*)

The river is a habitat, a very special habitat
It's where the freshest water's at
For people, fish, and muskrat
But when people dump their trash
Rivers take the biggest rap
The river is a habitat we depend on! (*Chorus*)

People are different than foxes and rabbits
Effect the whole world with their bad habits
Better to love it while we still have it
Or rat ta-tat-tat, our habitat's gone! (*Chorus*)
  (used with permission.)

Music, Movement, Rhythm, and Rhyme (CONT.)

Animal Charades

Cut out pictures from nature magazines of various animals that live in zoo. Glue the pictures onto squares of construction paper. Put them into a container. Select one student to begin the game. Have the student pull out an animal card and look at it without showing it to the rest of the class. The student then acts out the movements of the animal on the card. Whoever correctly identifies the animal is next.

Centers

Set up centers to encourage students to explore the theme further during a free choice period, or assign small groups to parent-guided centers while you work with other students.

Colors and Shapes Centers

Skills: identification and use of shapes and colors

Shape Pictures

Read *Color Zoo* by Lois Ehlert (Harper Collins, 1989). Provide shapes cut out of various colored construction paper. Students use the shapes to create images of animals and objects such as those used in *Color Zoo*.

Snacks

Be sure to check with parents about allergies before serving students any food.

Zoo Animal Sandwiches

Make sandwiches into the shapes of zoo animals for a fun and nutritious snack.

Ingredients/Materials:

- whole wheat bread
- animal cookie cutters
- filling: sliced cheese, peanut butter and jelly, cream cheese, etc.

Directions:

1. Assemble sandwiches.
2. Cut into animal shapes using cookie cutters.

Lion Faces

Make these fruit snacks into the face of a lion! Roar!

Ingredients:

- pineapple slices
- raisins
- shredded carrots

Directions:

1. Put pineapple slices on paper plates.
2. Provide each student with small containers (plastic bag) of shredded carrots and a dozen raisins.
3. Assist students with putting carrots around the pineapple "head" and raisins as mouth, nose and eyes.

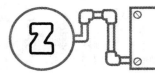

Zoo

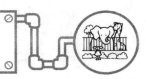

Zoo Alphabet Book

Use the following list with the Zoo Alphabet Book activity on page 288. Select one animal for each letter.

A: aardvark, antelope, armadillo, alligator

B: bat, baboon, butterfly

C: crab, cat

D: deer, dolphin

E: elephant, emu

F: flamingo, fox, frog, fish

G: gorilla, gibbon, goat, giraffe, goose

H: hippopotamus

I: iguana, insect

J: jaguar, jackal, jellyfish

K: koala, kangaroo

L: lion, lobster, lizard

M: monkey, mouse, manatee, moose

N: newt

O: octopus, ostrich, orangutan

P: pig, penguin, peacock, polar bear

Q: quail

R: rhinoceros, raccoon

S: snake, seal

T: turtle, tortoise, tiger

U: unicorn, underwater creatures

V: vulture

W: whales, walrus, wolf

X: fox

Y: yak

Z: zebra

Zoo

Zoo Counting Book Cover

Directions: Make one copy for each student. Use with Math Connections Activity on pages 289–290.

My *Zoo* Counting Book
by

_____

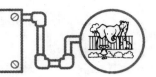
Zoo Counting Book First Page

Directions: Make one copy for each student. Use as the first page of the book, after the book cover on page 295 and before the student pages.

I went to the zoo today,

And what did I see?

All kinds of animals
looking at me!

I saw…

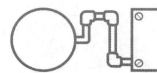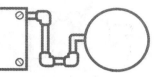

Read Aloud Tips

When children are allowed to experience the joy of a hearing a story read aloud, they develop a love of literature and the motivation to learn how to read. Consider using a "read aloud" as a time for pleasure. Focus on the story, the characters, and the emotion that is evoked by a wonderful book. Let the instructional time wait until after a read aloud session.

Setting the Stage

- Set aside at least one time, every day, for reading aloud.

- Read many different books. You don't have to tie every read-aloud book into the letter theme.

- Develop a read-aloud (or story-time) routine so that time is not lost with logistical tasks. For example, use a special signal (such as flicking the light switch on and off) to alert students that story-time has arrived. Students quietly gather carpet squares or pillows, and settle in for listening. Remind students to put on "listening ears."

- Create a special read aloud place in your classroom with pillows, couches, rugs, and stuffed animals.

- Remember that students may need time to learn how to listen to stories. Provide guidelines and reinforcement for appropriate behavior.

- Avoid using reading as a disciplinary action or threat. ("We won't be able to read a story today unless you all finish your math!") Books should never be used as weapons. The goal is to instill a love of reading, not to build negative associations.

- Practice reading aloud. Reading aloud comes naturally to few people. Read to yourself in front of the mirror, and tape record or videotape yourself reading aloud so you see and hear yourself as your students do.

- Allow reluctant readers or active students to quietly doodle with crayons and paper while listening. Sometimes students need to do something with their hands before they can listen with their minds and hearts.

Getting Ready

- Read the book to yourself. Make sure that you are familiar with the text and rhythm. Think about which features you are going to highlight during the read aloud session.

- Make sure students are comfortable and ready to listen, and are seated where they can see the book.

- Make sure that you are comfortable. Sit in a low chair, on the floor, or somewhere that every student can see you and the book.

- Allow time for the children to gather and settle in. Make sure each child is comfortable and ready to pay attention. A gentle reminder such as, "It is time to put on your listening ears," will help.

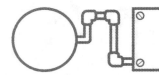 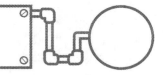

Read Aloud Tips *(CONT.)*

Before Reading

- Read the title, pointing to the words as you read.

- Read the author's, and the illustrator's names. If you have read other books by the same author or illustrator, say, "This book is written/illustrated by the same person who wrote/illustrated," and recall some of the details of the previously read books.

- Point out the illustrations on the front and back covers.

- Ask students to predict what they think the story might be about based on the title and cover illustrations.

- Relate the theme or story to students' previous knowledge.

- Set a purpose for the reading, particularly when the book is non-fiction, so that the students can focus on what they want to learn, and create networks of knowledge that connect prior information to newly acquired knowledge.

- When students say that they have already heard the book that you are going to read, respond positively and enthusiastically

During Reading

- As you read, make sure that each student can see the illustrations. Hold the book so that it is facing the students, and turn it slowly as you read.

- Be expressive. Your voice and facial expressions will draw students into the story.

- Slow down!

- Use props and/or costumes.

- Pause occasionally, to create suspense, to ask for predictions, or to reflect on what is being read. "What do you think will happen next?" "I wonder how she's feeling right now?"

- Initiate discussions about the characters, the setting, and the plot.

- Point to illustrations and words as you read. Incorporate motions with your hands and legs.

- Invite students to participate in reading stories that have repetitive or predictable text.

- Summarize what is happening in the story, particularly in a longer or more detailed book.

After Reading

- Allow time for students to articulate responses. Wait a few moments so they can think about what they would like to say. Good books evoke powerful responses—joy, laughter, fear, frustration. Allow these feelings to surface, and allow time for student responses.

- Respond to the story yourself. Your responses and questions will provide a good model for students. Responses can include comments or questions about characters or plot, the way the text was written, illustrations, and any other features of the book.

- When asking for a response to the literature, provide a variety of avenues for expression. Students could draw a picture of their favorite scenes, role play characters, or use music to express their reactions.

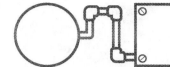

Assessment

Student Name:_____   Grade Level _____

Teacher Name: _____

Year: _____   School: _____

Track student's progress with number identification, number value, and number writing by marking "√" when the student can perform the skill.

	Identifies Letter	Identifies Sound	Writes Letter		Identifies Letter	Identifies Sound	Writes Letter
A				a			
B				b			
C				c			
D				d			
E				e			
F				r			
G				g			
H				h			
I				i			
J				j			
K				k			
L				l			
M				m			
N				n			
O				o			
P				p			
Q				q			
R				r			
S				s			
T				t			
U				u			
V				v			
W				w			
X				x			
Y				y			
Z				z			

Assessment

Student Name:_____   Grade Level _____

Teacher Name: _____

Year: _____   School: _____

Track student's progress with identyfying and forming shapes by marking "√" when the student can perform the skill.

	Identifies Shape	Forms Shape
Circle		
Square		
Triangle		
Rectangle		
Diamond		
Oval		

Track student's progress with identifying colors by marking "√" when the student can perform the skill.

	Identifies Color
Red	
Blue	
Yellow	
Green	
Orange	

	Identifies Color
White	
Black	
Brown	
Purple	
Pink	

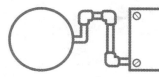
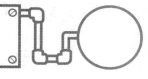

Index

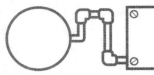
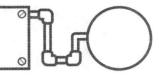

Index

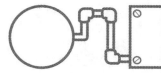

Index

Index